KUMA KUMA KUMA BEAR

STORY BY
Kumanano

ART BY
Sergei

CHAR.
DESIGN BY
029

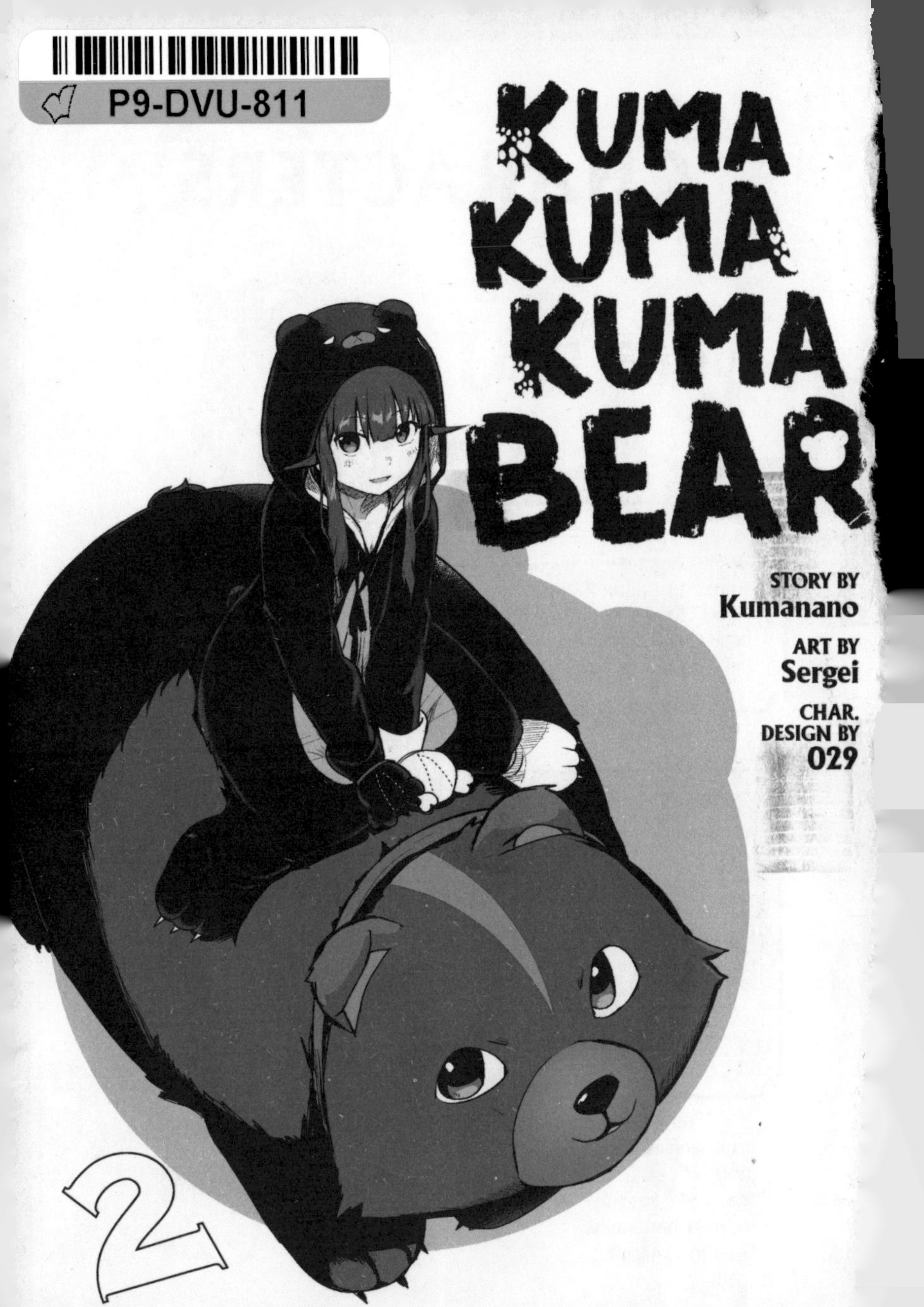

2

CHARACTERS

【 Yuna & Fina 】

YUNA

A shut-in gamer. One day someone calling themselves "God" forces Yuna into OP bear gear, and transports her into another world!

FINA

A girl Yuna saved from wolves. Her mother is sick, so she works hard to support her family. Lives in Crimonia.

【Rulina's Party】

RULINA

Rank D Adventuer.
Deboranay's party member,
but now she's off with Yuna
to slay a goblin horde?!

LANZ

Idolizes Deboranay,
hates Yuna.

GIL

Strong but sensitive.

DEBORANAY

Picked a fight with
Yuna and got
wrecked.

【Adventurers' Guild】

GENTZ

Nice guy who runs
the Adventurers'
Guild trading post.

HELEN

Adventurers' Guild
receptionist. Yuna's
overseer.

LAROC

Guild Master of the
Adventurers' Guild
in Crimonia.

CONTENTS

Chapter 11............ 5

Chapter 12............ 21

Chapter 13............ 37

Chapter 14............ 53

Chapter 15............ 69

Chapter 16............ 85

Chapter 17............ 101

Chapter 18............ 117

Chapter 19............ 133

Chapter 20............ 149

Short Story: Bear House 165

Bonus Manga 172

STORY

Recluse gamer girl Yuna was given OP bear gear and then transported to another world. Yuna departs on a quest with Rulina to slay a goblin horde, and they find themselves up against a force larger than anticipated!

KUMA KUMA KUMA BEAR
VOLUME. 2

Chapter 11

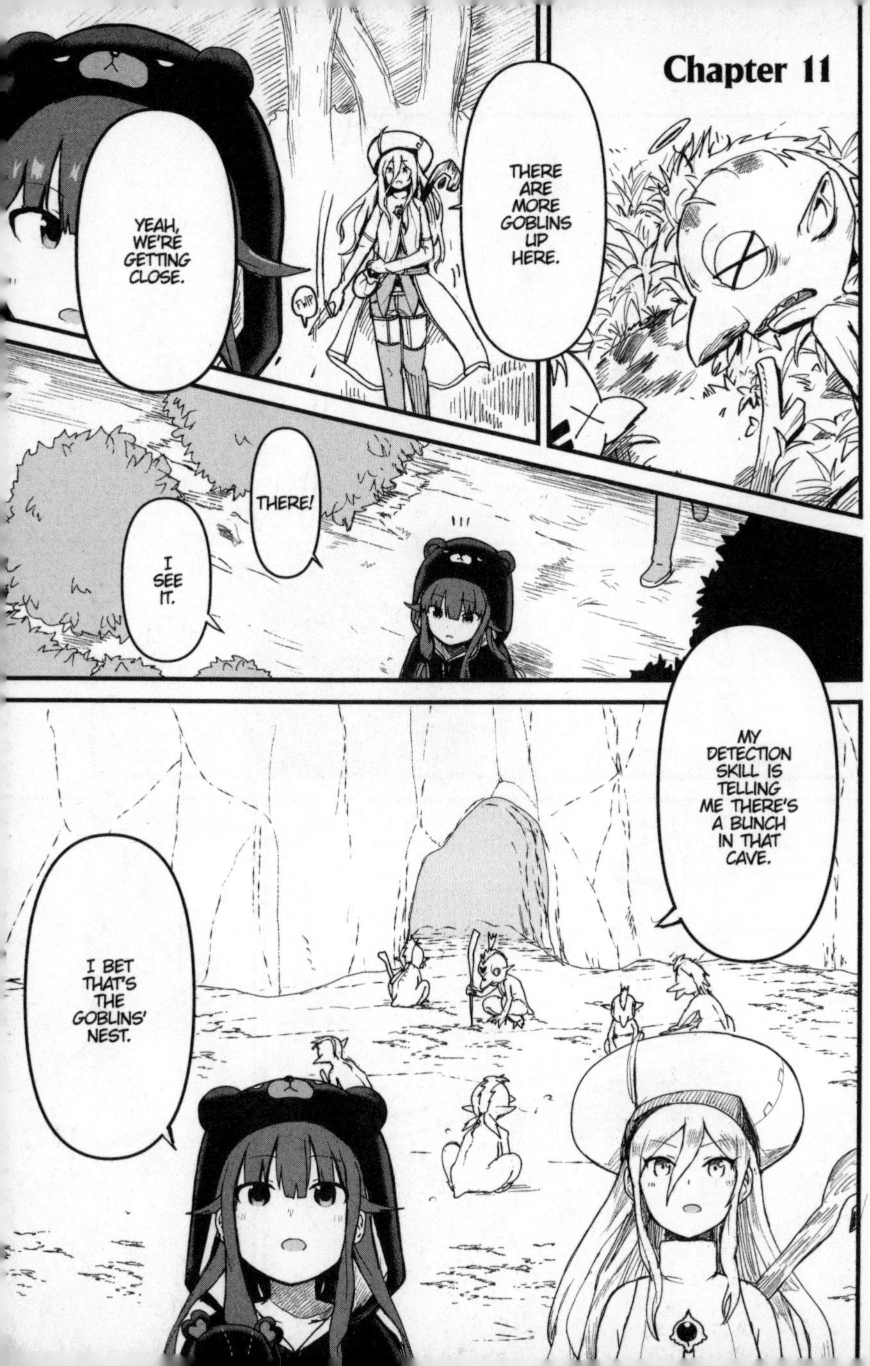
THERE ARE MORE GOBLINS UP HERE.
FWIP
YEAH, WE'RE GETTING CLOSE.
THERE!
I SEE IT.
MY DETECTION SKILL IS TELLING ME THERE'S A BUNCH IN THAT CAVE.
I BET THAT'S THE GOBLINS' NEST.

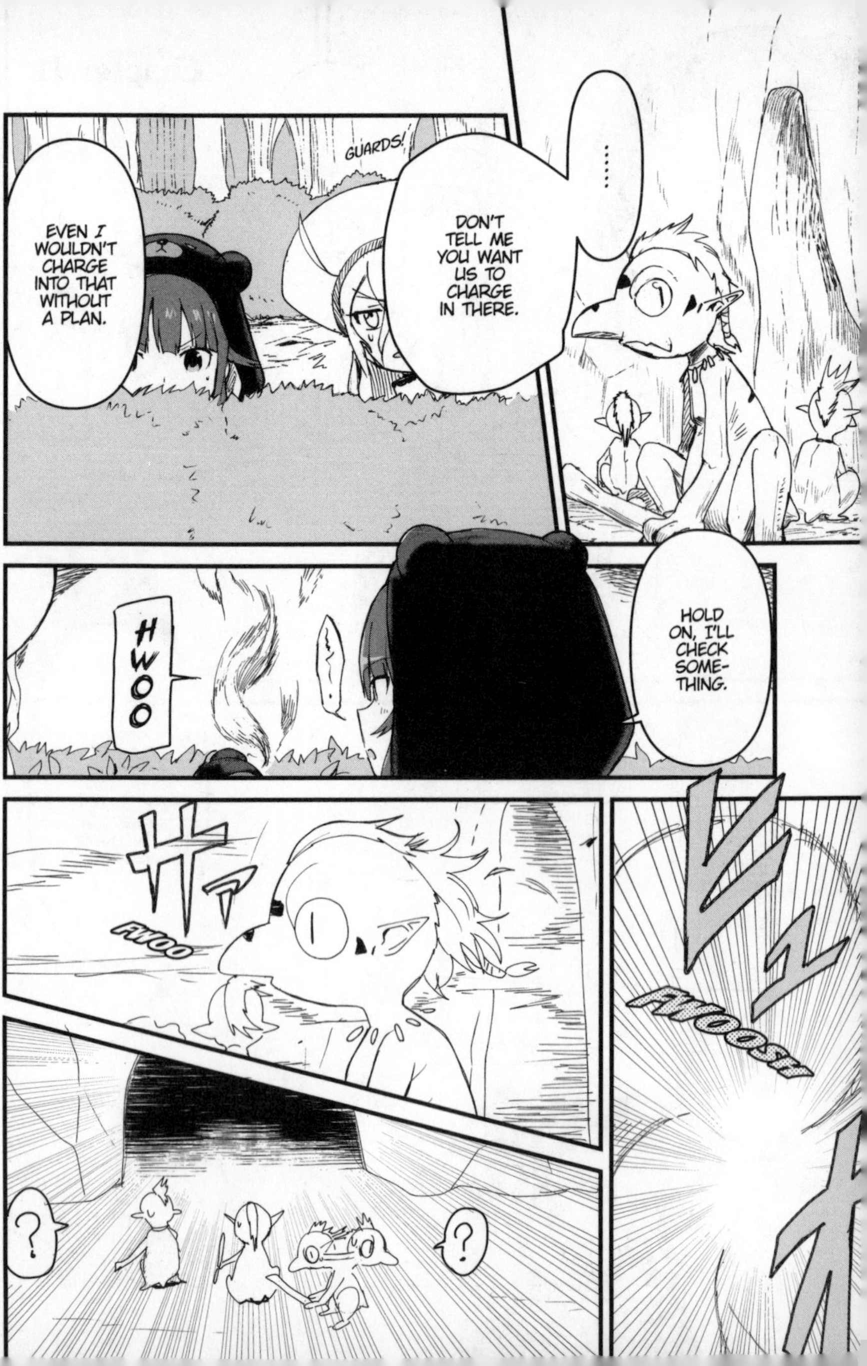
......
DON'T TELL ME YOU WANT US TO CHARGE IN THERE.
GUARDS!
EVEN I WOULDN'T CHARGE INTO THAT WITHOUT A PLAN.
HOLD ON, I'LL CHECK SOMETHING.
HWOO
FWOOSH
FWOO
?
?

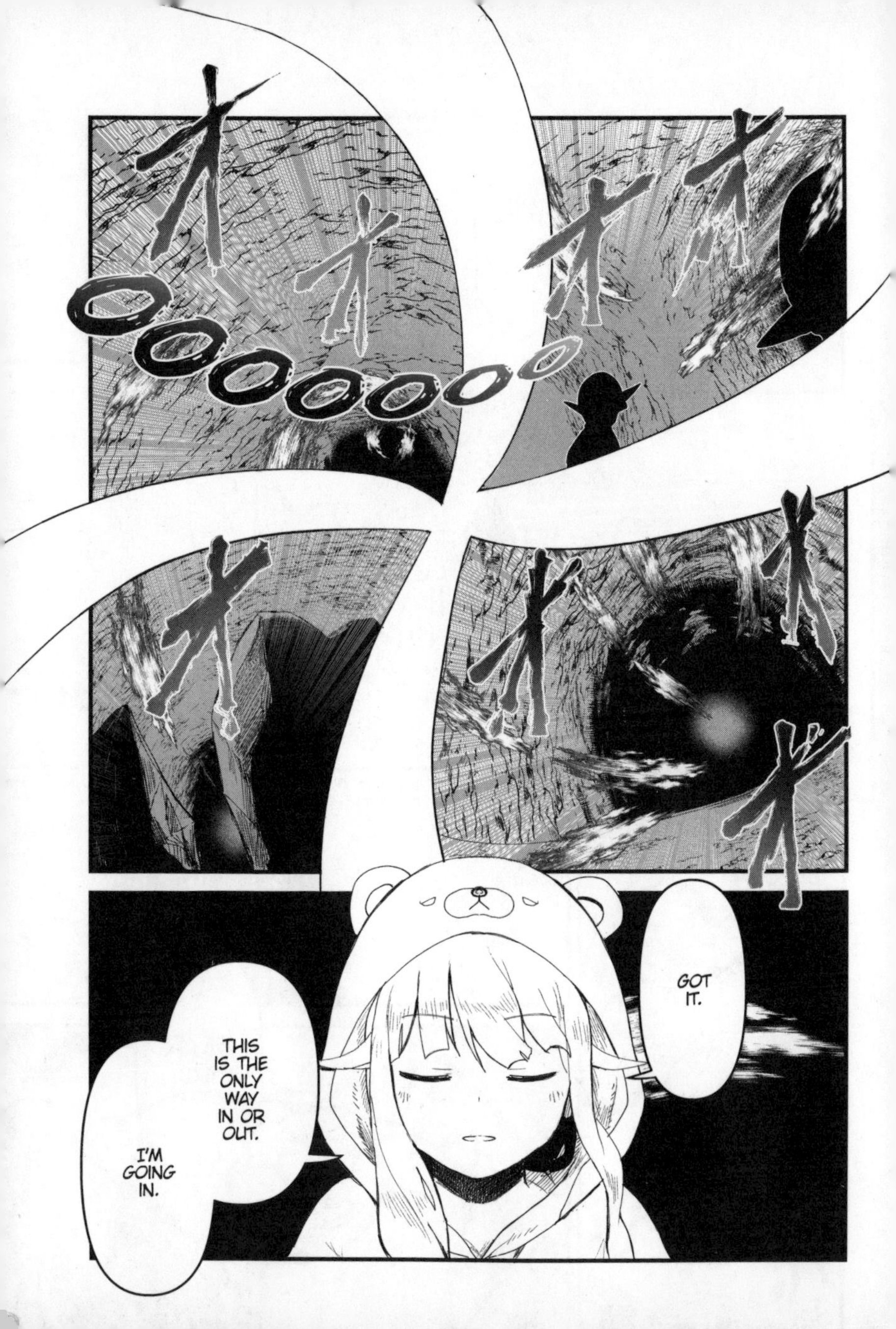
OOOOOOOO
GOT IT.
THIS IS THE ONLY WAY IN OR OUT.
I'M GOING IN.

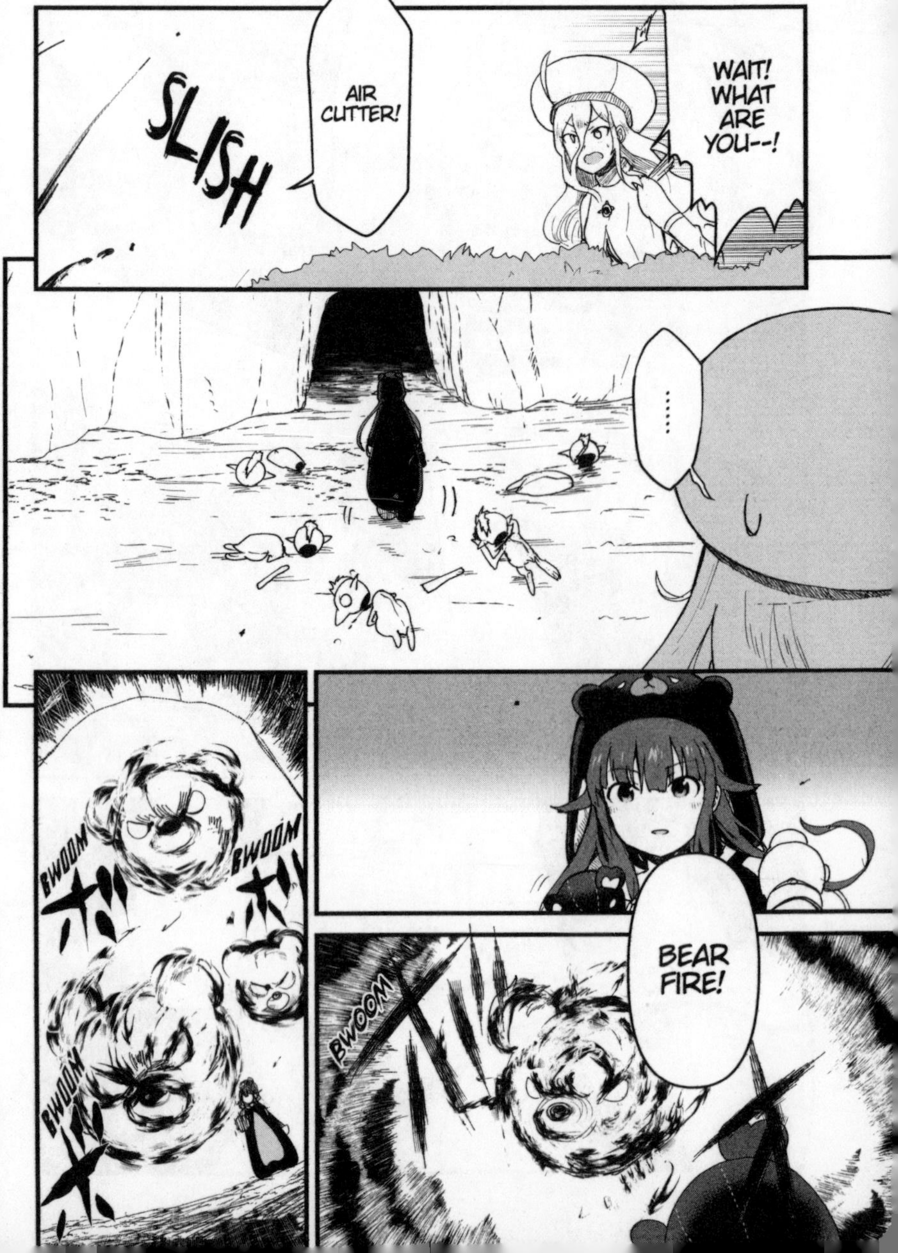
WAIT! WHAT ARE YOU--!
AIR CUTTER!
SLISH
......
BEAR FIRE!
BWOOM
BWOOM
BWOOM
BWOOM

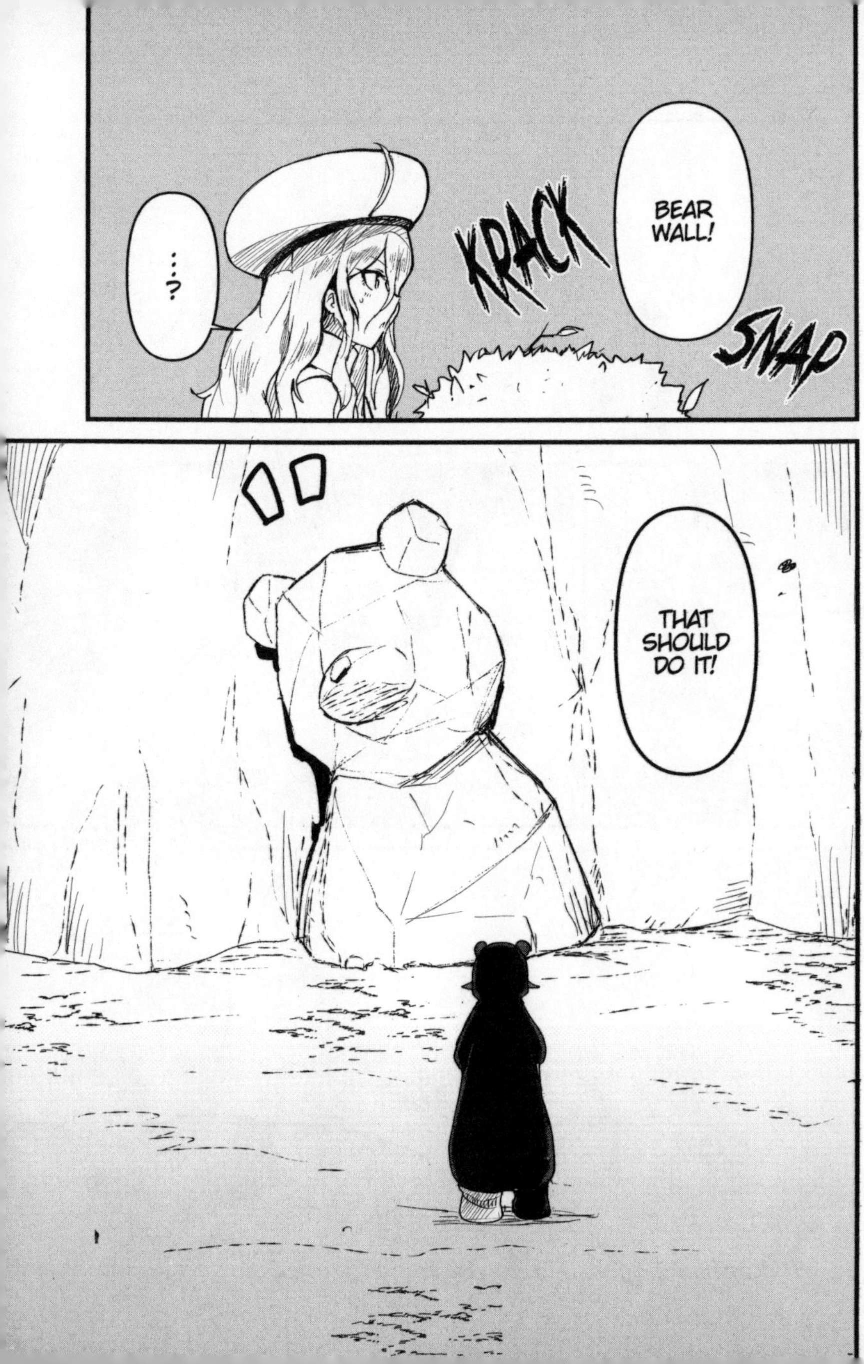
BEAR WALL!
KRACK
SNAP
...?
THAT SHOULD DO IT!

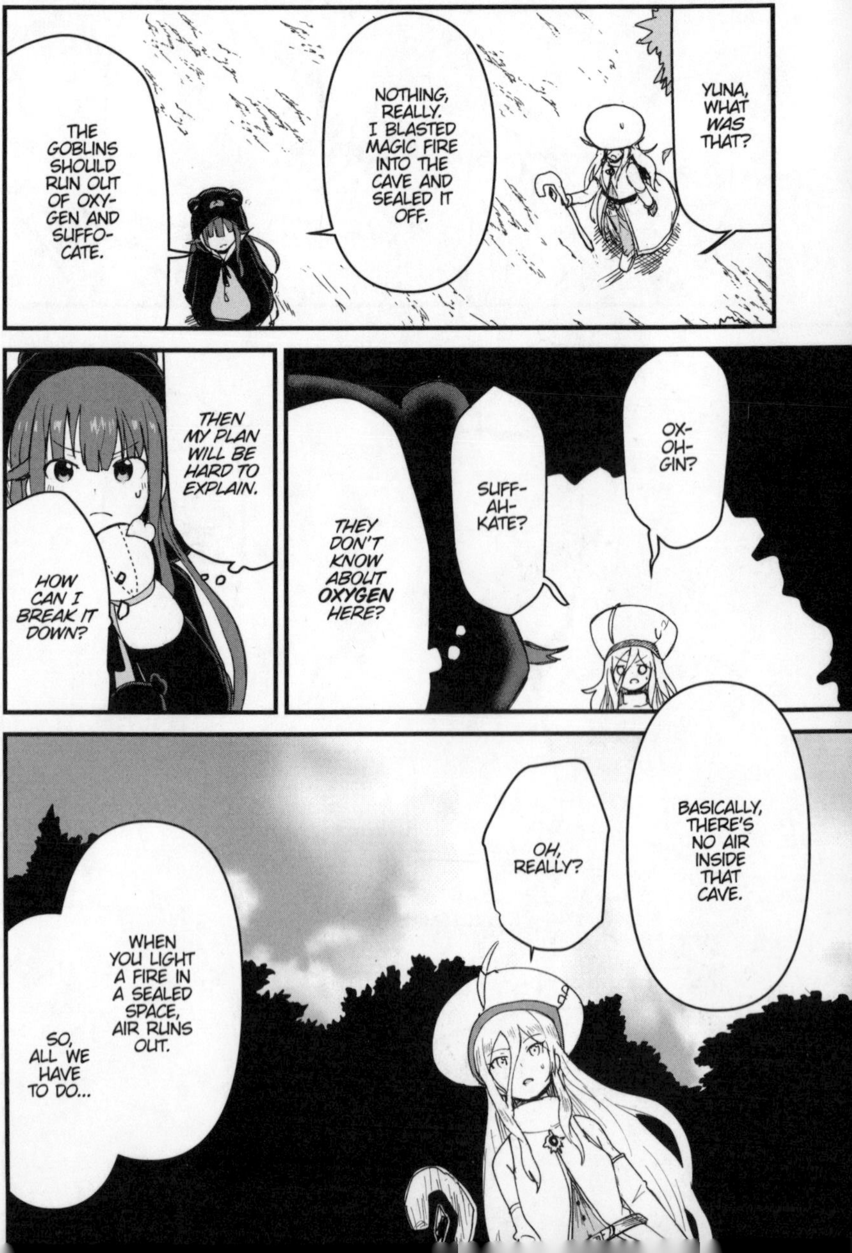
YUNA, WHAT WAS THAT?
NOTHING, REALLY. I BLASTED MAGIC FIRE INTO THE CAVE AND SEALED IT OFF.
THE GOBLINS SHOULD RUN OUT OF OXYGEN AND SUFFOCATE.
OX-OH-GIN?
SUFF-AH-KATE?
THEY DON'T KNOW ABOUT OXYGEN HERE?
THEN MY PLAN WILL BE HARD TO EXPLAIN.
HOW CAN I BREAK IT DOWN?
BASICALLY, THERE'S NO AIR INSIDE THAT CAVE.
OH, REALLY?
WHEN YOU LIGHT A FIRE IN A SEALED SPACE, AIR RUNS OUT.
SO, ALL WE HAVE TO DO...

IS WAIT FOR THE GOBLINS TO RUN OUT OF STRENGTH.

IT MIGHT TAKE SOME TIME, THOUGH.

HOW MUCH TIME?

A FEW MINUTES?

I'LL USE MY DETECTION MAGIC TO WATCH THEM UNTIL THEY'RE DOWN.

I'LL COLLECT THE GOBLINS' MANA GEMS WHILE WE WAIT.

A FEW MIN-LITES?

GROSS!

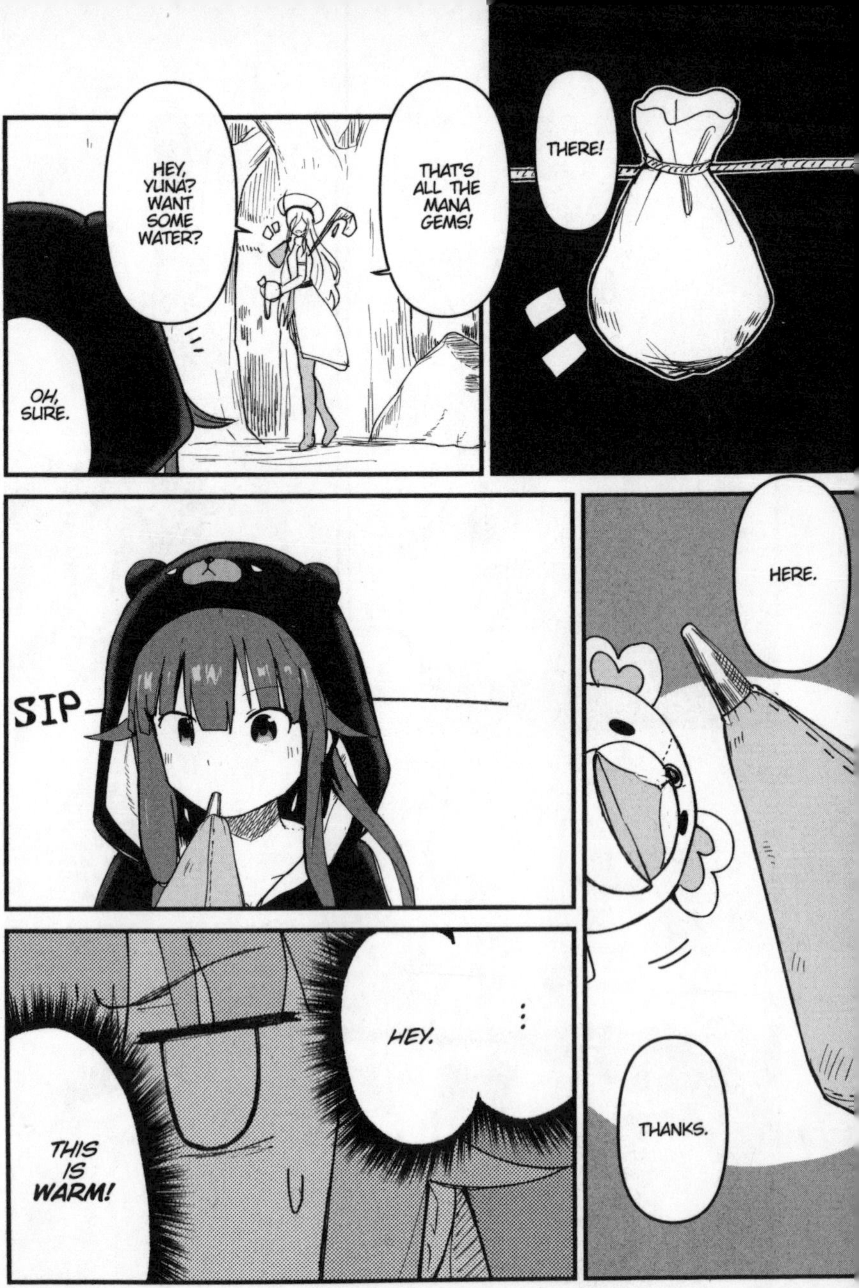
THERE!
THAT'S ALL THE MANA GEMS!
HEY, YUNA? WANT SOME WATER?
OH, SURE.
HERE.
THANKS.
SIP—
...
HEY.
THIS IS WARM!

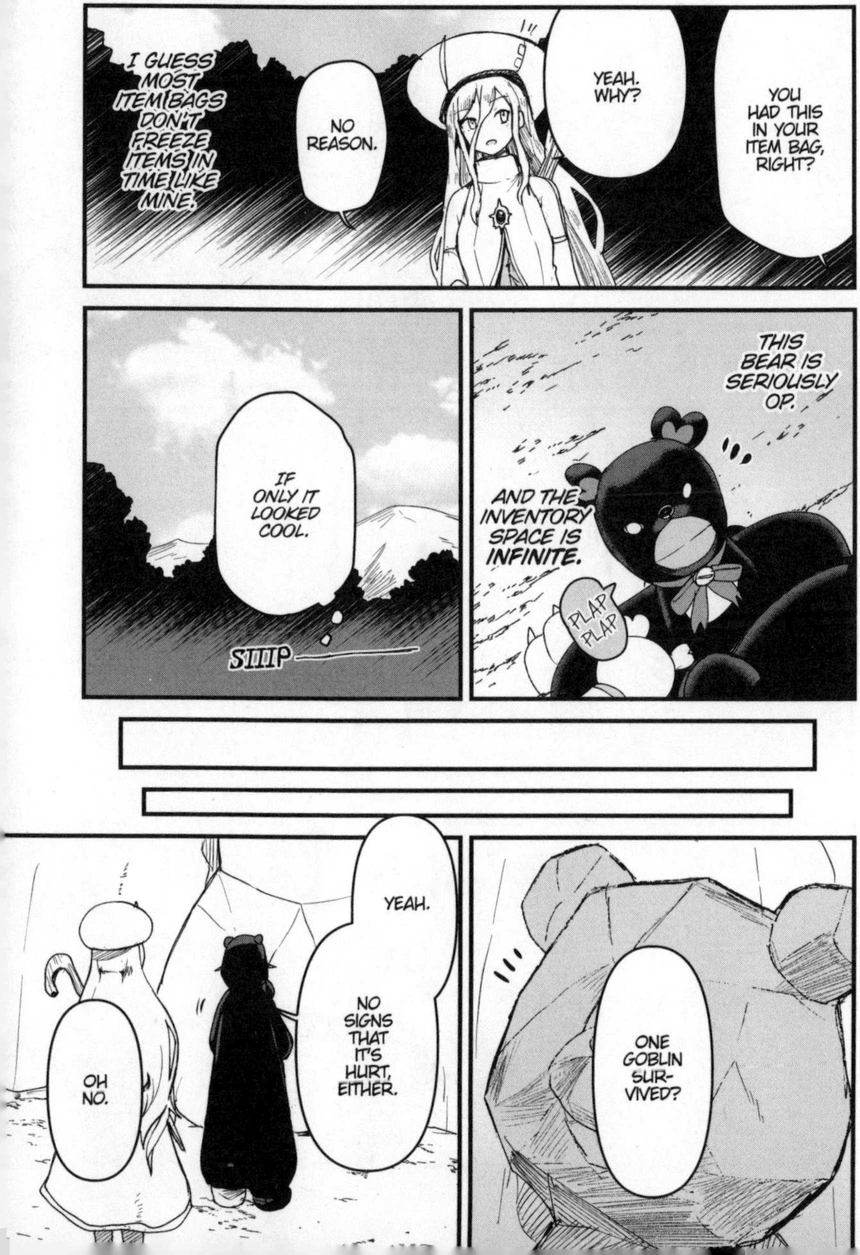
YOU HAD THIS IN YOUR ITEM BAG, RIGHT?
YEAH. WHY?
NO REASON.
I GUESS MOST ITEM BAGS DON'T FREEZE ITEMS IN TIME LIKE MINE.
THIS BEAR IS SERIOUSLY OP.
AND THE INVENTORY SPACE IS INFINITE.
PLAP PLAP
IF ONLY IT LOOKED COOL.
SIIIP
ONE GOBLIN SUR-VIVED?
YEAH.
NO SIGNS THAT IT'S HURT, EITHER.
OH NO.

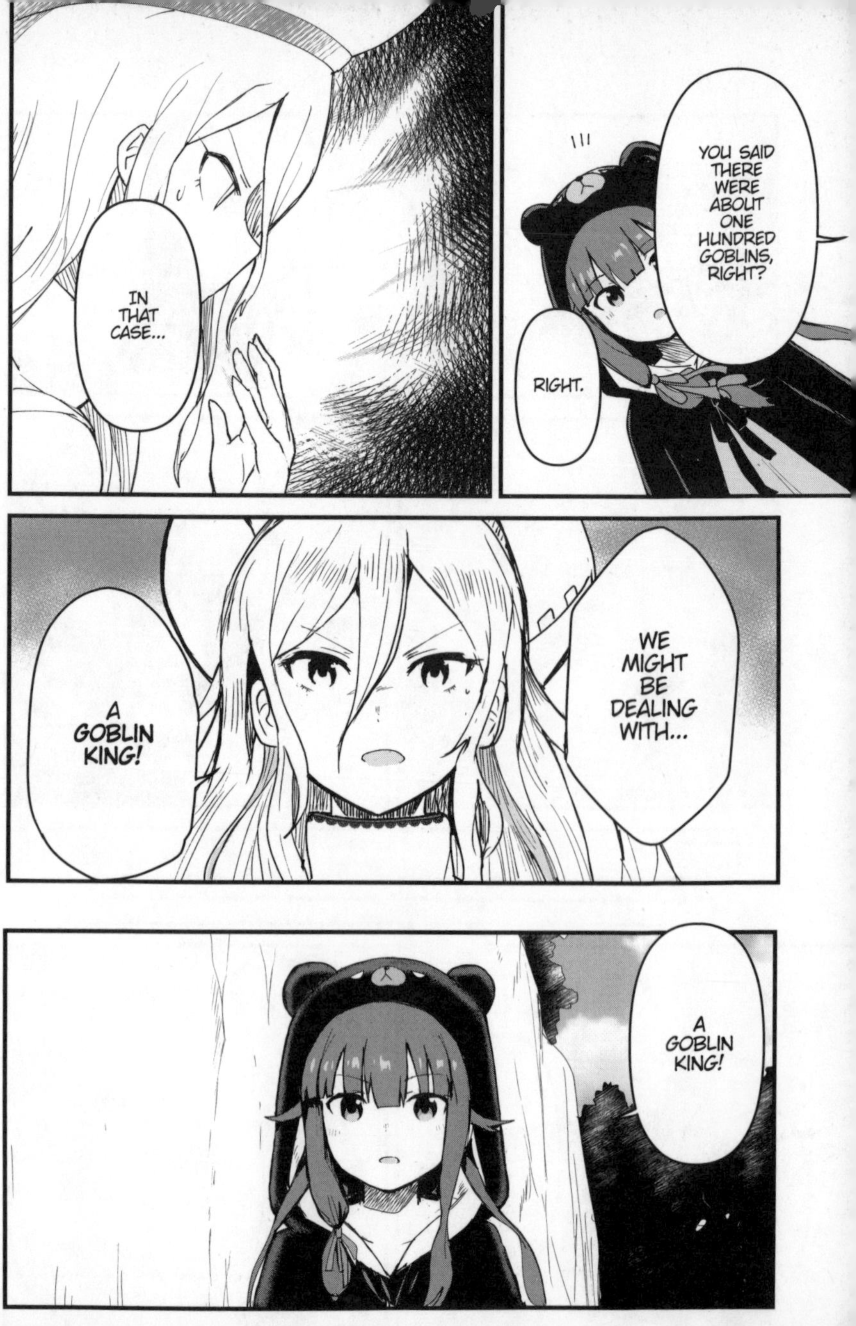
!!!
YOU SAID THERE WERE ABOUT ONE HUNDRED GOBLINS, RIGHT?
RIGHT.
IN THAT CASE...
WE MIGHT BE DEALING WITH...
A GOBLIN KING!
A GOBLIN KING!

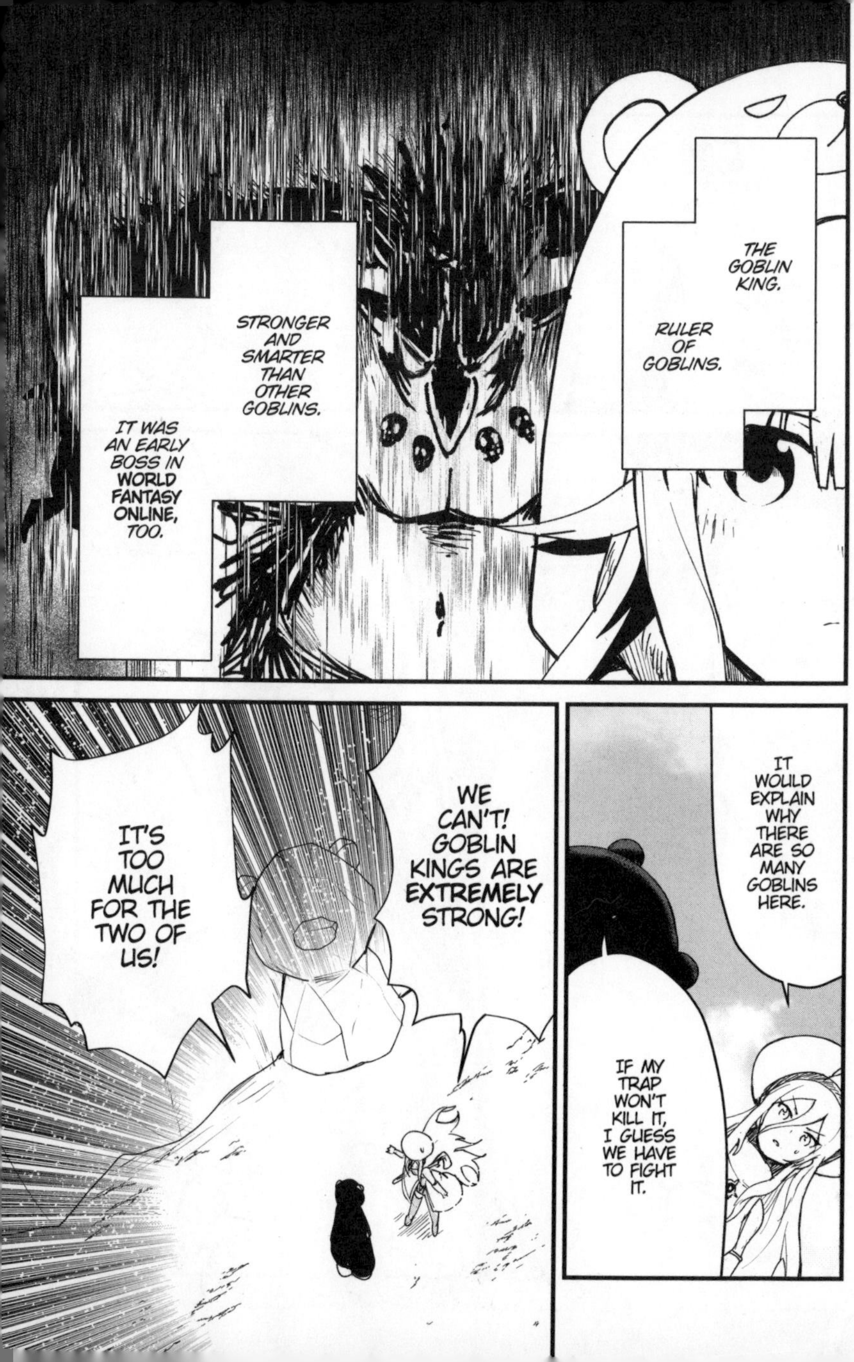
THE GOBLIN KING.
RULER OF GOBLINS.
STRONGER AND SMARTER THAN OTHER GOBLINS.
IT WAS AN EARLY BOSS IN WORLD FANTASY ONLINE, TOO.
IT WOULD EXPLAIN WHY THERE ARE SO MANY GOBLINS HERE.
IF MY TRAP WON'T KILL IT, I GUESS WE HAVE TO FIGHT IT.
WE CAN'T! GOBLIN KINGS ARE EXTREMELY STRONG!
IT'S TOO MUCH FOR THE TWO OF US!

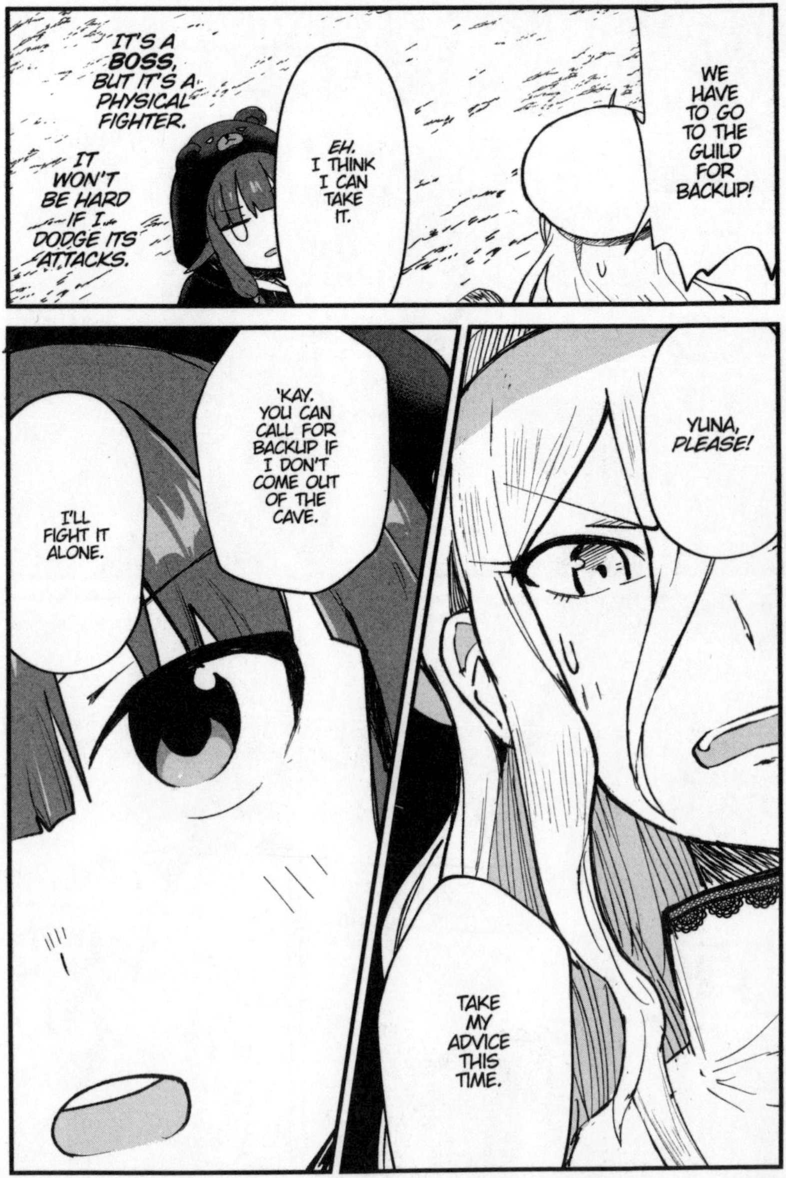
WE HAVE TO GO TO THE GUILD FOR BACKUP!
EH. I THINK I CAN TAKE IT.
IT'S A BOSS, BUT IT'S A PHYSICAL FIGHTER.
IT WON'T BE HARD IF I... DODGE ITS ATTACKS.
YUNA, PLEASE!
TAKE MY ADVICE THIS TIME.
'KAY. YOU CAN CALL FOR BACKUP IF I DON'T COME OUT OF THE CAVE.
I'LL FIGHT IT ALONE.

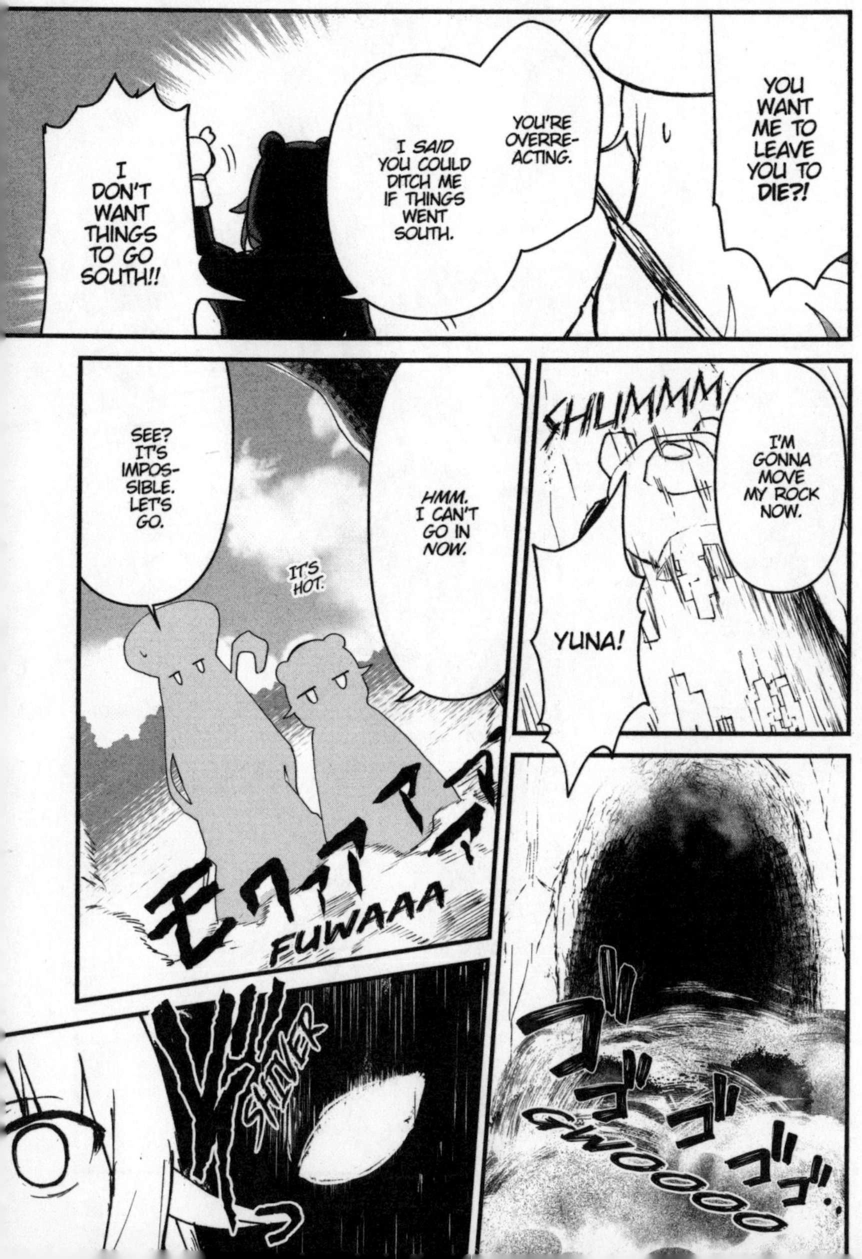

YOU WANT ME TO LEAVE YOU TO DIE?!
YOU'RE OVERRE-ACTING.
I SAID YOU COULD DITCH ME IF THINGS WENT SOUTH.
I DON'T WANT THINGS TO GO SOUTH!!
SHUMMM
I'M GONNA MOVE MY ROCK NOW.
YUNA!
HMM. I CAN'T GO IN NOW.
IT'S HOT.
SEE? IT'S IMPOS-SIBLE. LET'S GO.
FUWAAA
GWOOOOOO
SHIVER

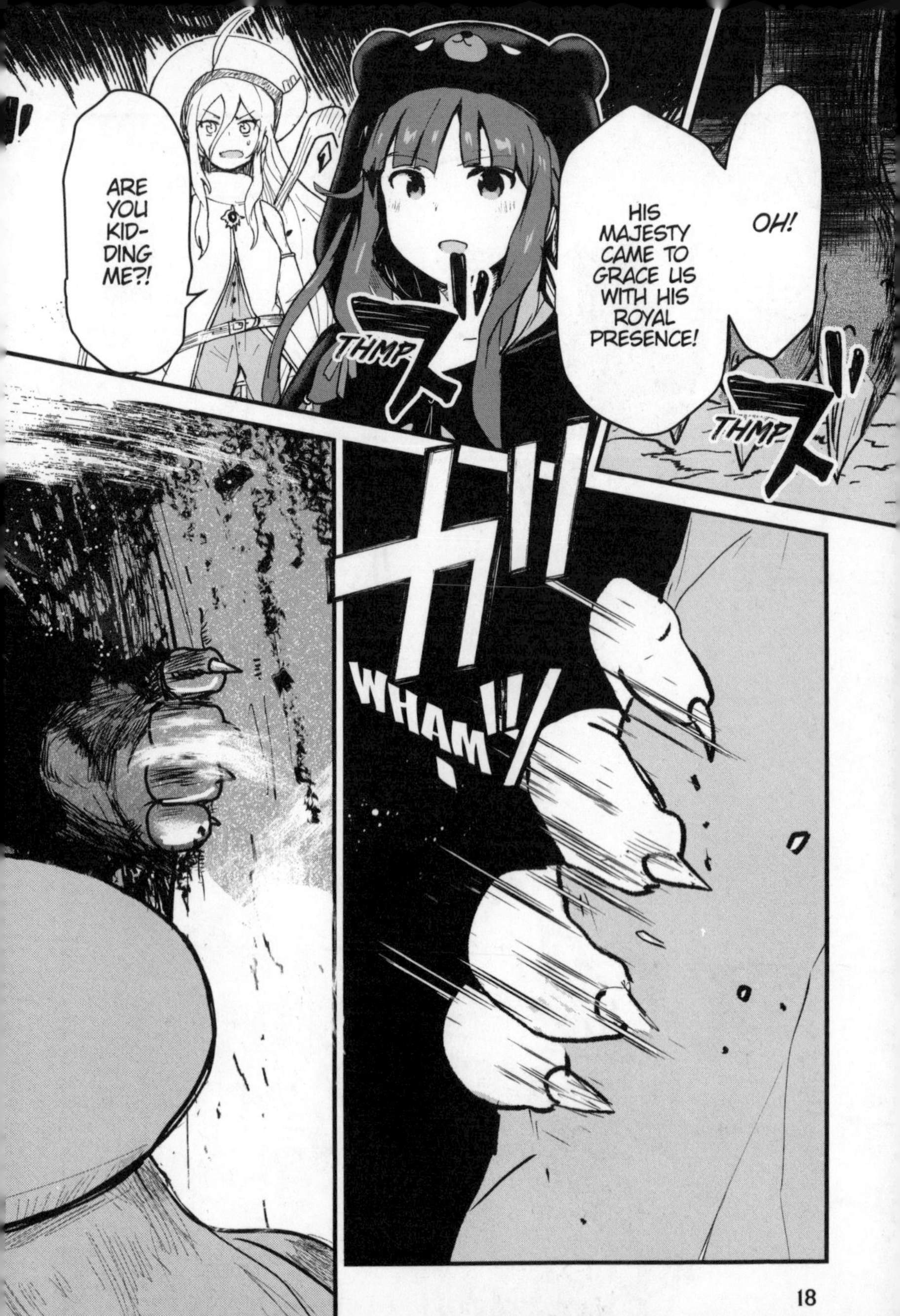
OH!
HIS MAJESTY CAME TO GRACE US WITH HIS ROYAL PRESENCE!
THMP
THMP
ARE YOU KID-DING ME?!
WHAM!!

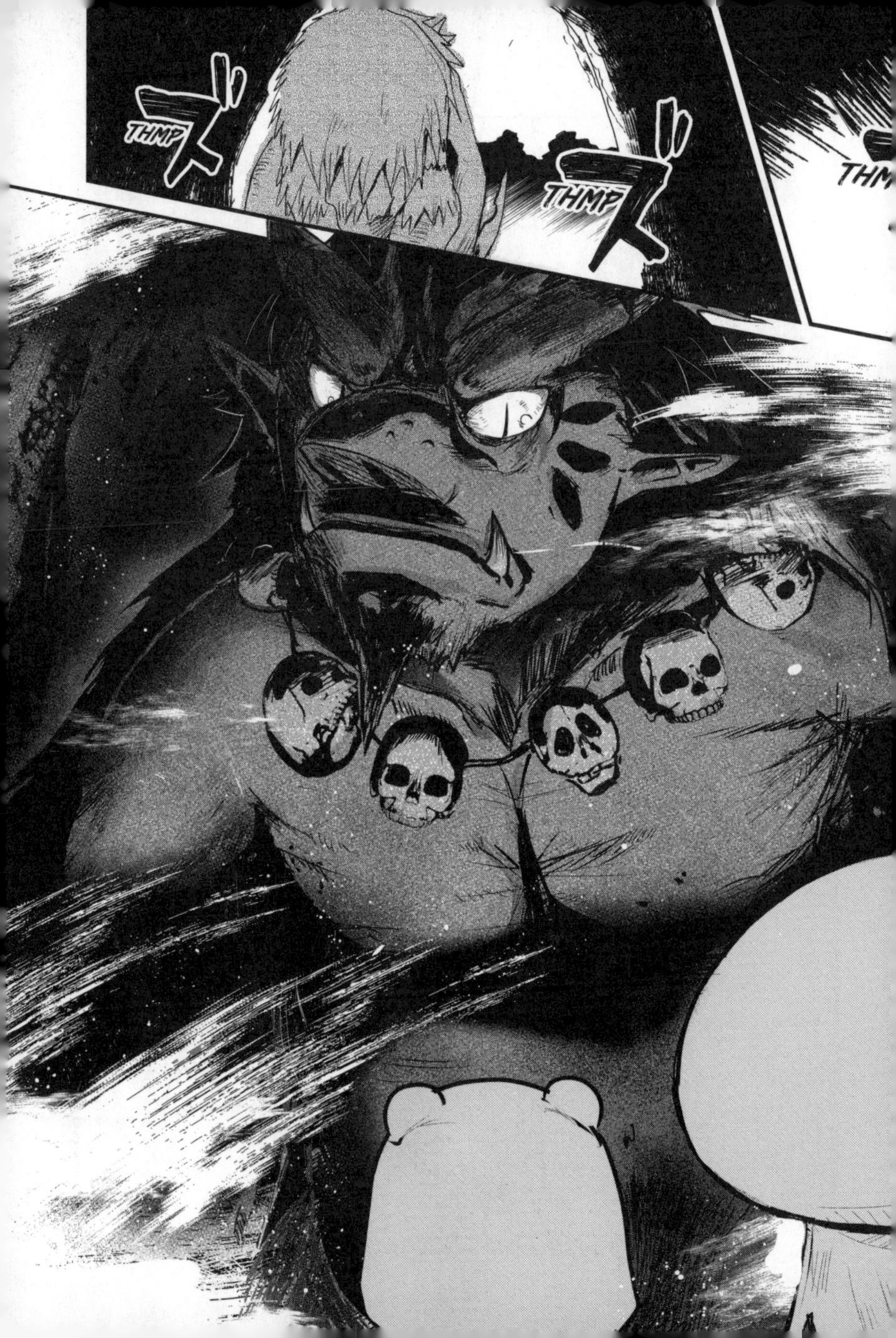
THM
THMP
THMP

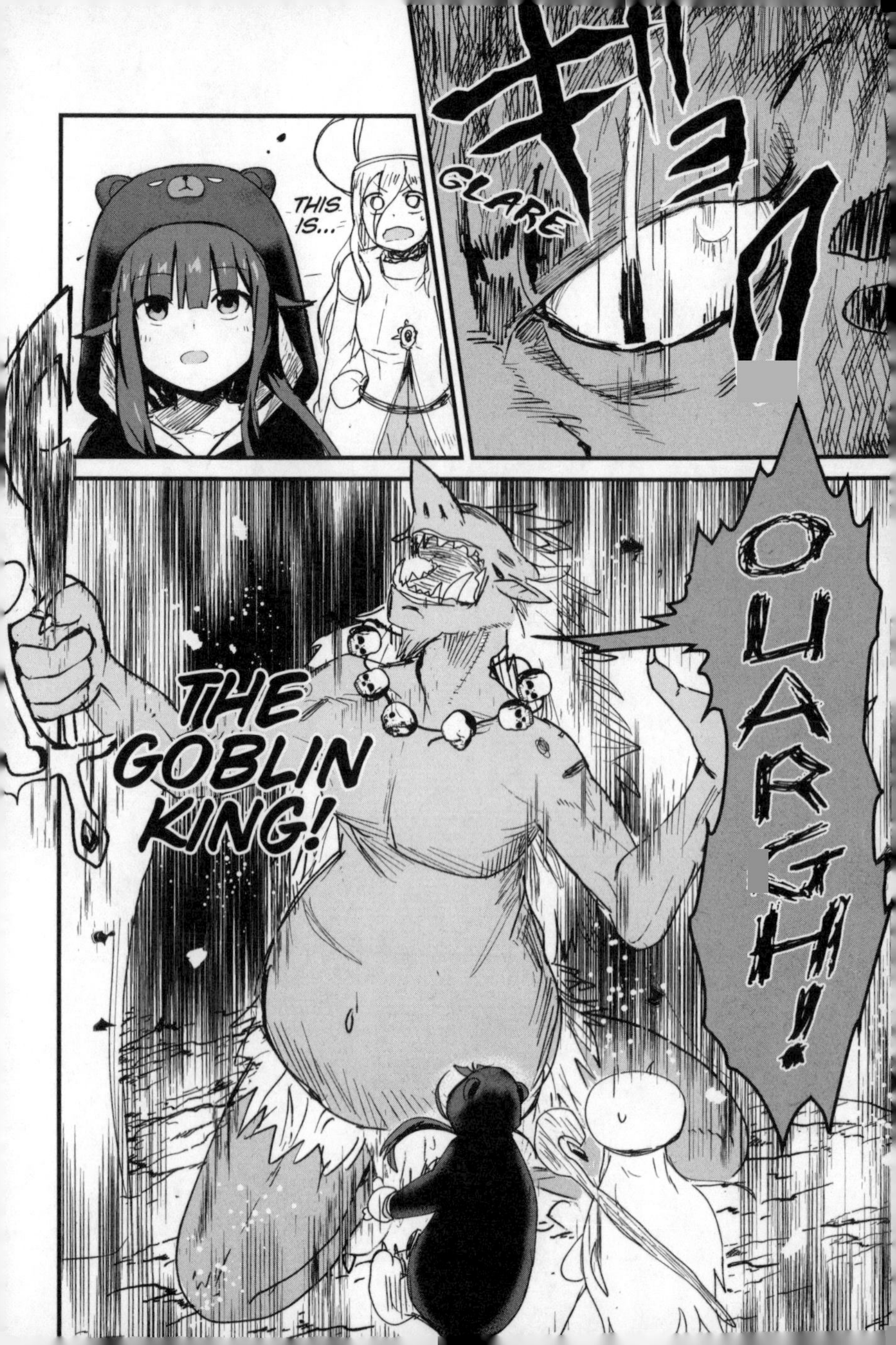
ギョロ
GLARE
THIS IS...
OUARGH!!
THE GOBLIN KING!

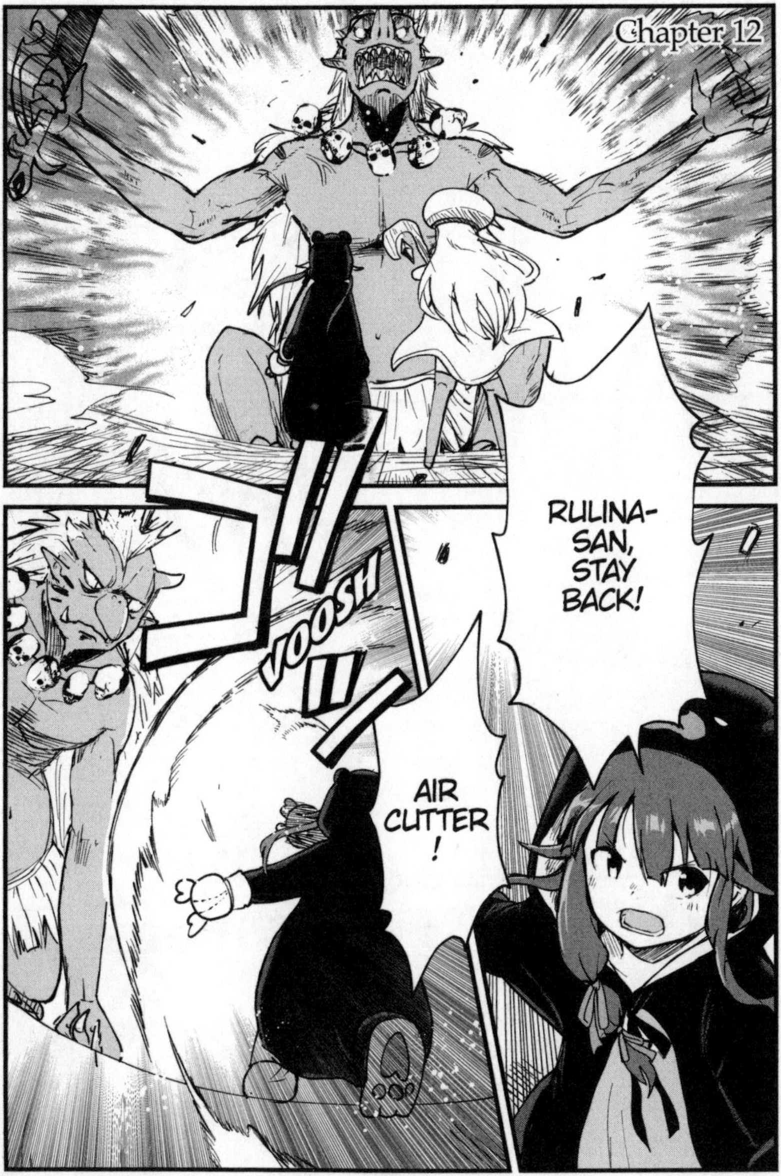
Chapter 12
RULINA-SAN, STAY BACK!
VOOSH
AIR CUTTER!

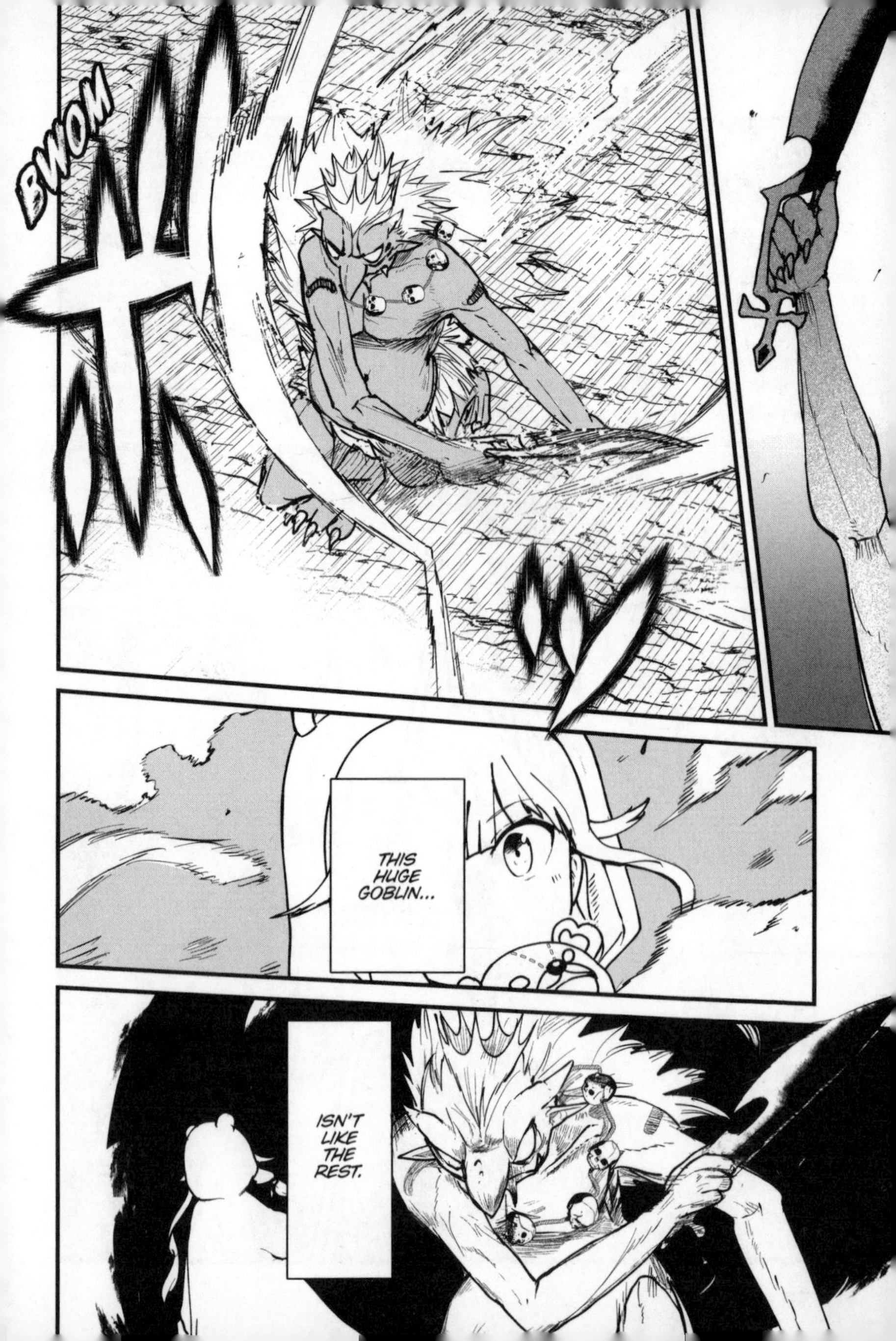
BWOM
THIS HUGE GOBLIN...
ISN'T LIKE THE REST.

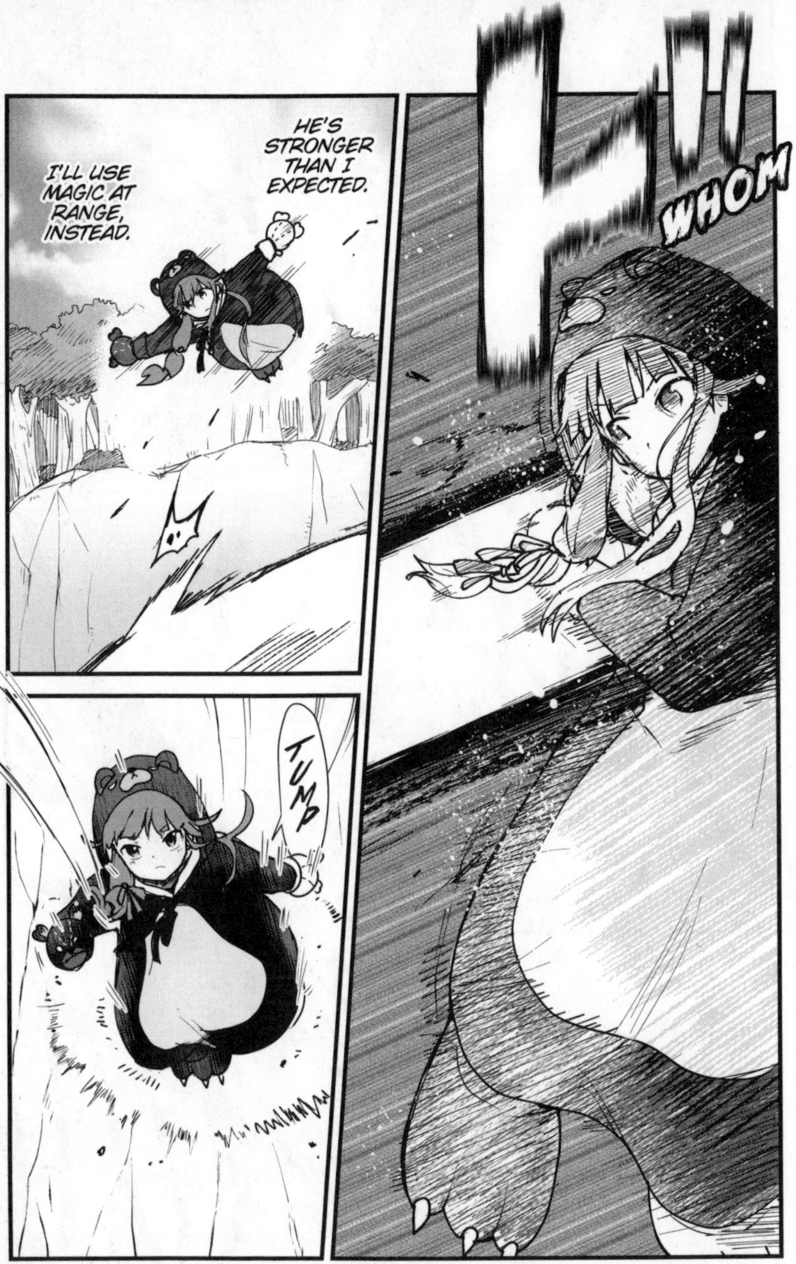
WHOM
HE'S STRONGER THAN I EXPECTED.
I'LL USE MAGIC AT RANGE, INSTEAD.
TUMP

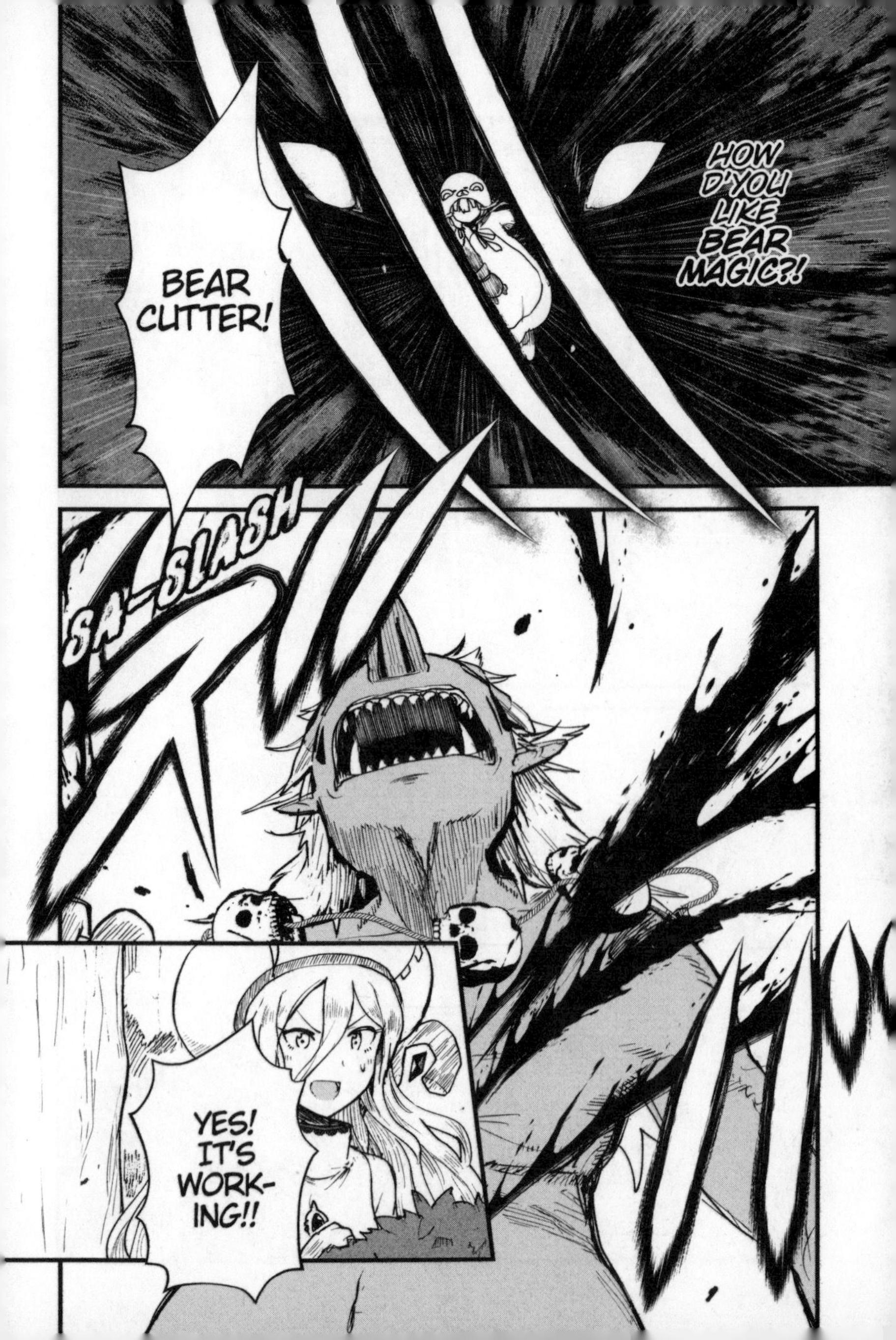
HOW D'YOU LIKE BEAR MAGIC?!
BEAR CUTTER!
SA-SLASH
YES! IT'S WORK-ING!!

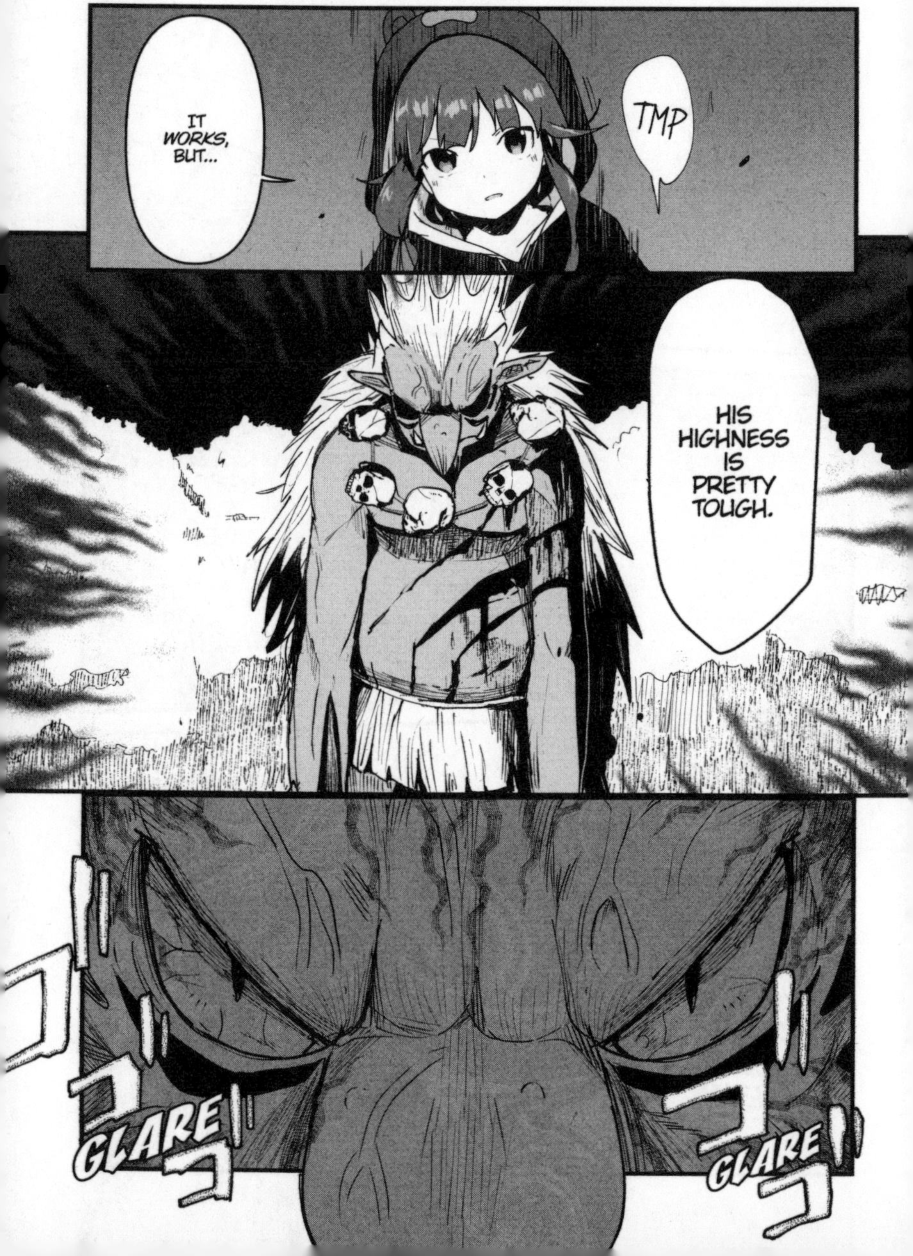
TMP
IT WORKS, BUT...
HIS HIGHNESS IS PRETTY TOUGH.
GLARE
GLARE

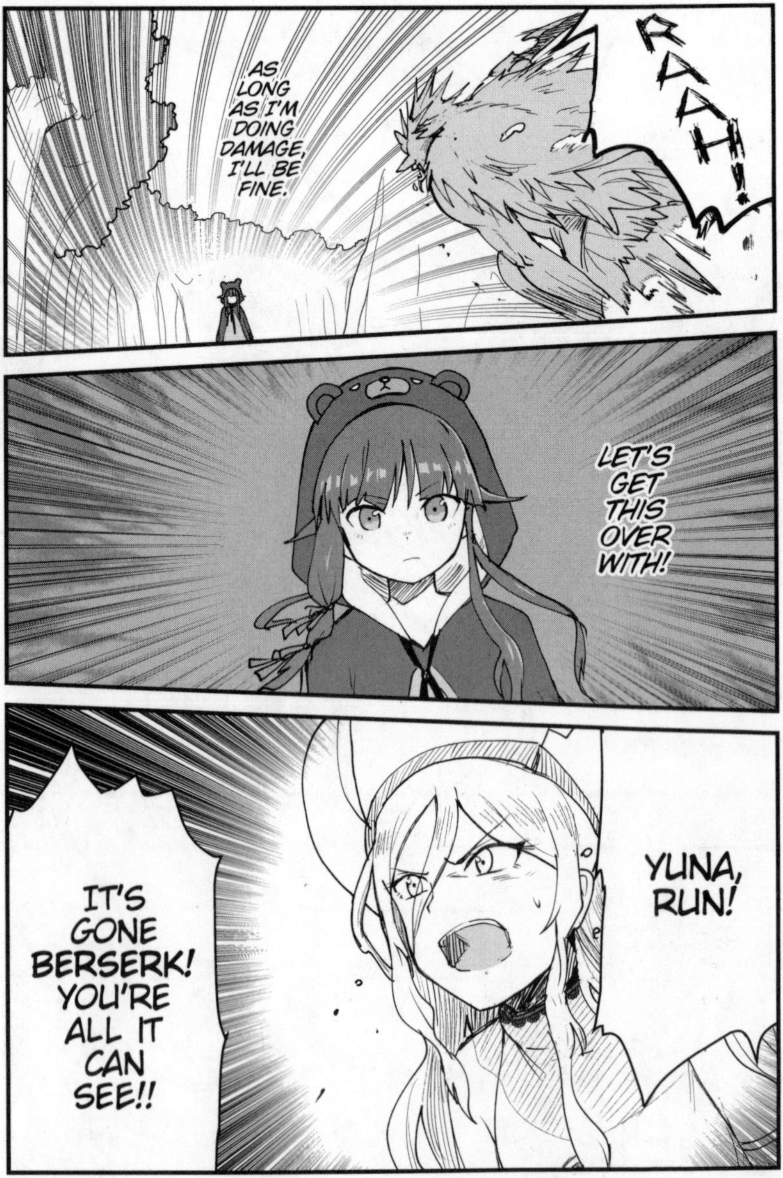
RAAH!
AS LONG AS I'M DOING DAMAGE, I'LL BE FINE.
LET'S GET THIS OVER WITH!
YUNA, RUN!
IT'S GONE BERSERK! YOU'RE ALL IT CAN SEE!!

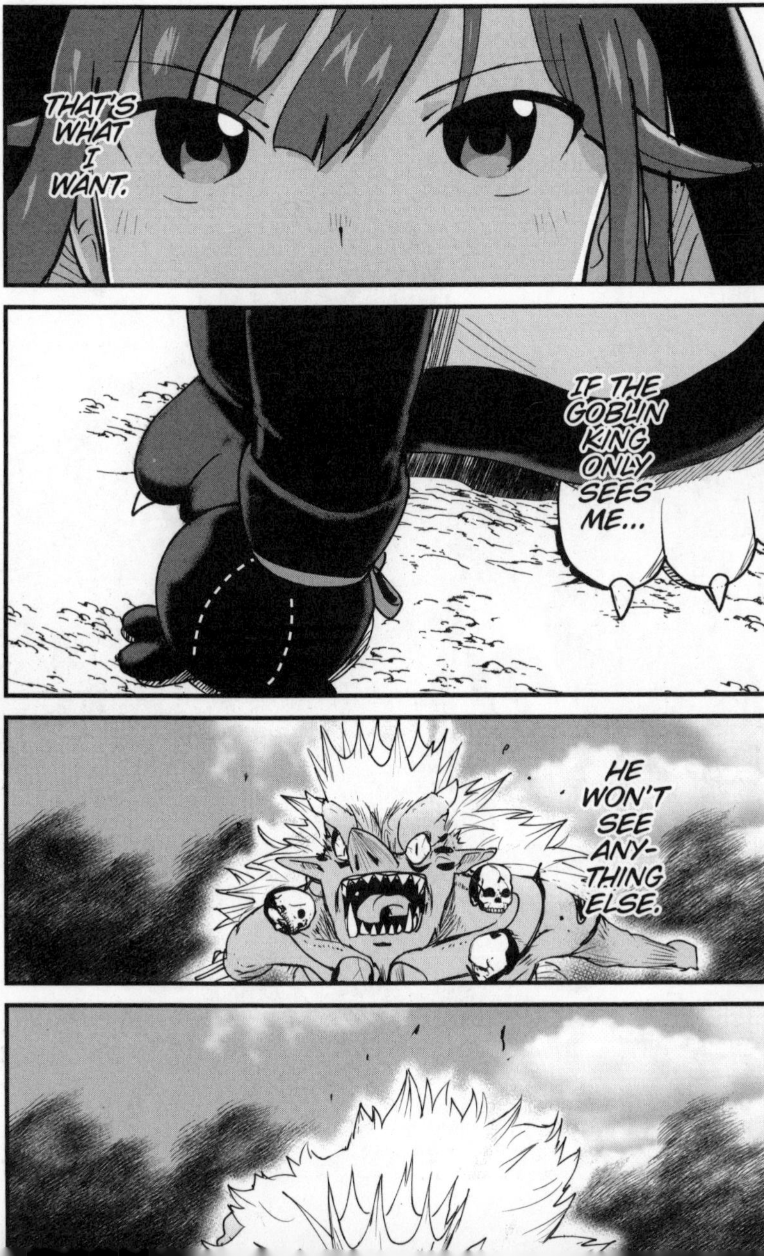
THAT'S WHAT I WANT.
IF THE GOBLIN KING ONLY SEES ME...
HE WON'T SEE ANYTHING ELSE.

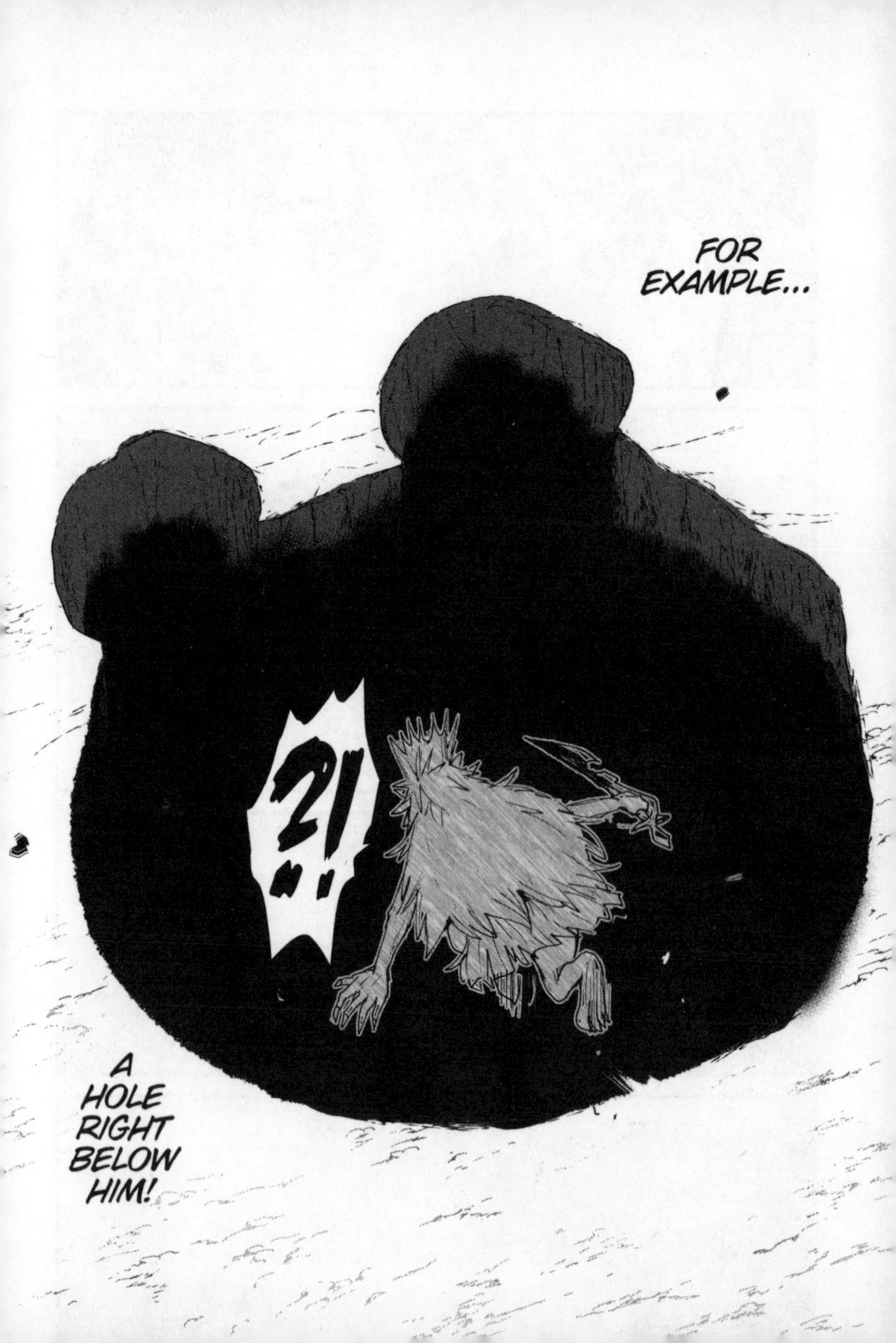
FOR EXAMPLE...
?!
A HOLE RIGHT BELOW HIM!

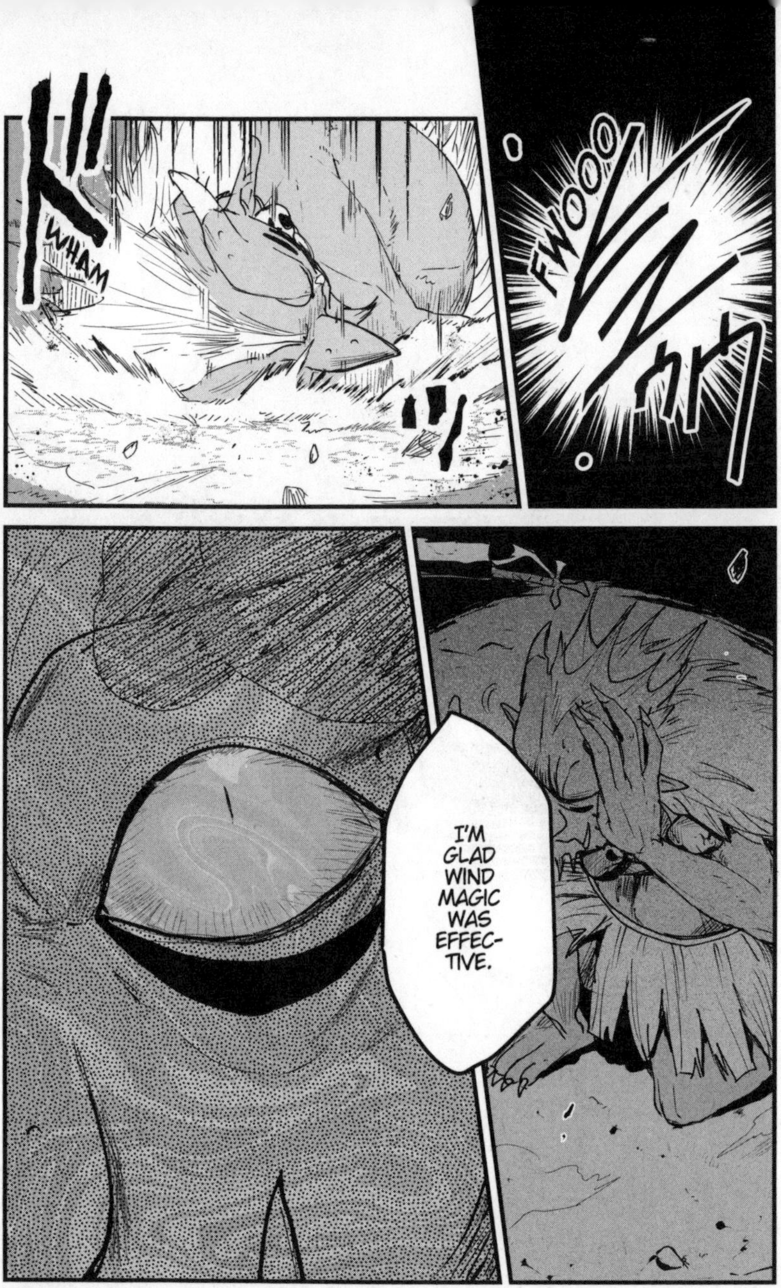
FWOOOM
WHAM
I'M GLAD WIND MAGIC WAS EFFECTIVE.

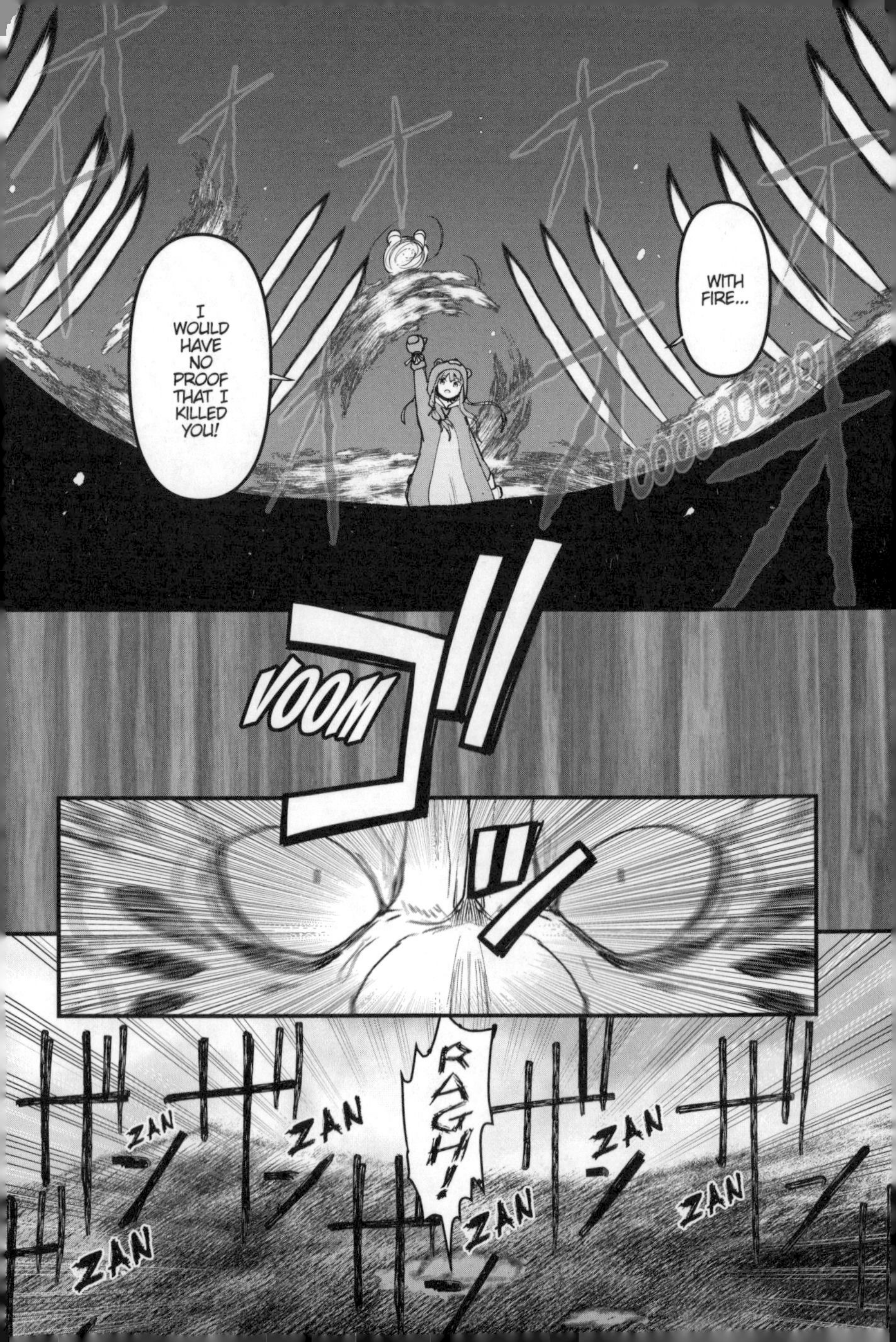
WITH FIRE...
I WOULD HAVE NO PROOF THAT I KILLED YOU!
VOOM
RAGH!
ZAN
ZAN
ZAN
ZAN
ZAN
ZAN
ZAN

......
I CAN'T BELIEVE YOU KILLED A GOBLIN KING!
WOW!
I WAS SURPRISED BY HOW STRONG IT WAS.
STEP BACK. I'LL FILL IN THE HOLE.

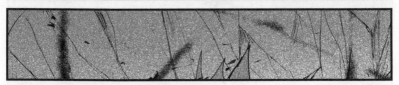

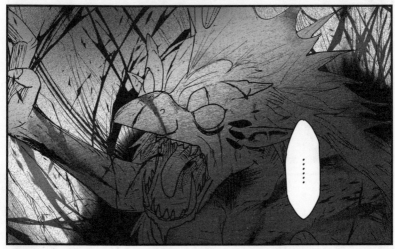

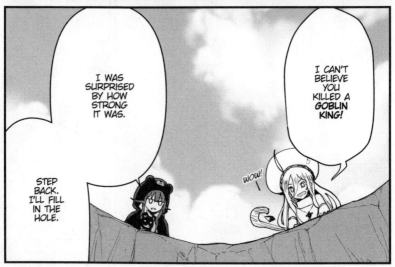

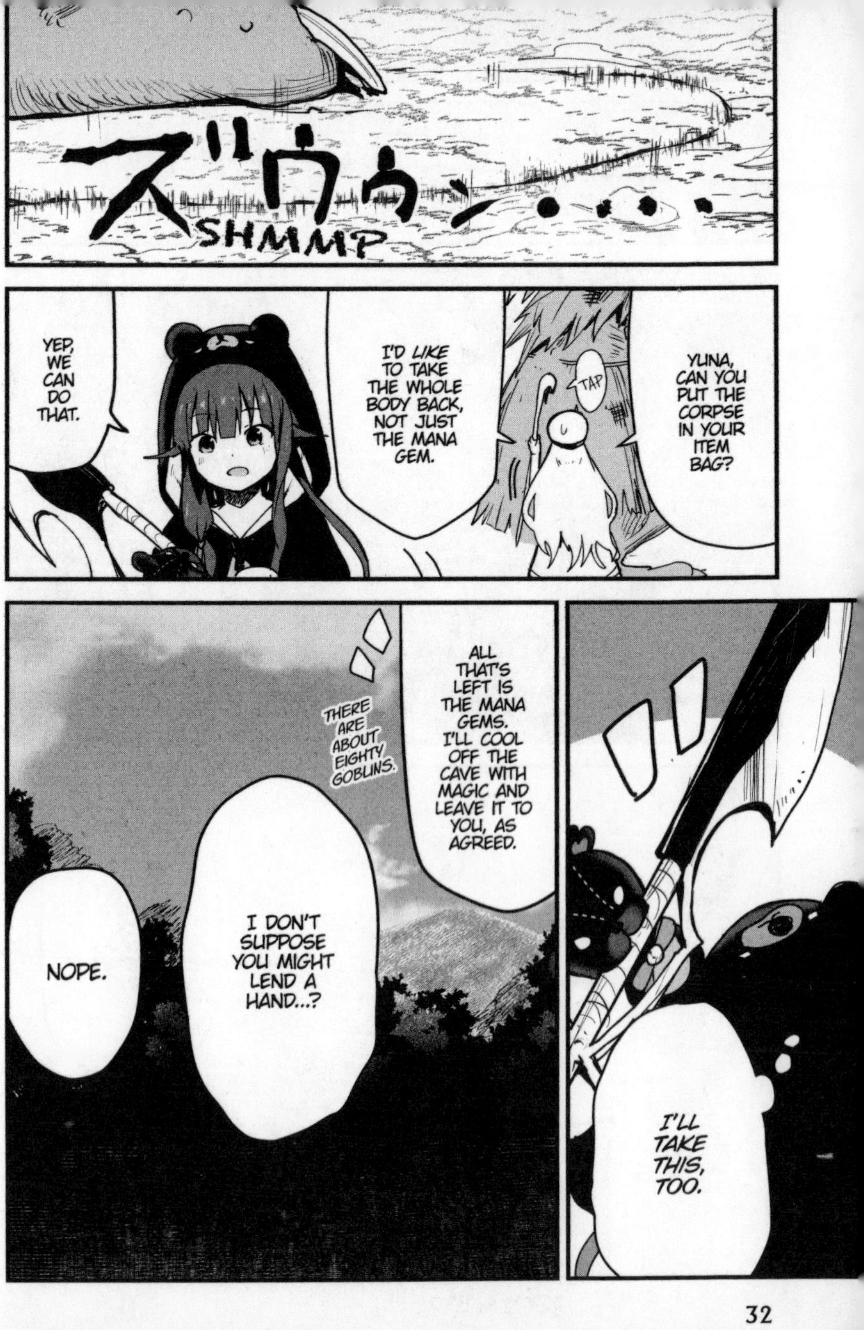
SHMMP
YUNA, CAN YOU PUT THE CORPSE IN YOUR ITEM BAG?
TAP
I'D *LIKE* TO TAKE THE WHOLE BODY BACK, NOT JUST THE MANA GEM.
YEP, WE CAN DO THAT.
I'LL TAKE THIS, TOO.
ALL THAT'S LEFT IS THE MANA GEMS. I'LL COOL OFF THE CAVE WITH MAGIC AND LEAVE IT TO YOU, AS AGREED.
THERE ARE ABOUT EIGHTY GOBLINS.
I DON'T SUPPOSE YOU MIGHT LEND A HAND...?
NOPE.

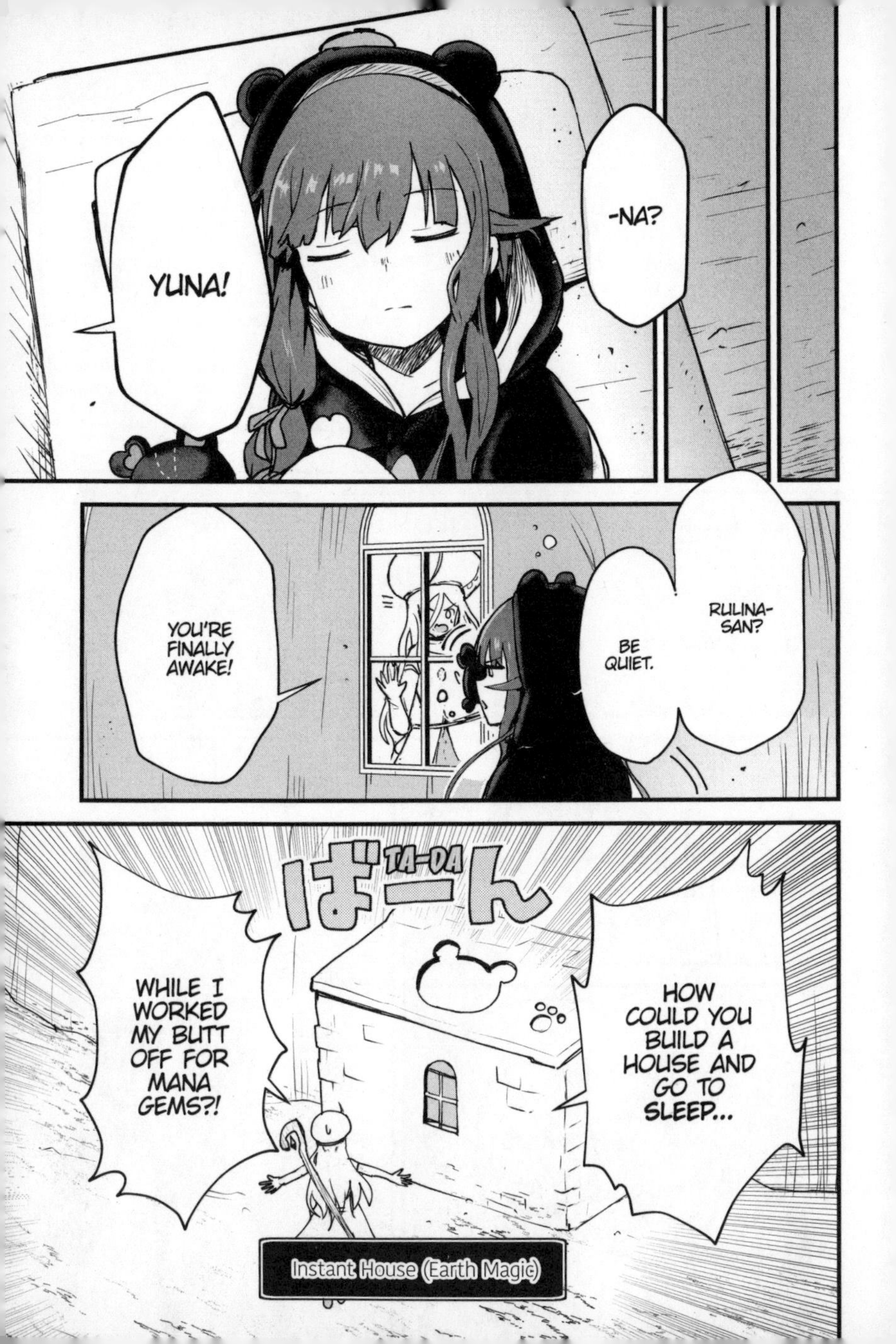
-NA?
YUNA!
RULINA-SAN?
BE QUIET.
YOU'RE FINALLY AWAKE!
ばーん
TA-DA
HOW COULD YOU BUILD A HOUSE AND GO TO SLEEP...
WHILE I WORKED MY BUTT OFF FOR MANA GEMS?!
Instant House (Earth Magic)

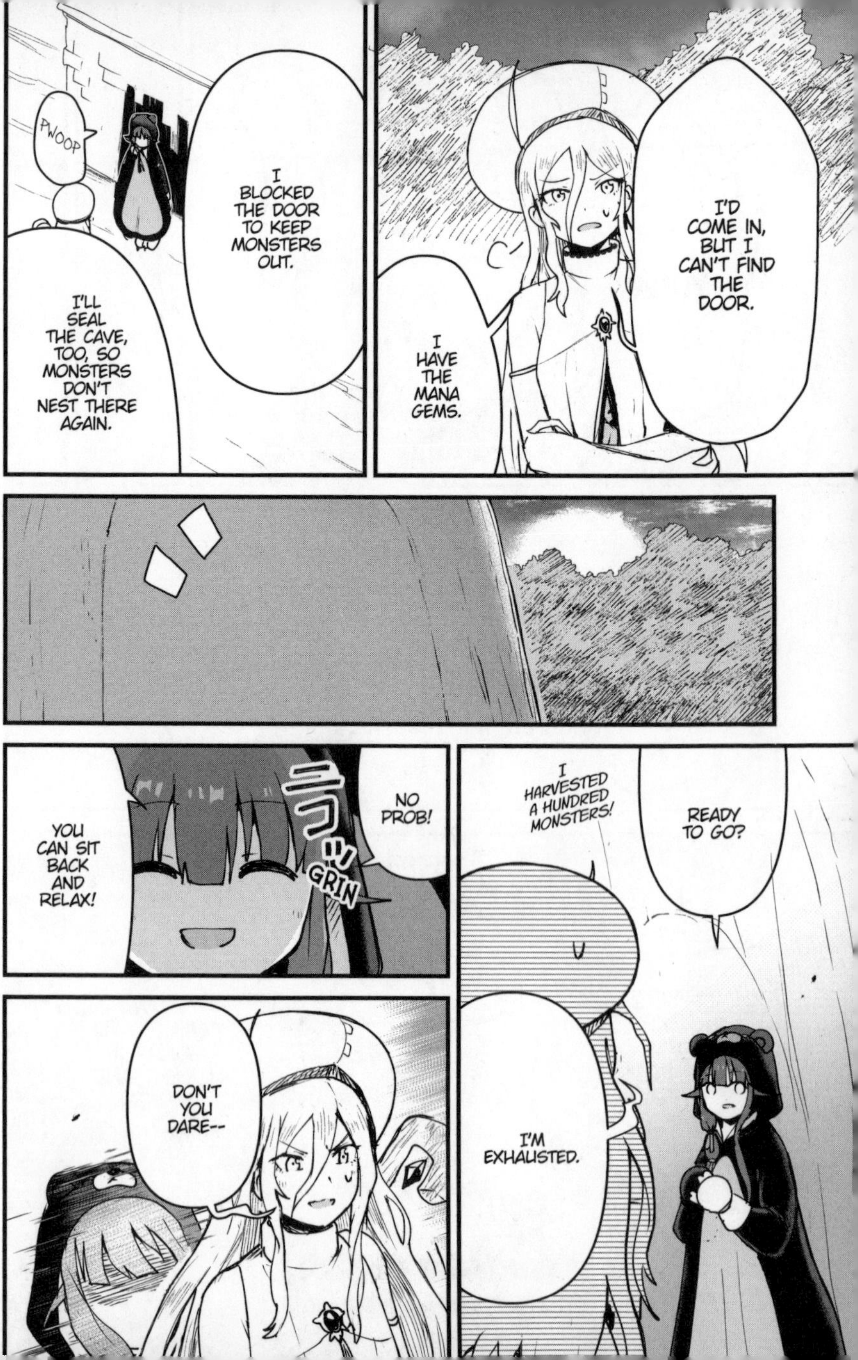
I'D COME IN, BUT I CAN'T FIND THE DOOR.
I HAVE THE MANA GEMS.
I BLOCKED THE DOOR TO KEEP MONSTERS OUT.
PWOOP
I'LL SEAL THE CAVE, TOO, SO MONSTERS DON'T NEST THERE AGAIN.
READY TO GO?
I HARVESTED A HUNDRED MONSTERS!
I'M EXHAUSTED.
NO PROB!
GRIN
YOU CAN SIT BACK AND RELAX!
DON'T YOU DARE--

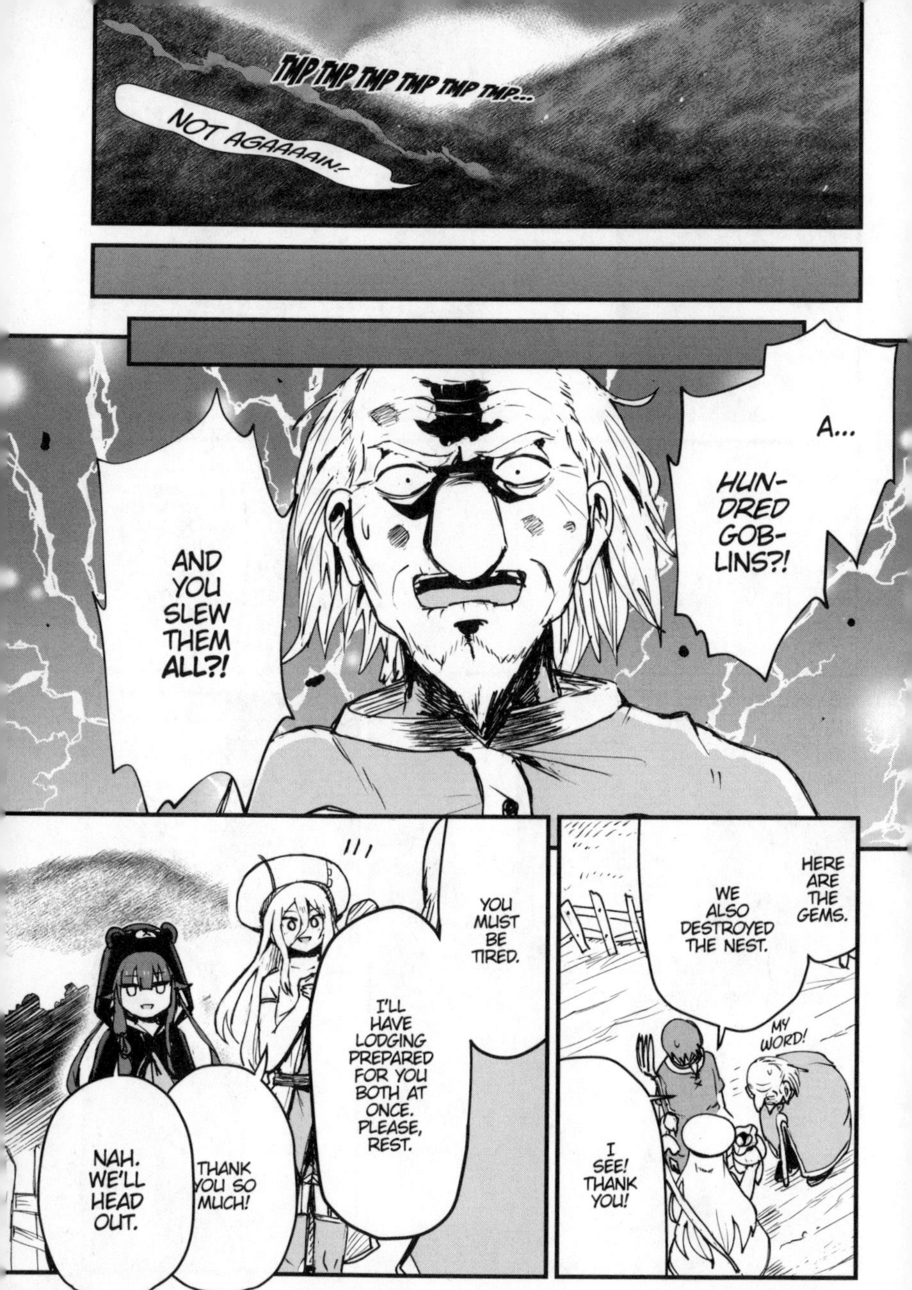
TMP TMP TMP TMP TMP TMP...
NOT AGAAAAAIN!
A... HUN-DRED GOB-LINS?!
AND YOU SLEW THEM ALL?!
HERE ARE THE GEMS.
WE ALSO DESTROYED THE NEST.
MY WORD!
I SEE! THANK YOU!
YOU MUST BE TIRED.
I'LL HAVE LODGING PREPARED FOR YOU BOTH AT ONCE. PLEASE, REST.
THANK YOU SO MUCH!
NAH. WE'LL HEAD OUT.

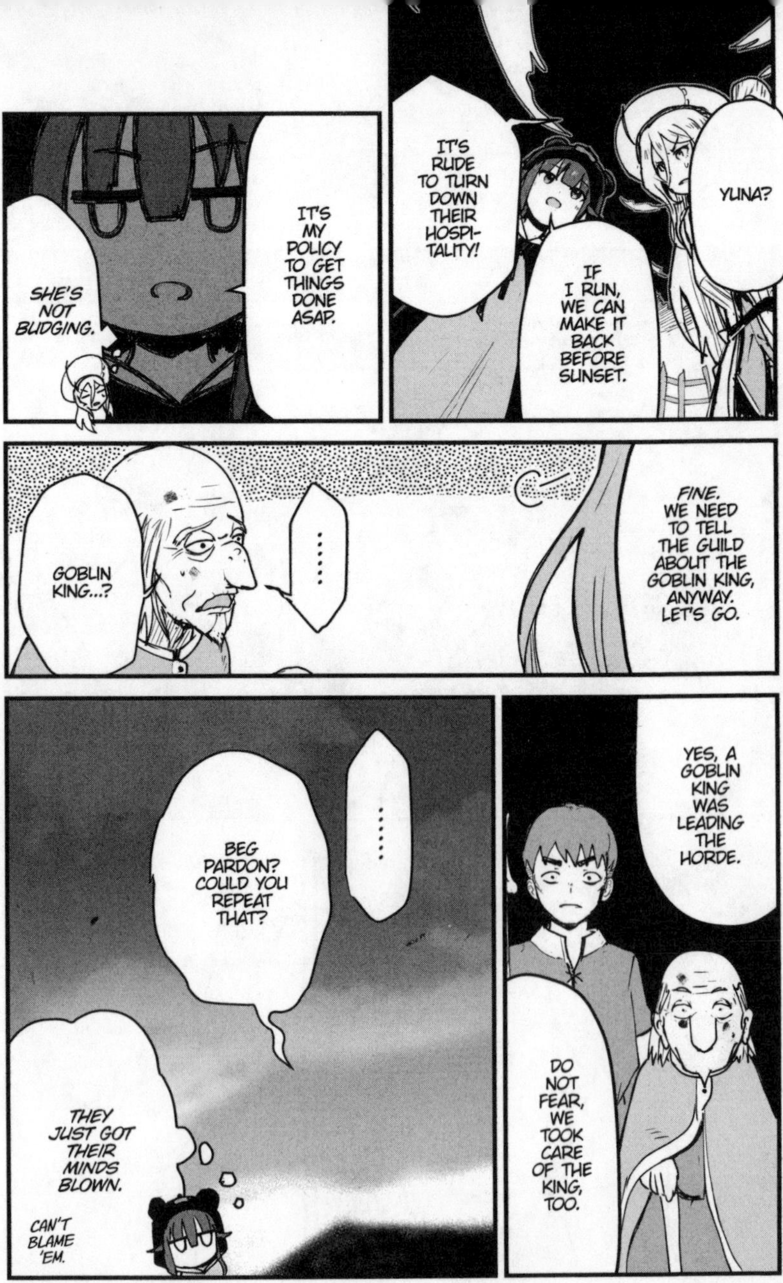
YUNA?
IT'S RUDE TO TURN DOWN THEIR HOSPITALITY!
IF I RUN, WE CAN MAKE IT BACK BEFORE SUNSET.
IT'S MY POLICY TO GET THINGS DONE ASAP.
SHE'S NOT BUDGING.
FINE. WE NEED TO TELL THE GUILD ABOUT THE GOBLIN KING, ANYWAY. LET'S GO.
......
GOBLIN KING...?
YES, A GOBLIN KING WAS LEADING THE HORDE.
DO NOT FEAR, WE TOOK CARE OF THE KING, TOO.
......
BEG PARDON? COULD YOU REPEAT THAT?
THEY JUST GOT THEIR MINDS BLOWN.
CAN'T BLAME 'EM.

Chapter 13

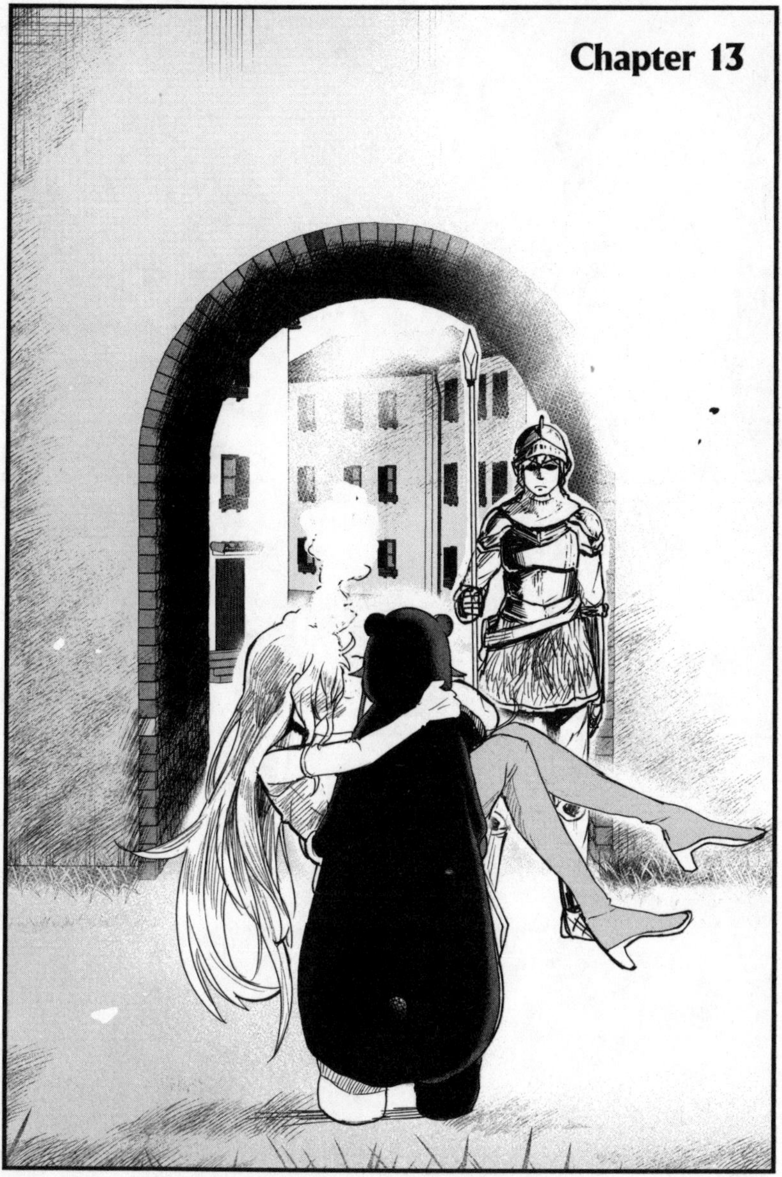

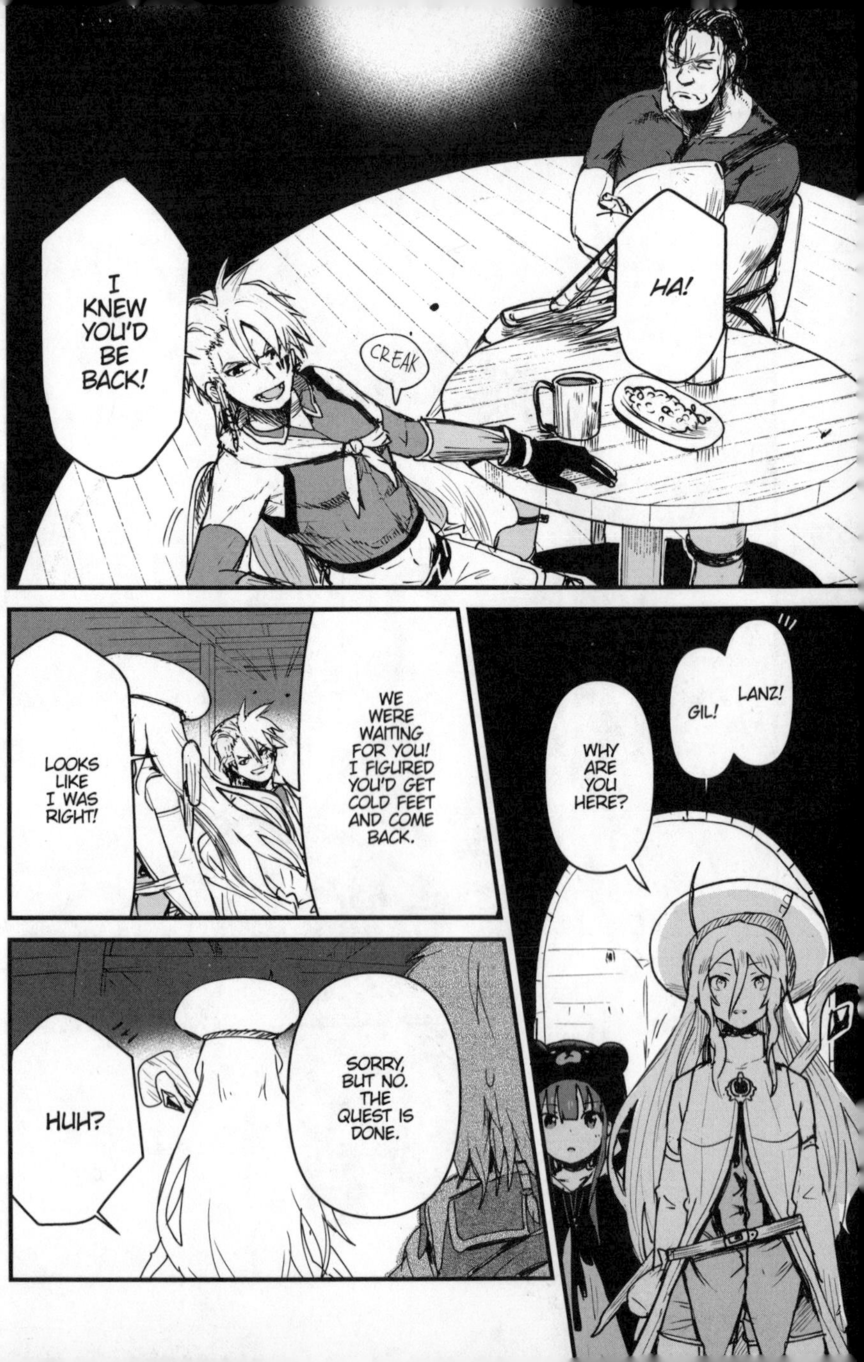
HA!
CREAK
I KNEW YOU'D BE BACK!
LANZ!
GIL!
WHY ARE YOU HERE?
WE WERE WAITING FOR YOU! I FIGURED YOU'D GET COLD FEET AND COME BACK.
LOOKS LIKE I WAS RIGHT!
SORRY, BUT NO. THE QUEST IS DONE.
HUH?

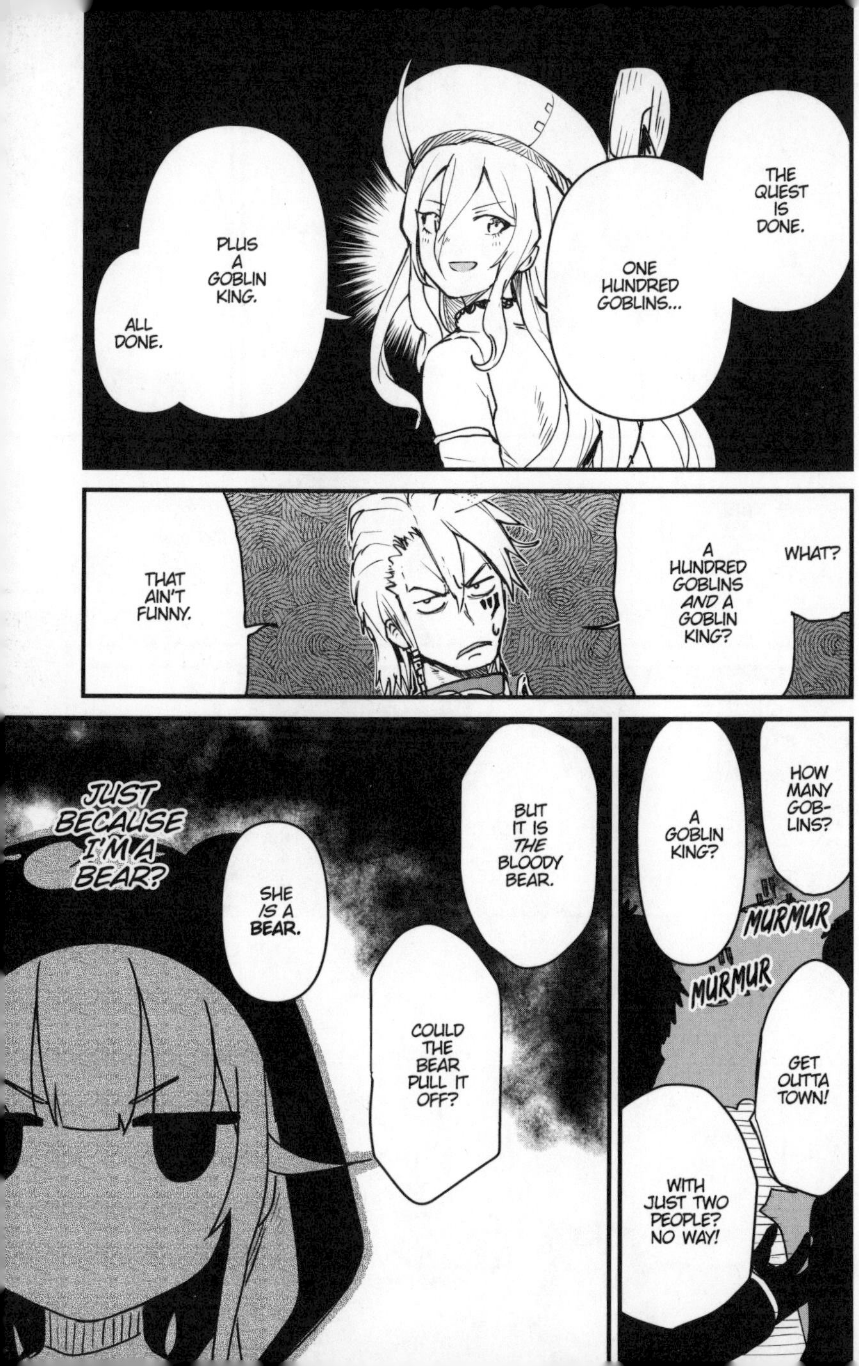
THE QUEST IS DONE.
ONE HUNDRED GOBLINS...
PLUS A GOBLIN KING.
ALL DONE.
WHAT?
A HUNDRED GOBLINS AND A GOBLIN KING?
THAT AIN'T FUNNY.
HOW MANY GOB-LINS?
A GOBLIN KING?
MURMUR
MURMUR
GET OUTTA TOWN!
WITH JUST TWO PEOPLE? NO WAY!
BUT IT IS THE BLOODY BEAR.
SHE IS A BEAR.
COULD THE BEAR PULL IT OFF?
JUST BECAUSE I'M A BEAR?

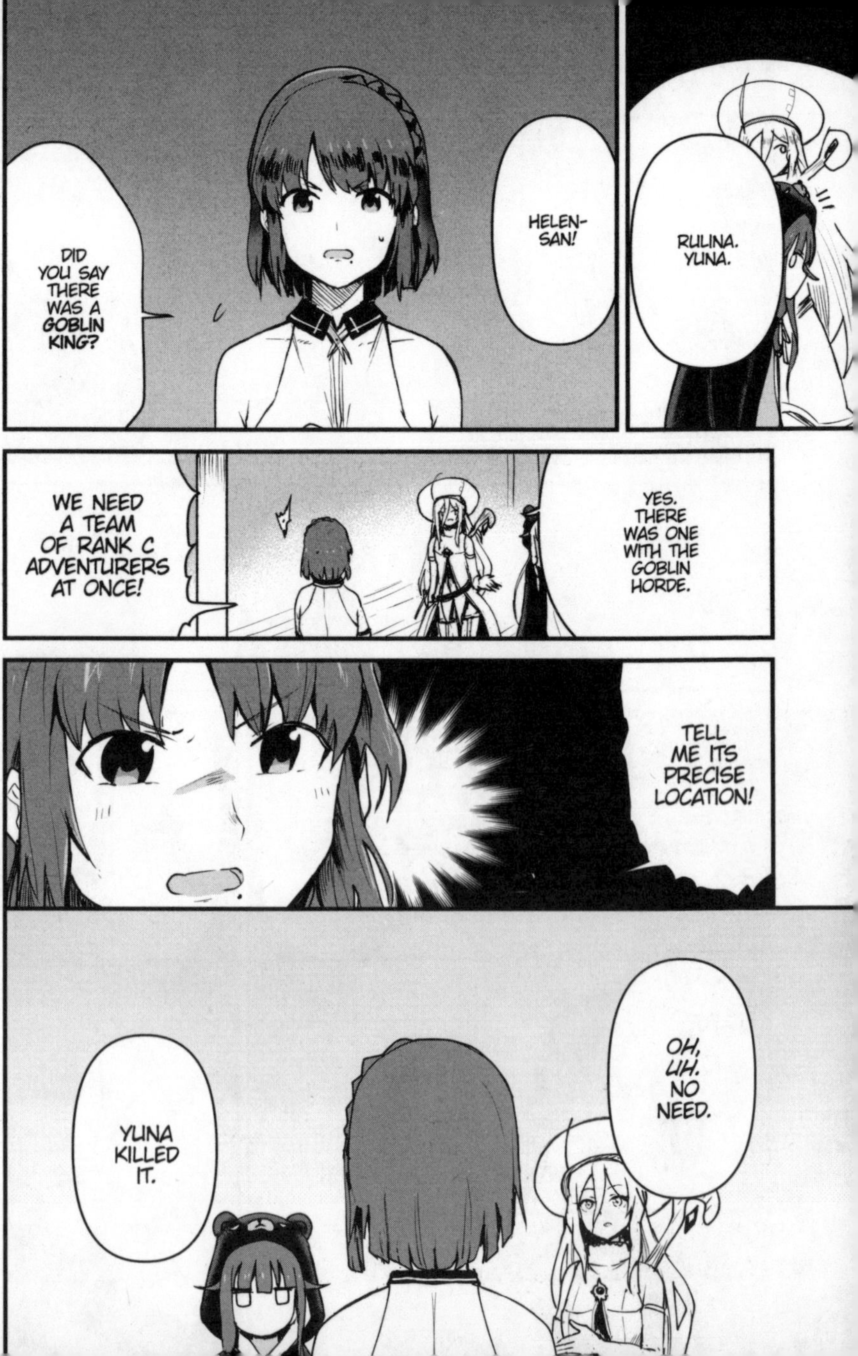
RULINA. YUNA.
HELEN-SAN!
DID YOU SAY THERE WAS A GOBLIN KING?
YES. THERE WAS ONE WITH THE GOBLIN HORDE.
WE NEED A TEAM OF RANK C ADVENTURERS AT ONCE!
TELL ME ITS PRECISE LOCATION!
OH, UH. NO NEED.
YUNA KILLED IT.

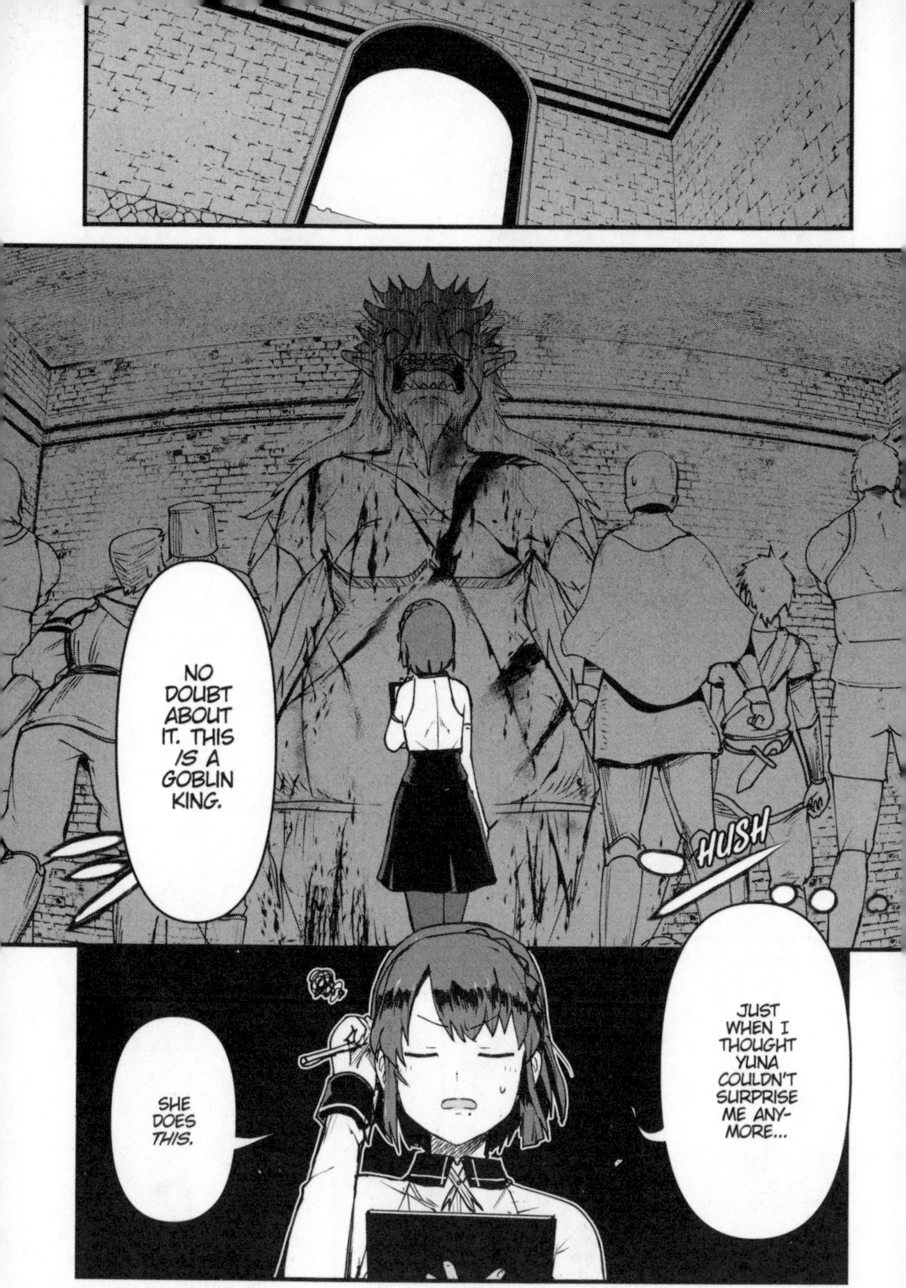
HUSH
NO DOUBT ABOUT IT. THIS IS A GOBLIN KING.
JUST WHEN I THOUGHT YUNA COULDN'T SURPRISE ME ANY-MORE...
SHE DOES THIS.

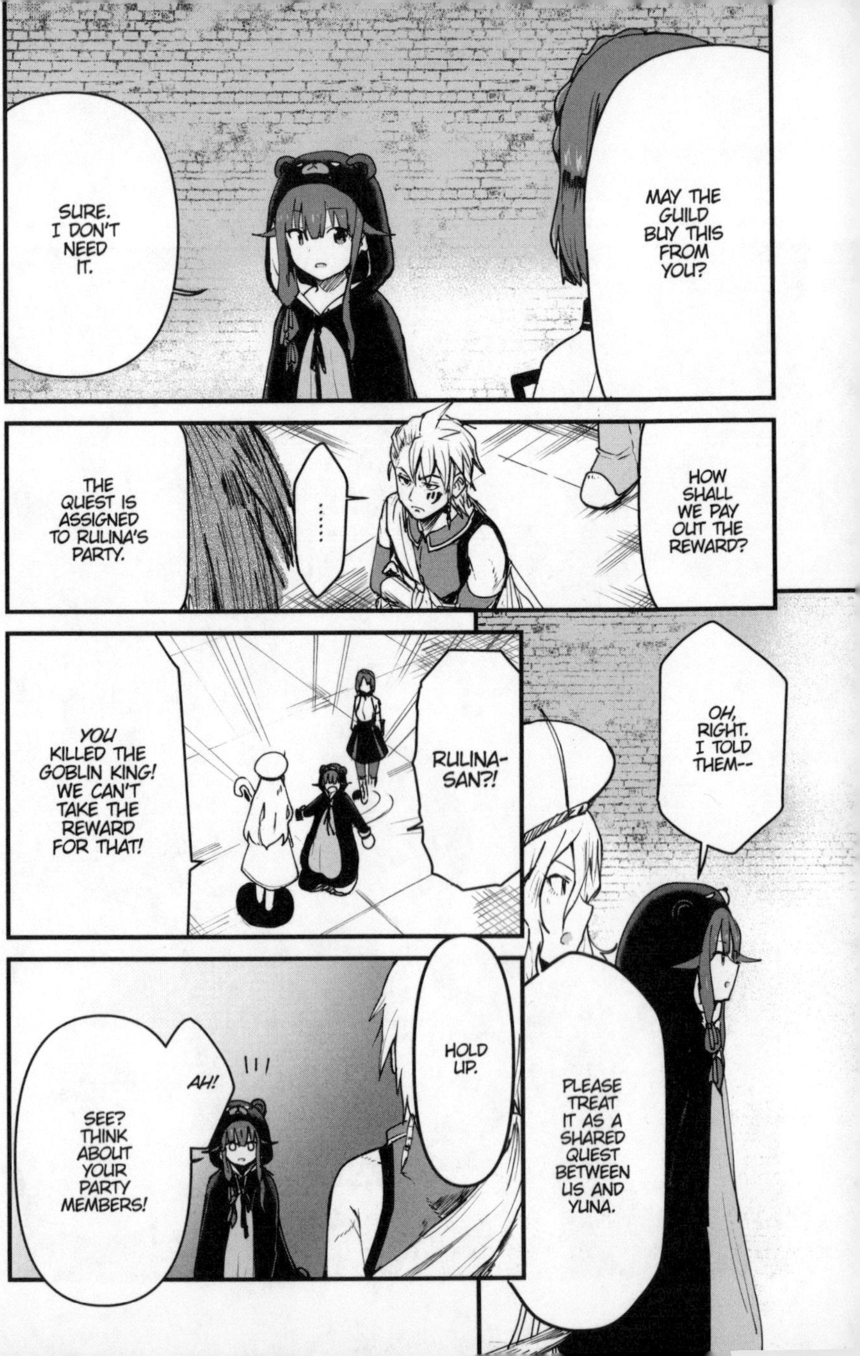
MAY THE GUILD BUY THIS FROM YOU?
SURE. I DON'T NEED IT.
HOW SHALL WE PAY OUT THE REWARD?
......
THE QUEST IS ASSIGNED TO RULINA'S PARTY.
OH, RIGHT. I TOLD THEM--
RULINA-SAN?!
YOU KILLED THE GOBLIN KING! WE CAN'T TAKE THE REWARD FOR THAT!
HOLD UP.
PLEASE TREAT IT AS A SHARED QUEST BETWEEN US AND YUNA.
AH!
SEE? THINK ABOUT YOUR PARTY MEMBERS!

I DON'T WANT MY CUT.

ALL I DID WAS SIT ON THE SIDELINES, THINKING SHE'D COME RUNNING BACK.

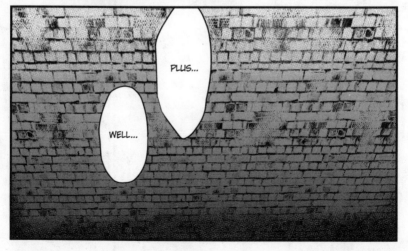

PLUS...

WELL...

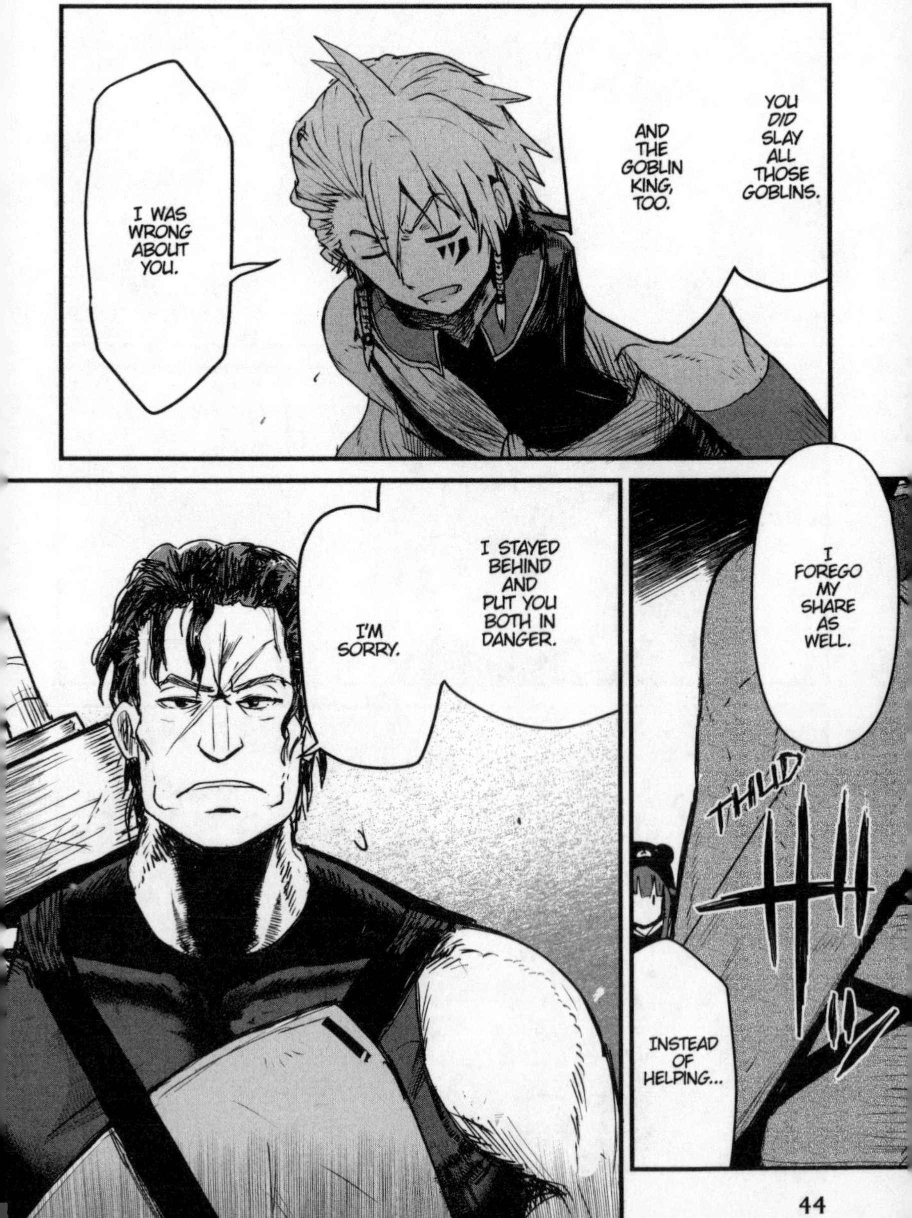
YOU DID SLAY ALL THOSE GOBLINS.
AND THE GOBLIN KING, TOO.
I WAS WRONG ABOUT YOU.
I FOREGO MY SHARE AS WELL.
THUD
INSTEAD OF HELPING...
I STAYED BEHIND AND PUT YOU BOTH IN DANGER.
I'M SORRY.

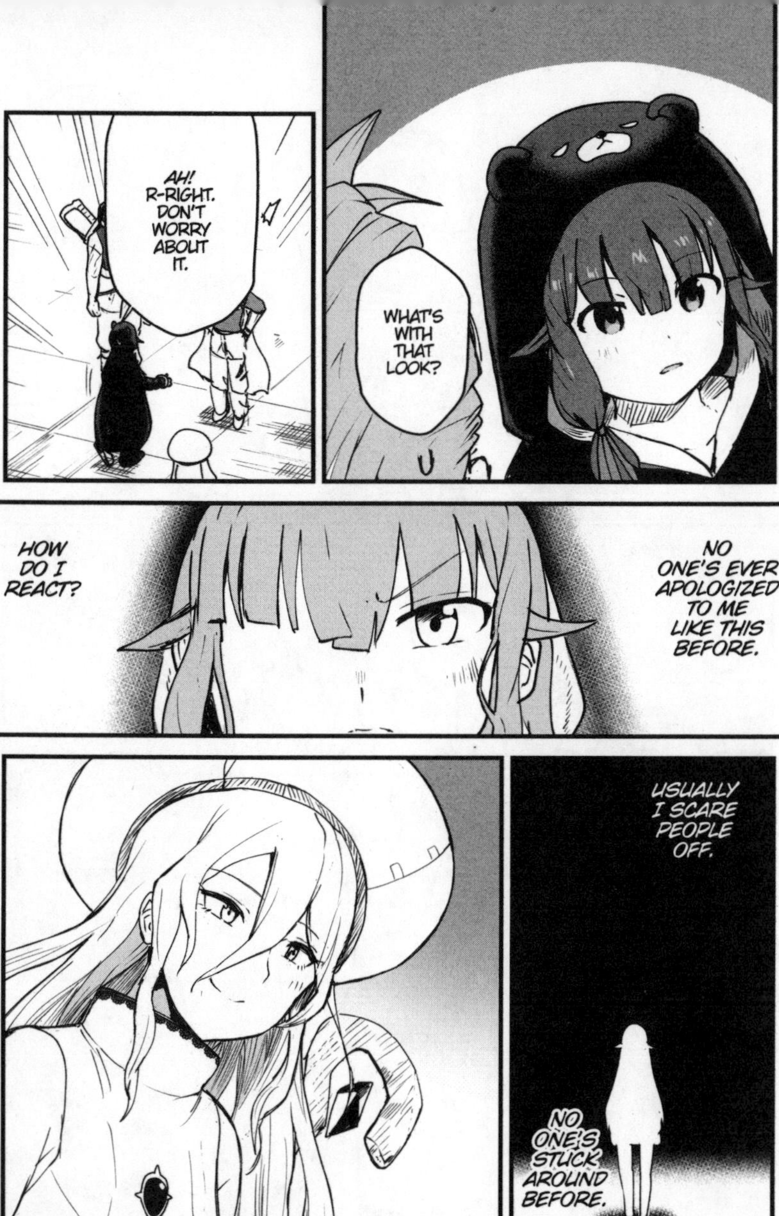
WHAT'S WITH THAT LOOK?
AH! R-RIGHT. DON'T WORRY ABOUT IT.
NO ONE'S EVER APOLOGIZED TO ME LIKE THIS BEFORE.
HOW DO I REACT?
USUALLY I SCARE PEOPLE OFF.
NO ONE'S STUCK AROUND BEFORE.

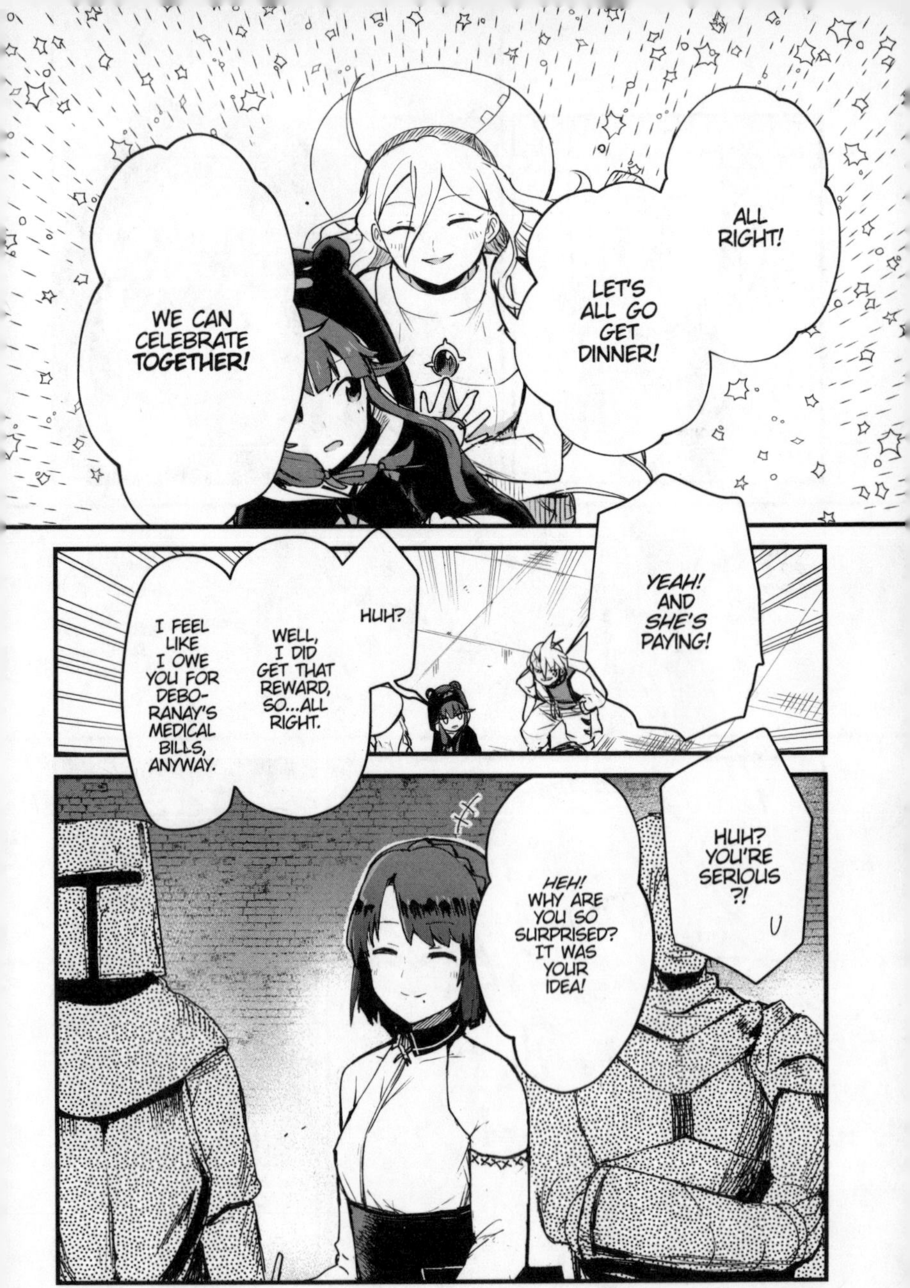
ALL RIGHT!
LET'S ALL GO GET DINNER!
WE CAN CELEBRATE TOGETHER!
YEAH! AND SHE'S PAYING!
HUH?
WELL, I DID GET THAT REWARD, SO...ALL RIGHT.
I FEEL LIKE I OWE YOU FOR DEBO-RANAY'S MEDICAL BILLS, ANYWAY.
HUH? YOU'RE SERIOUS?!
HEH! WHY ARE YOU SO SURPRISED? IT WAS YOUR IDEA!

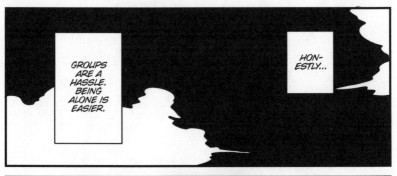

GROUPS ARE A HASSLE. BEING ALONE IS EASIER.

HON-ESTLY...

BUT...

EATING WITH PEOPLE LIKE THIS...

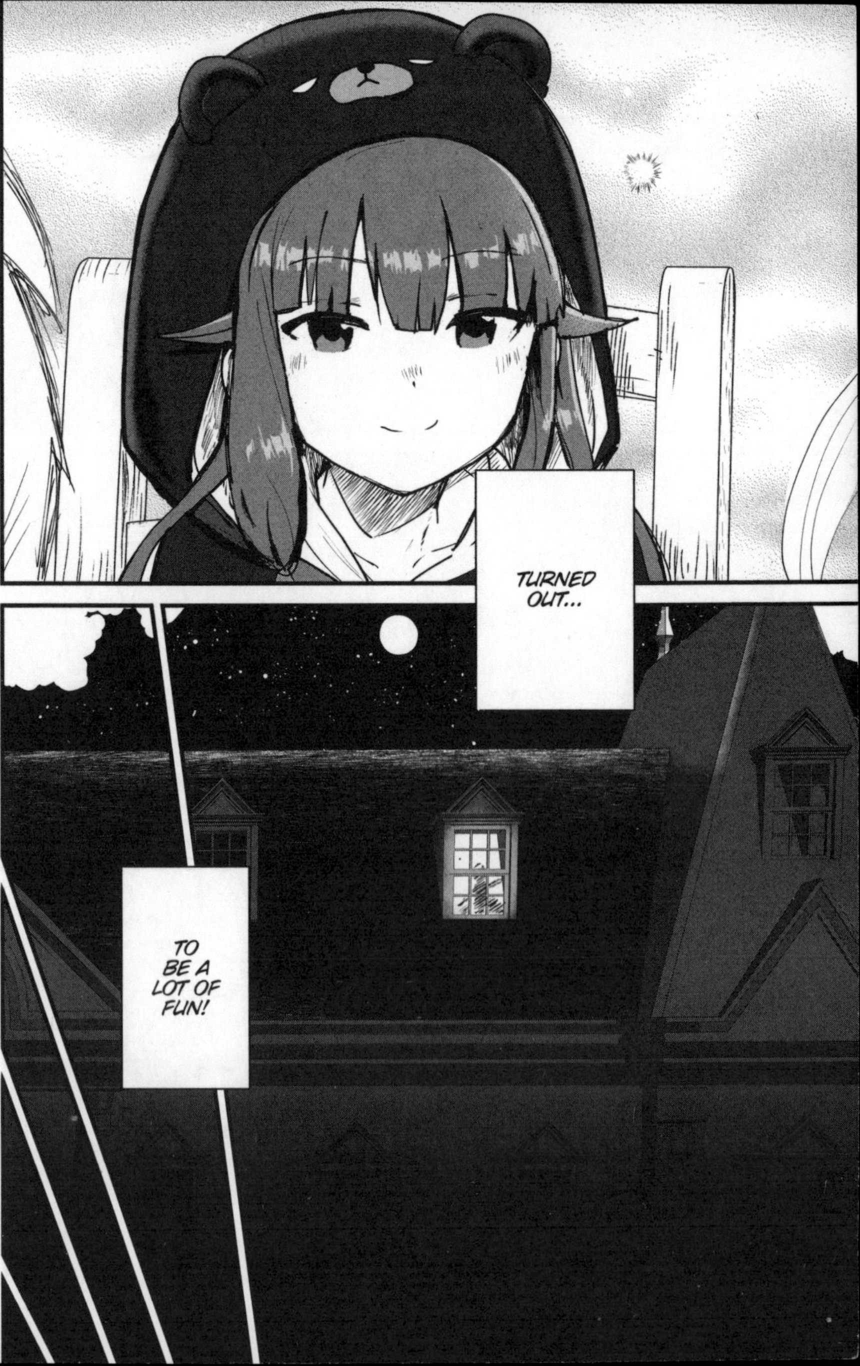
TURNED OUT...
TO BE A LOT OF FUN!

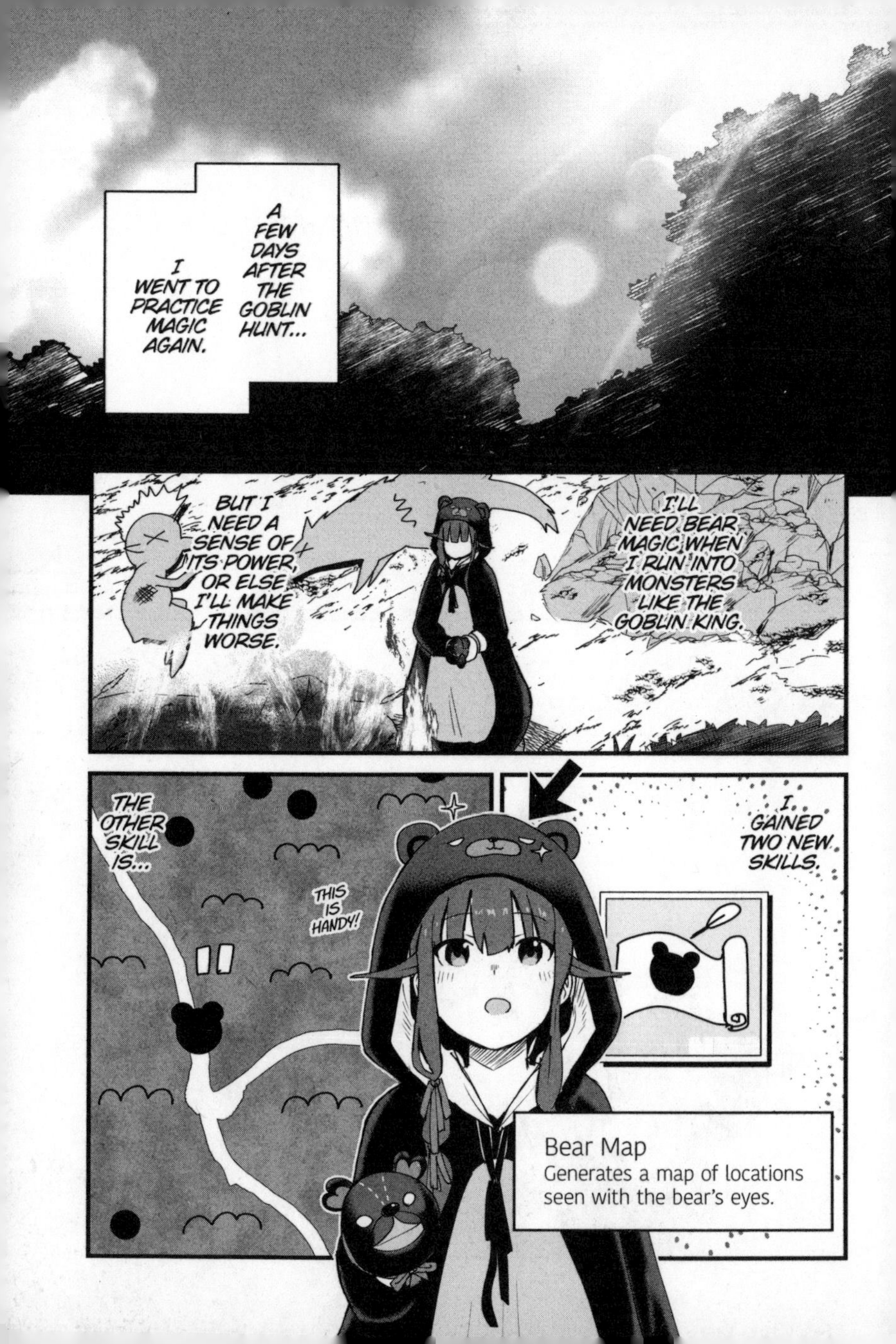
A FEW DAYS AFTER THE GOBLIN HUNT...
I WENT TO PRACTICE MAGIC AGAIN.
I'LL NEED BEAR MAGIC WHEN I RUN INTO MONSTERS LIKE THE GOBLIN KING.
BUT I NEED A SENSE OF ITS POWER, OR ELSE I'LL MAKE THINGS WORSE.
I GAINED TWO NEW SKILLS.
Bear Map
Generates a map of locations seen with the bear's eyes.
THE OTHER SKILL IS...
THIS IS HANDY!

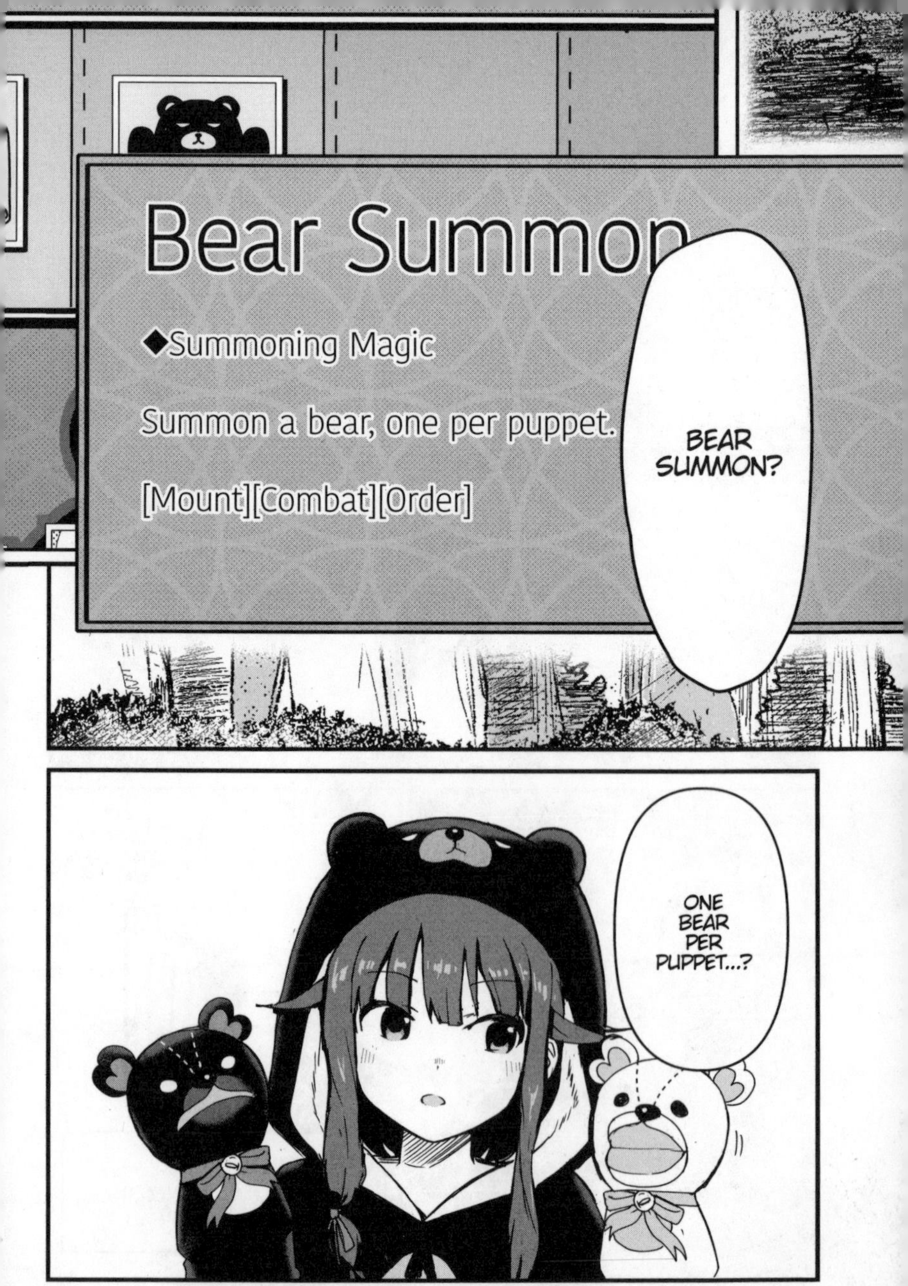
Bear Summon
◆Summoning Magic
Summon a bear, one per puppet.
[Mount][Combat][Order]
BEAR SUMMON?
ONE BEAR PER PUPPET...?

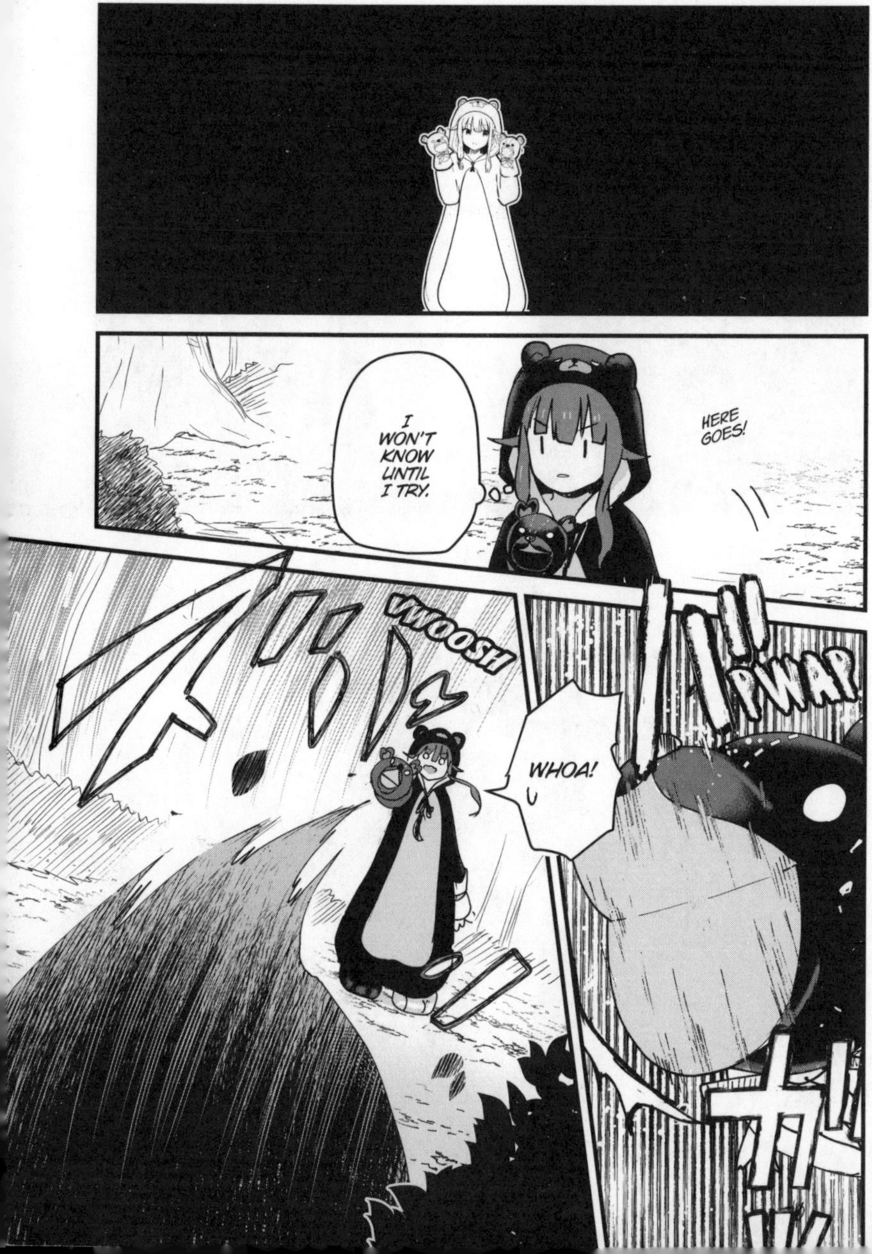
HERE GOES!
I WON'T KNOW UNTIL I TRY.
PWAP
WHOA!
VWOOSH

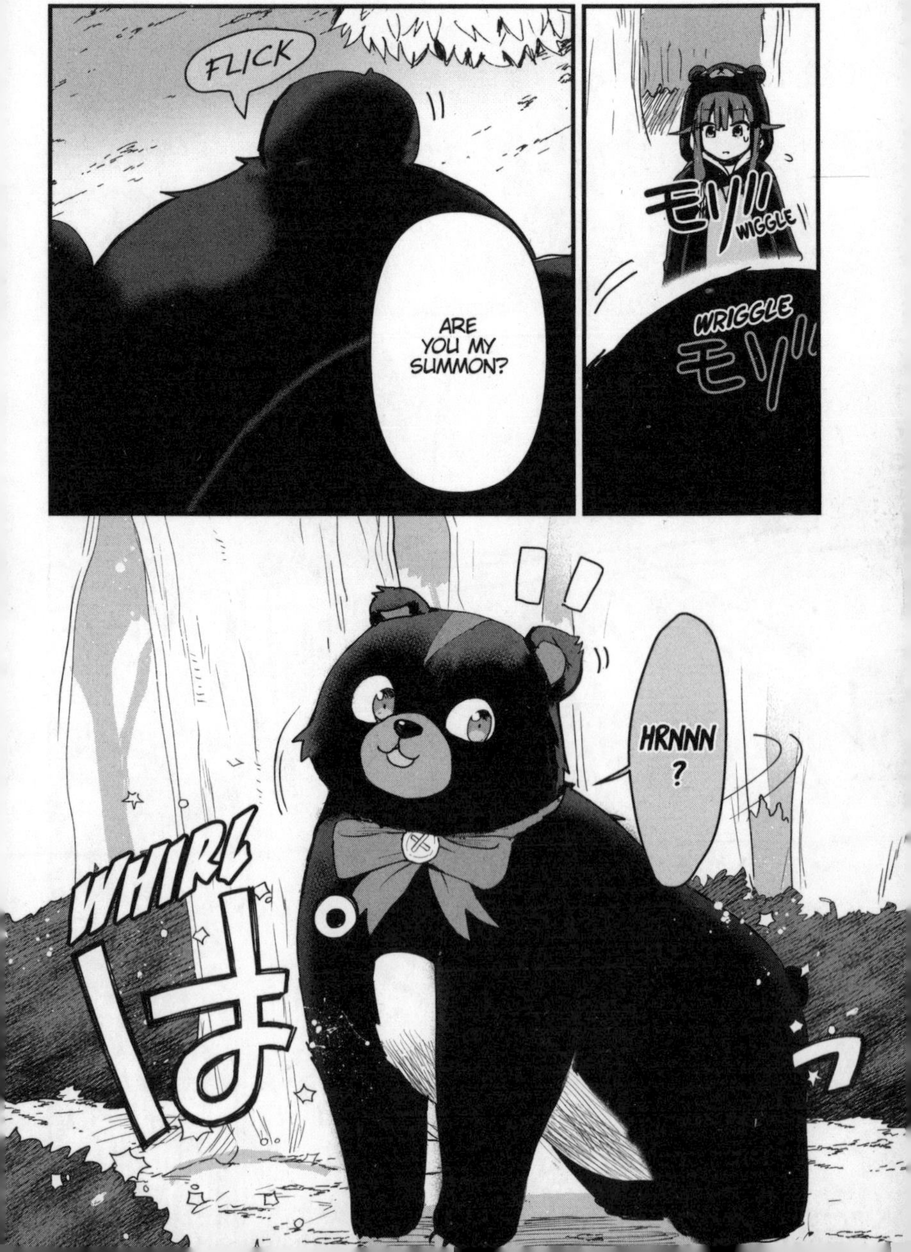
WIGGLE
WRIGGLE
FLICK
ARE YOU MY SUMMON?
HRNNN?
WHIRL

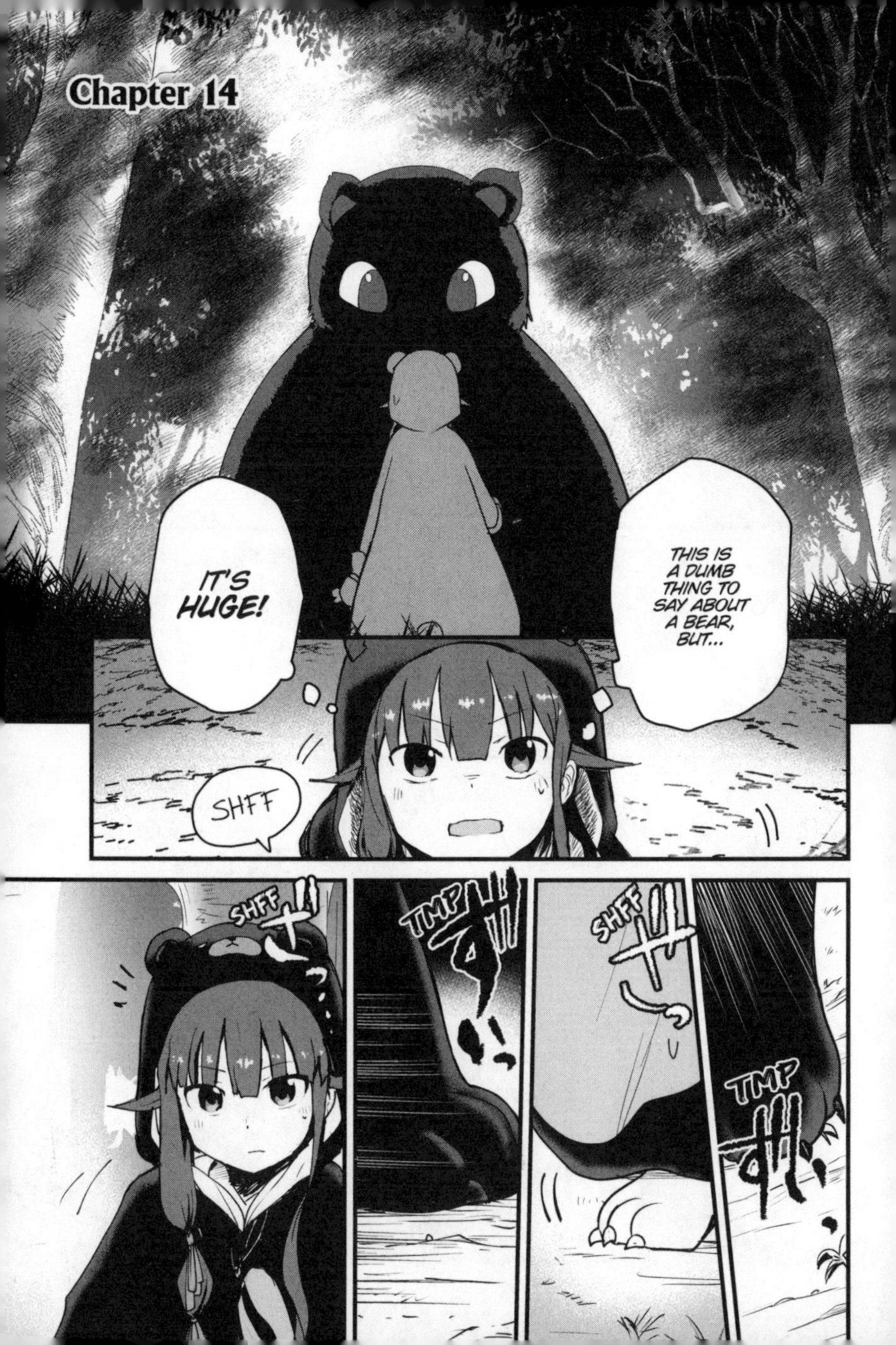
Chapter 14
THIS IS A DUMB THING TO SAY ABOUT A BEAR, BUT...
IT'S HUGE!
SHFF
SHFF
TMP
TMP
SHFF

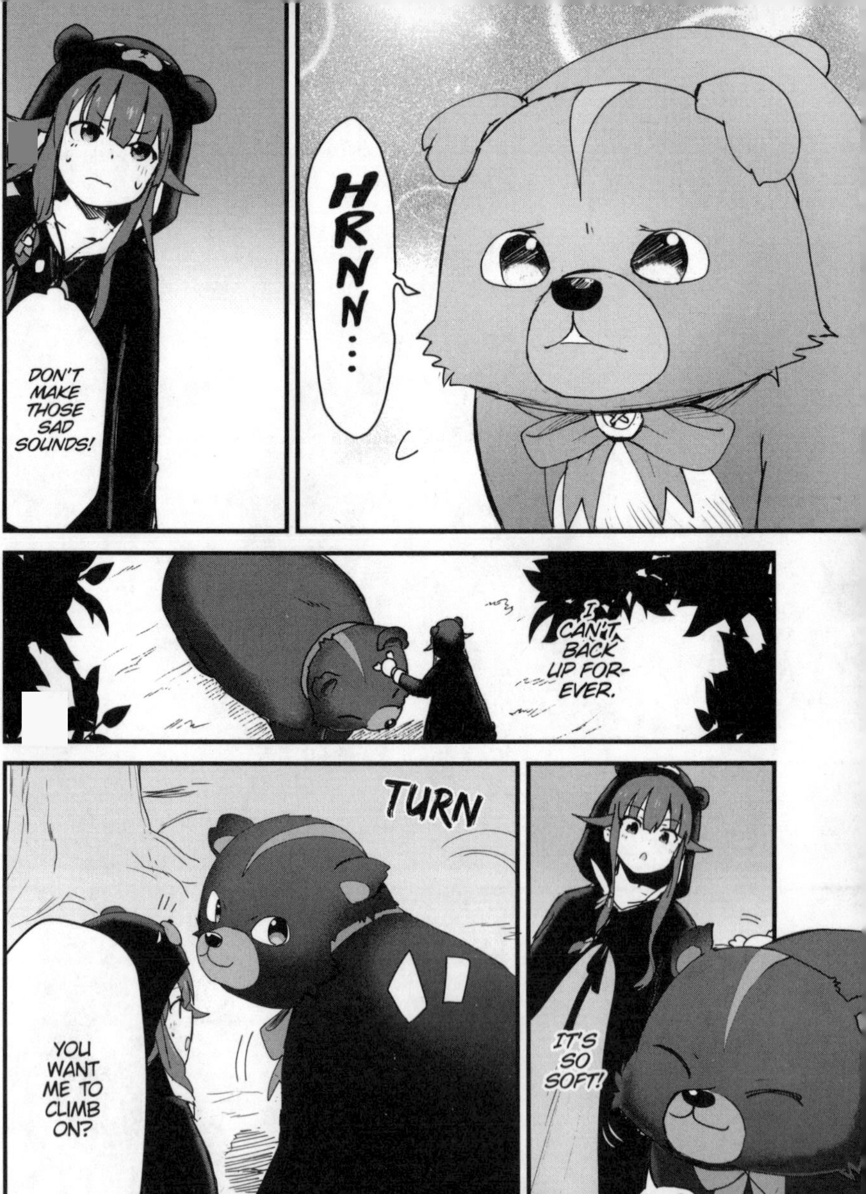
HRNN...
DON'T MAKE THOSE SAD SOUNDS!
I CAN'T BACK UP FOR-EVER.
IT'S SO SOFT!
RUB
TURN
YOU WANT ME TO CLIMB ON?

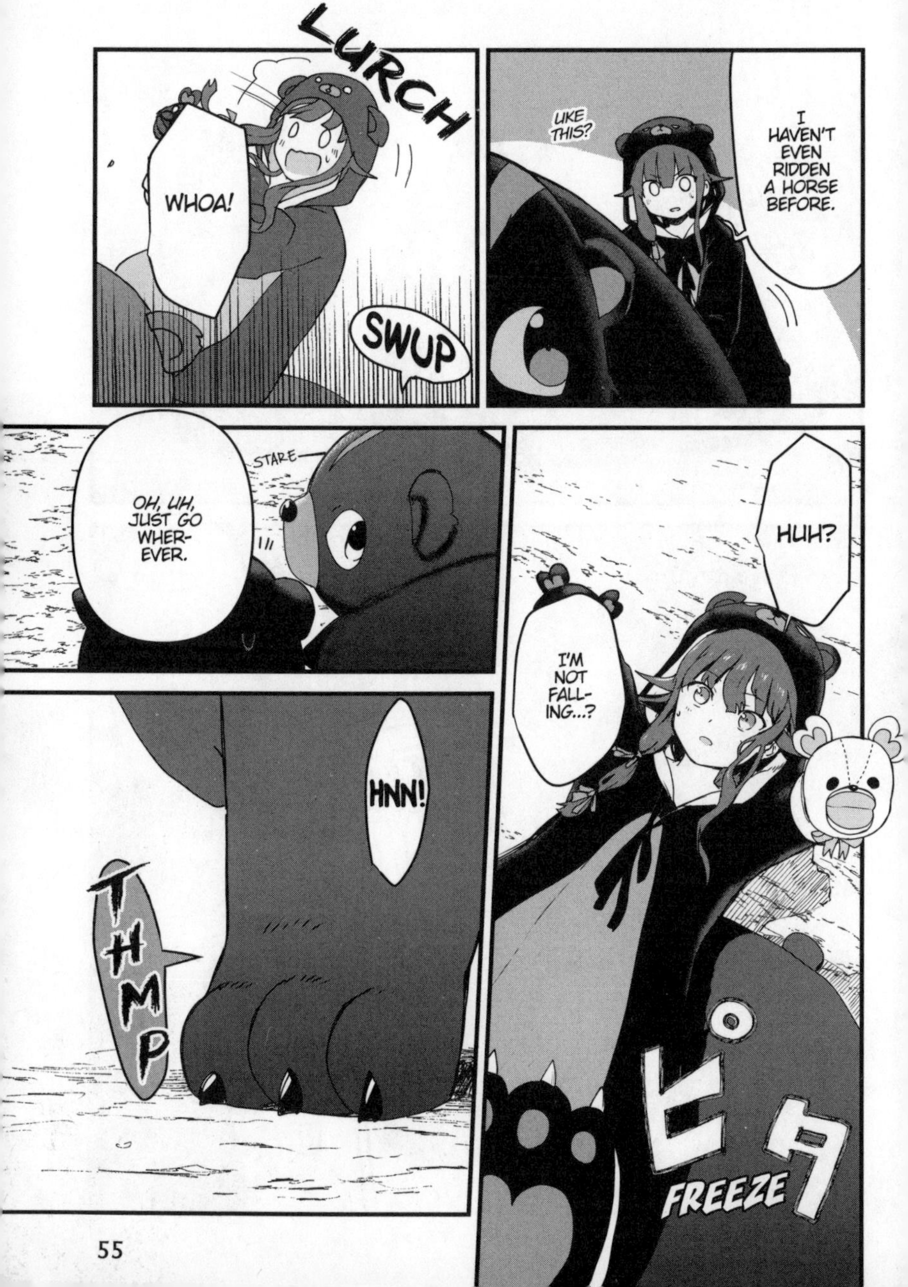
I HAVEN'T EVEN RIDDEN A HORSE BEFORE.
LIKE THIS?
LURCH
WHOA!
SWUP
HUH?
I'M NOT FALL-ING...?
ピタ
FREEZE
OH, UH, JUST GO WHER-EVER.
STARE
HNN!
THMP

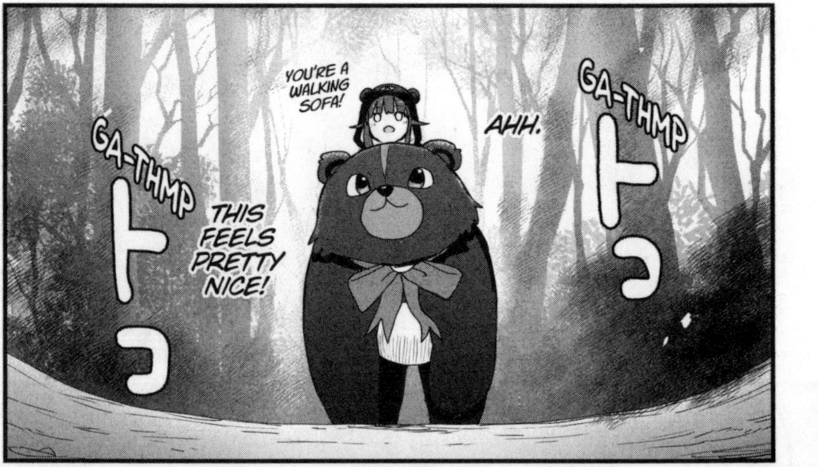
GA-THMP
トッ
AHH.
YOU'RE A WALKING SOFA!
THIS FEELS PRETTY NICE!
GA-THMP
トッ

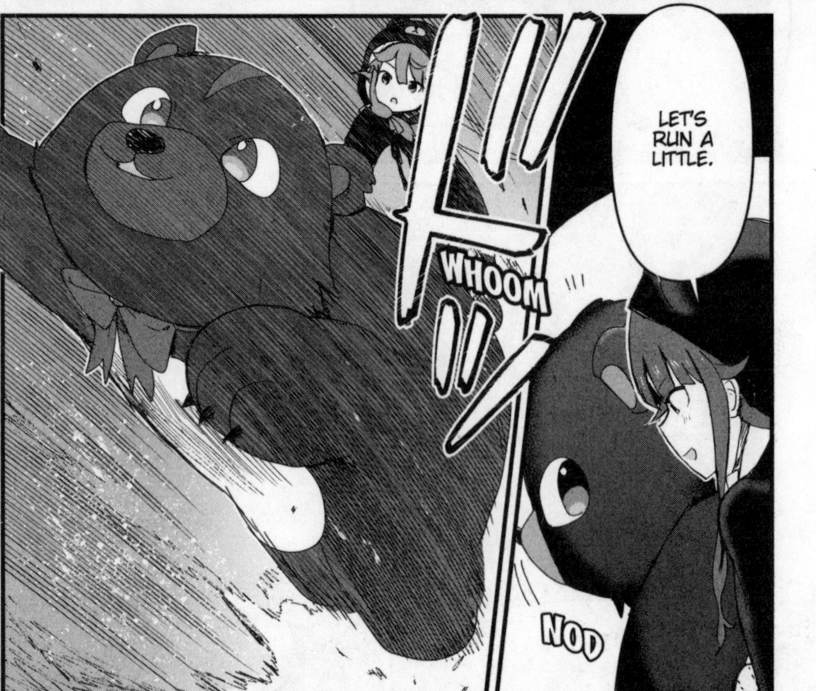
LET'S RUN A LITTLE.
NOD
WHOOM

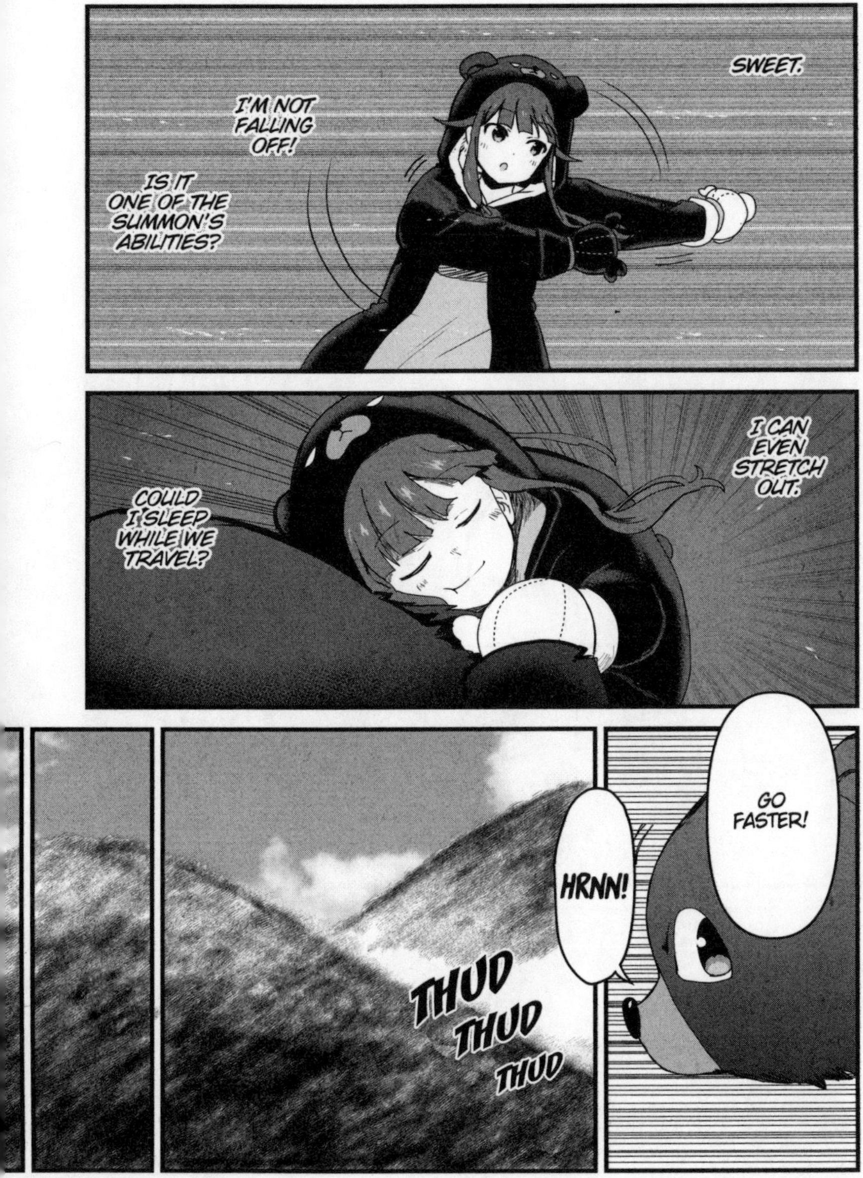
SWEET.
I'M NOT FALLING OFF!
IS IT ONE OF THE SUMMON'S ABILITIES?
I CAN EVEN STRETCH OUT.
COULD I SLEEP WHILE WE TRAVEL?
GO FASTER!
HRNN!
THUD THUD THUD

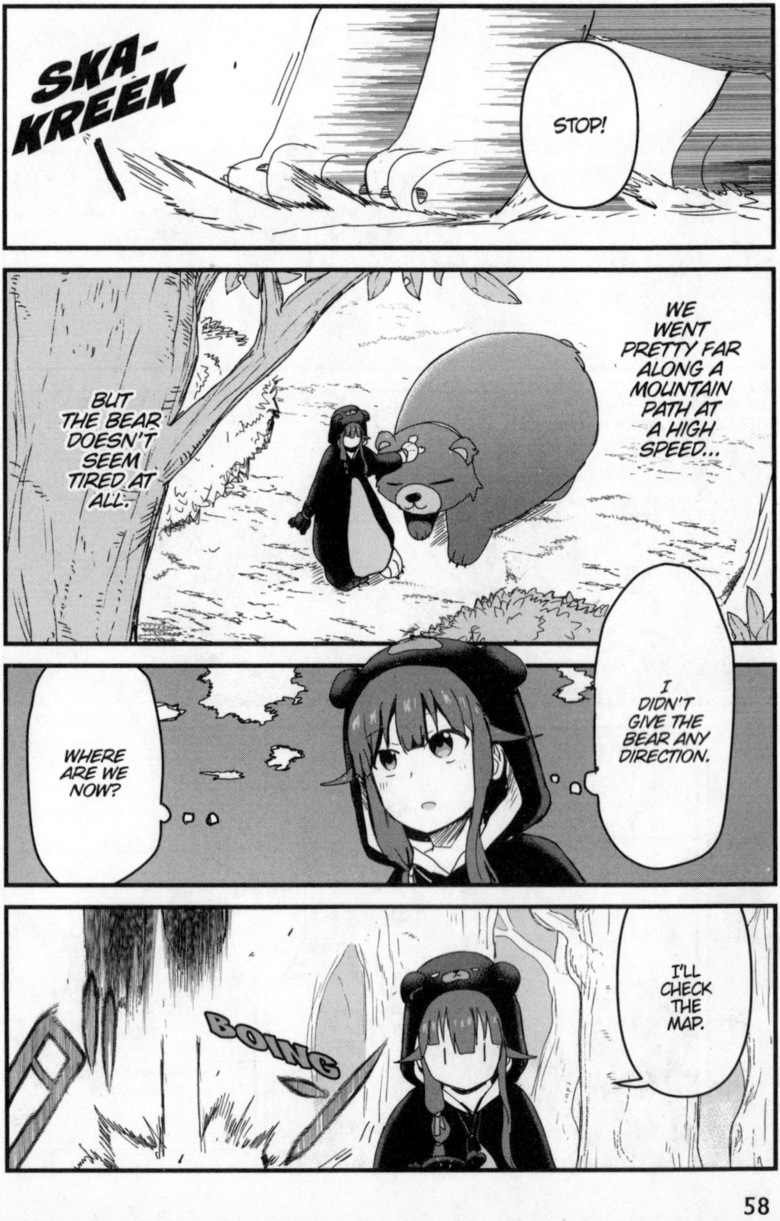
STOP!
SKA-KREEK
WE WENT PRETTY FAR ALONG A MOUNTAIN PATH AT A HIGH SPEED...
BUT THE BEAR DOESN'T SEEM TIRED AT ALL.
I DIDN'T GIVE THE BEAR ANY DIRECTION.
WHERE ARE WE NOW?
I'LL CHECK THE MAP.
BOING

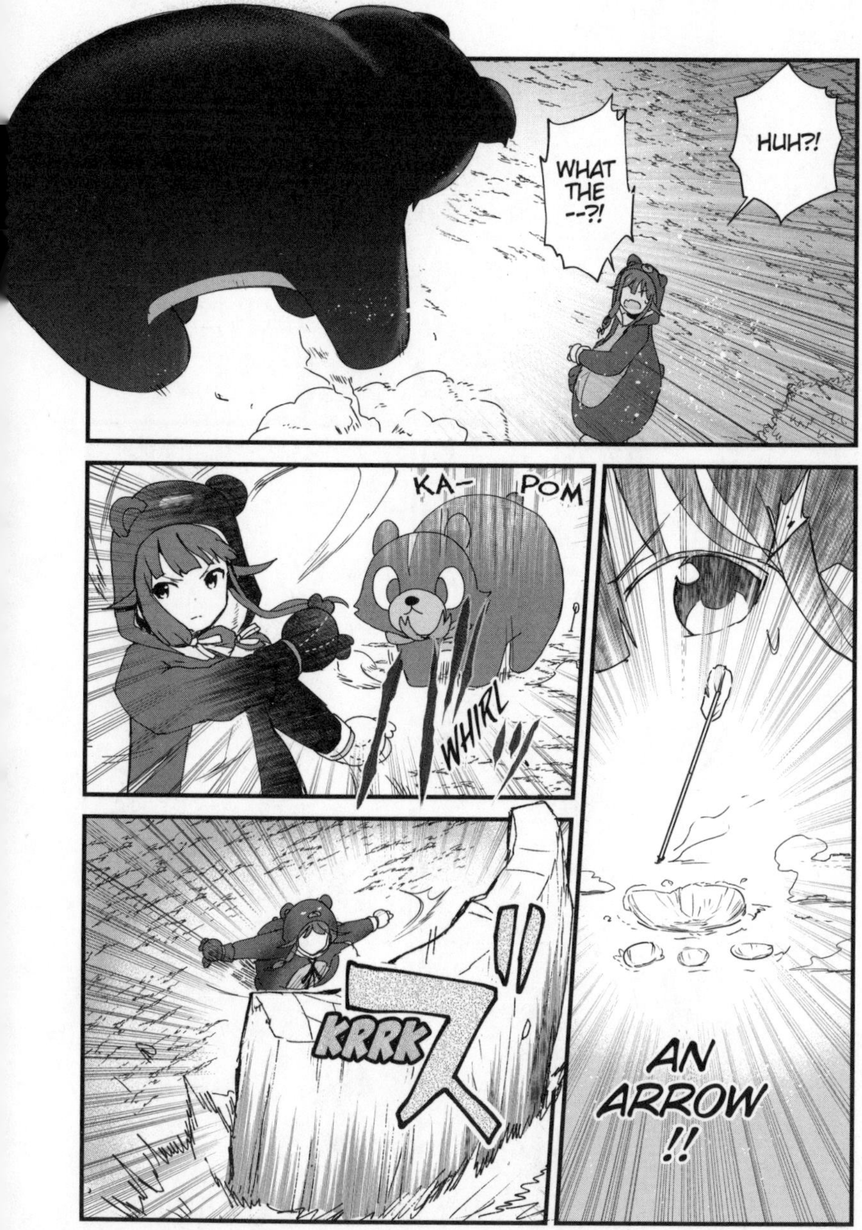
HUH?!
WHAT THE --?!
AN ARROW !!
KA- POM
WHIRL
ズ
KRRK

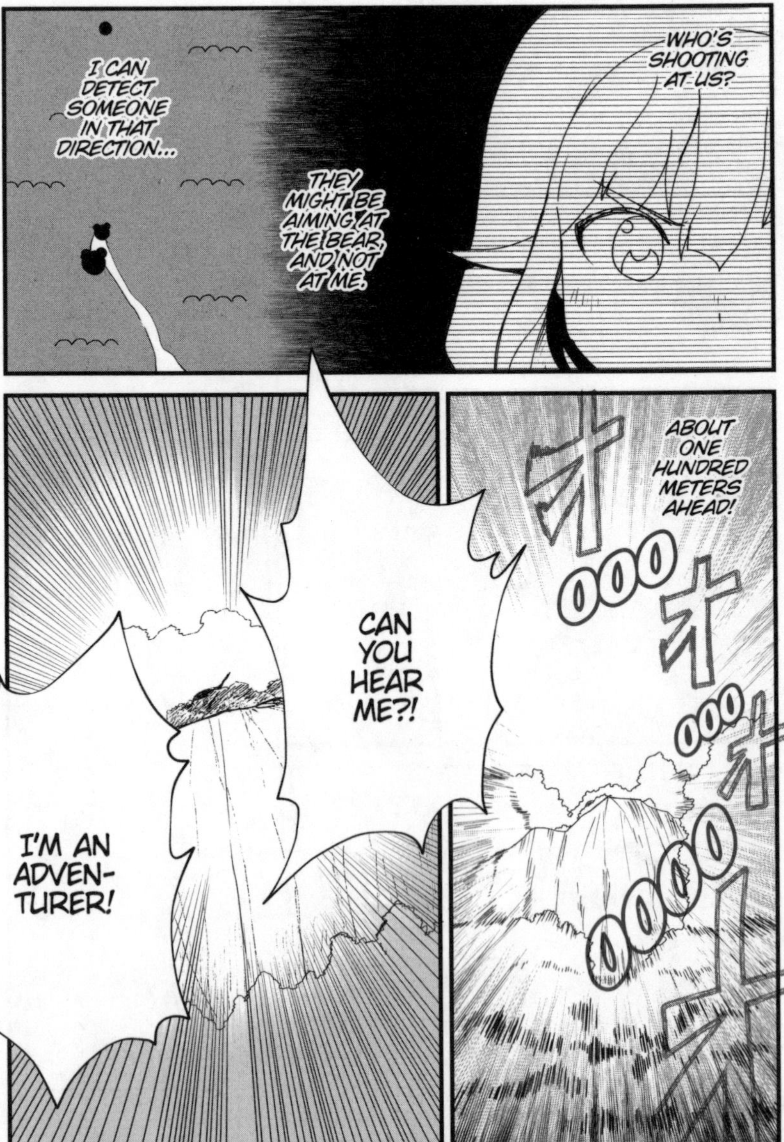
WHO'S SHOOTING AT US?
THEY MIGHT BE AIMING AT THE BEAR, AND NOT AT ME.
I CAN DETECT SOMEONE IN THAT DIRECTION...
ABOUT ONE HUNDRED METERS AHEAD!
OOO
OOO
OOOO
CAN YOU HEAR ME?!
I'M AN ADVENTURER!

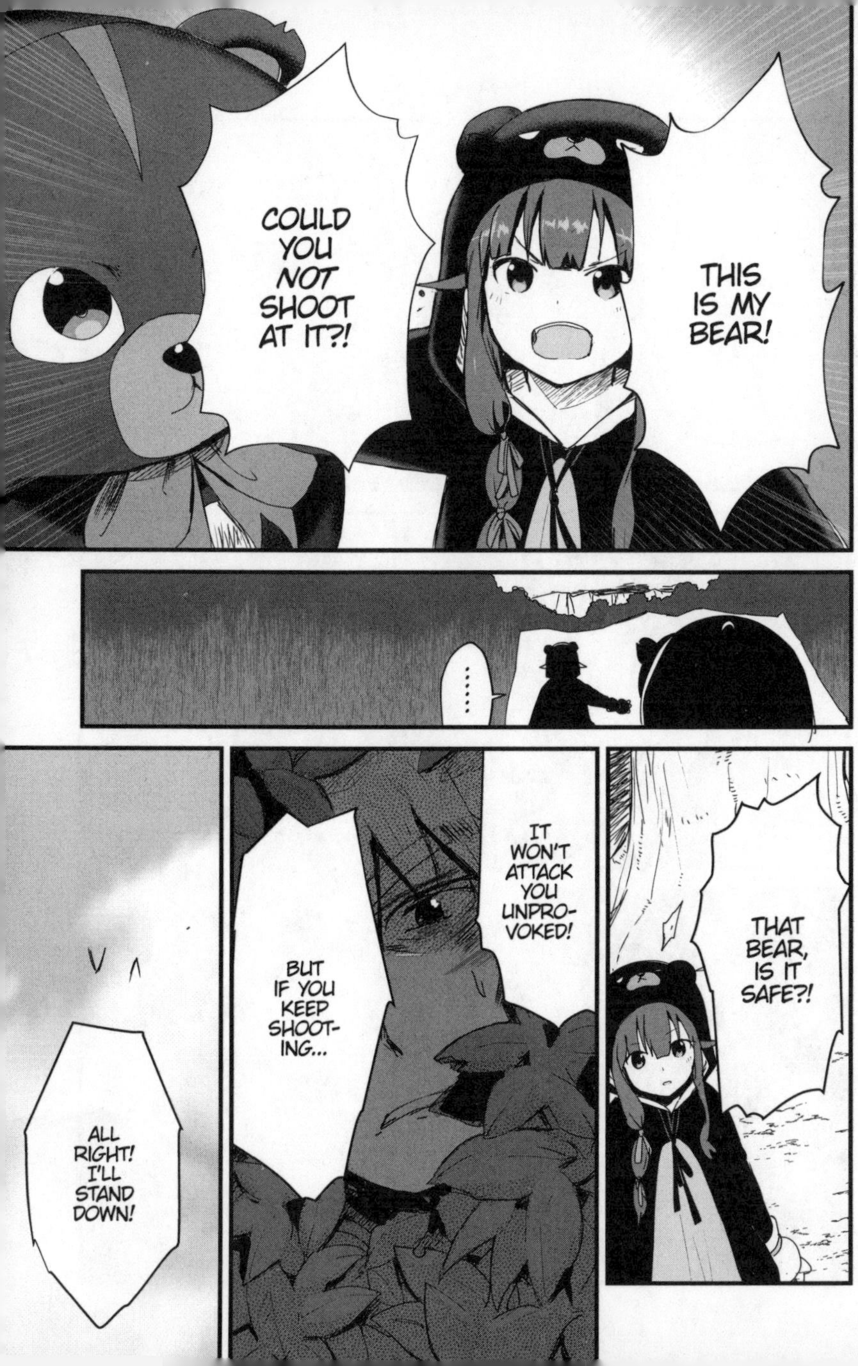
THIS IS MY BEAR!
COULD YOU NOT SHOOT AT IT?!
......
THAT BEAR, IS IT SAFE?!
IT WON'T ATTACK YOU UNPROVOKED!
BUT IF YOU KEEP SHOOTING...
ALL RIGHT! I'LL STAND DOWN!

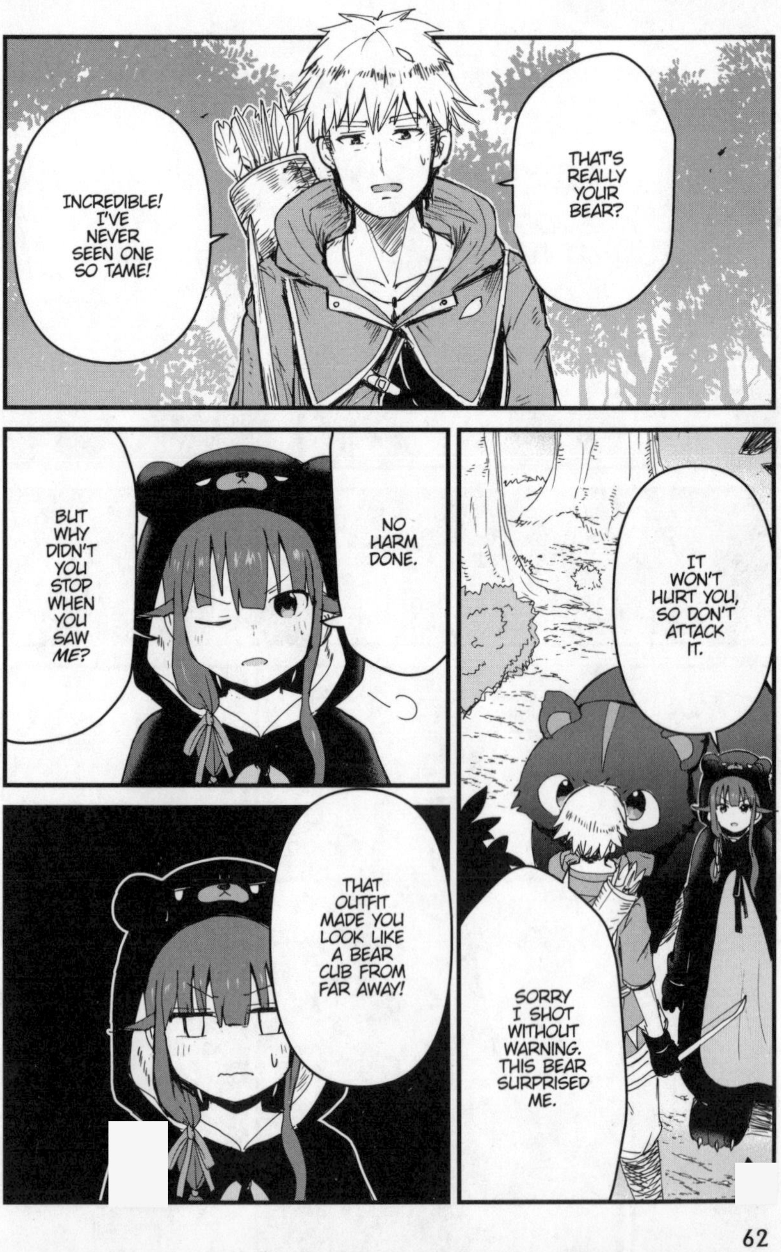
THAT'S REALLY YOUR BEAR?
INCREDIBLE! I'VE NEVER SEEN ONE SO TAME!
IT WON'T HURT YOU, SO DON'T ATTACK IT.
SORRY I SHOT WITHOUT WARNING. THIS BEAR SURPRISED ME.
NO HARM DONE.
BUT WHY DIDN'T YOU STOP WHEN YOU SAW ME?
THAT OUTFIT MADE YOU LOOK LIKE A BEAR CUB FROM FAR AWAY!

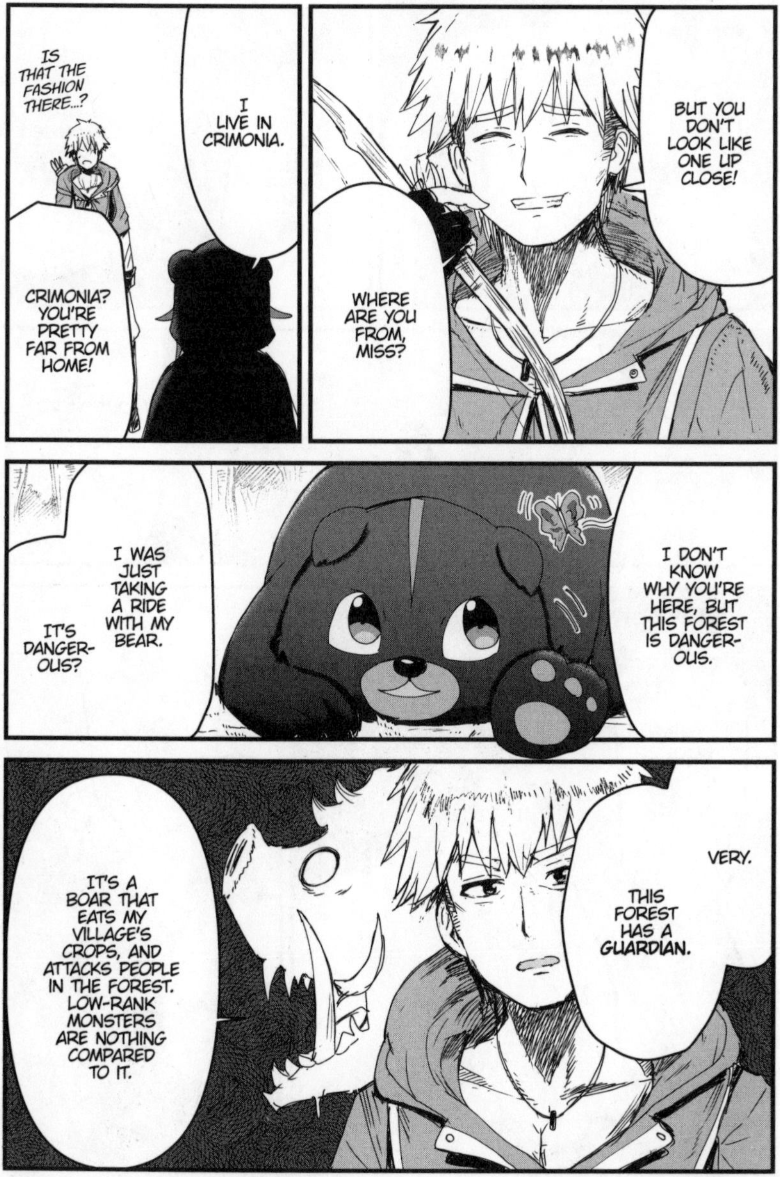
BUT YOU DON'T LOOK LIKE ONE UP CLOSE!
WHERE ARE YOU FROM, MISS?
I LIVE IN CRIMONIA.
IS THAT THE FASHION THERE...?
CRIMONIA? YOU'RE PRETTY FAR FROM HOME!
I DON'T KNOW WHY YOU'RE HERE, BUT THIS FOREST IS DANGER-OUS.
I WAS JUST TAKING A RIDE WITH MY BEAR.
IT'S DANGER-OUS?
VERY.
THIS FOREST HAS A GUARDIAN.
IT'S A BOAR THAT EATS MY VILLAGE'S CROPS, AND ATTACKS PEOPLE IN THE FOREST. LOW-RANK MONSTERS ARE NOTHING COMPARED TO IT.

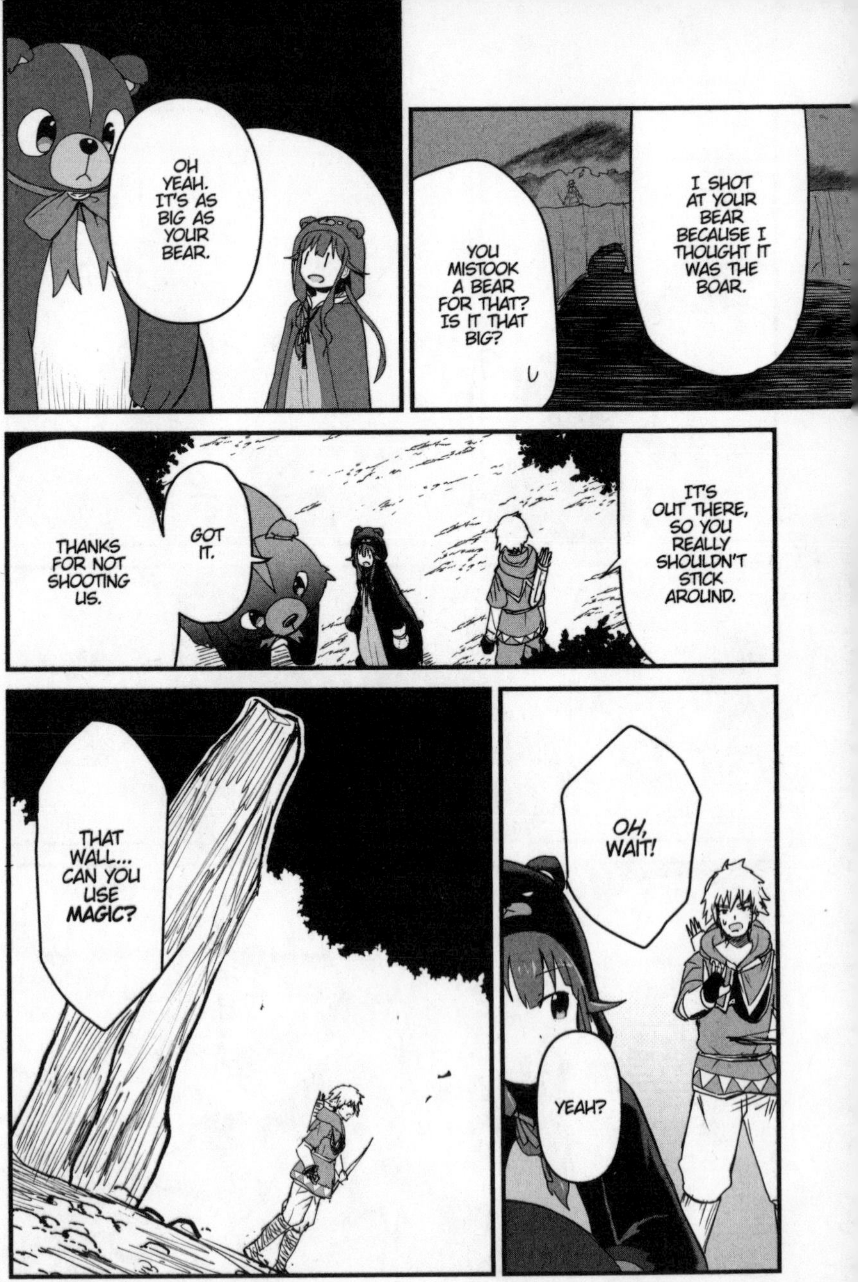
I SHOT AT YOUR BEAR BECAUSE I THOUGHT IT WAS THE BOAR.
YOU MISTOOK A BEAR FOR THAT? IS IT THAT BIG?
OH YEAH. IT'S AS BIG AS YOUR BEAR.
IT'S OUT THERE, SO YOU REALLY SHOULDN'T STICK AROUND.
GOT IT.
THANKS FOR NOT SHOOTING US.
OH, WAIT!
YEAH?
THAT WALL... CAN YOU USE MAGIC?

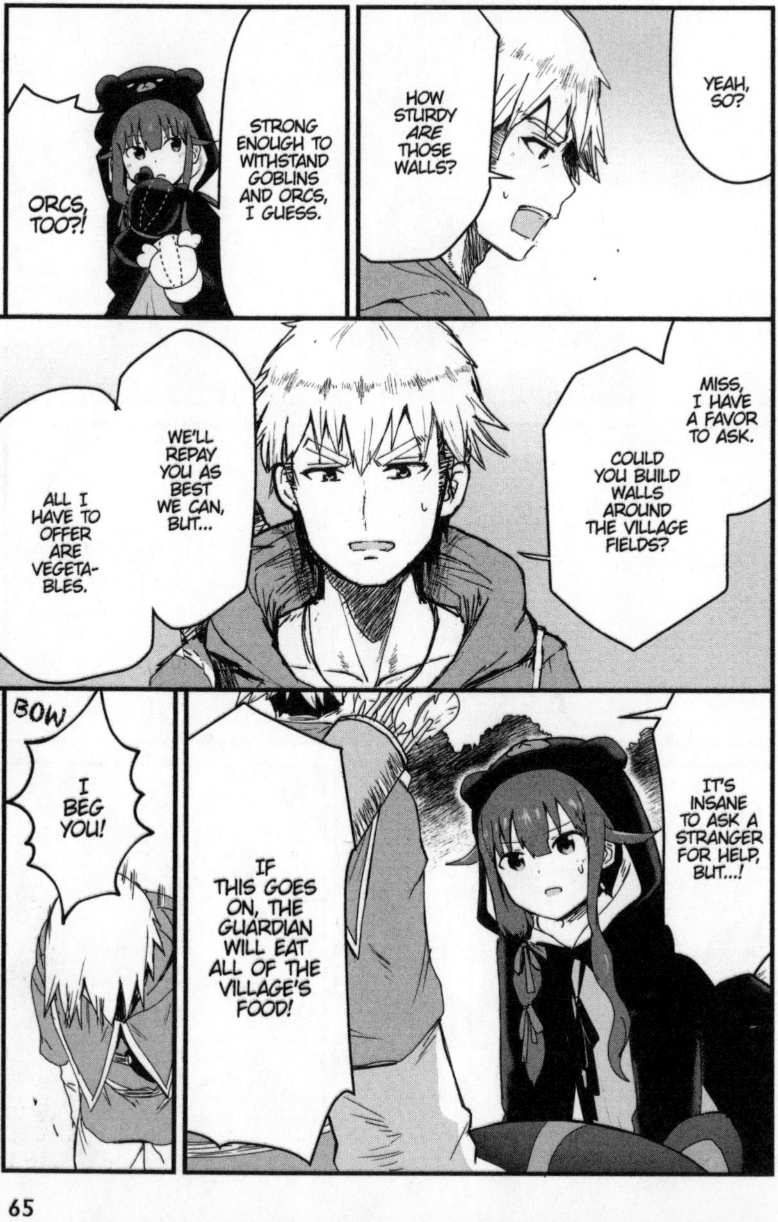
YEAH, SO?
HOW STURDY ARE THOSE WALLS?
STRONG ENOUGH TO WITHSTAND GOBLINS AND ORCS, I GUESS.
ORCS, TOO?!
MISS, I HAVE A FAVOR TO ASK.
COULD YOU BUILD WALLS AROUND THE VILLAGE FIELDS?
WE'LL REPAY YOU AS BEST WE CAN, BUT...
ALL I HAVE TO OFFER ARE VEGETA-BLES.
IT'S INSANE TO ASK A STRANGER FOR HELP, BUT...!
IF THIS GOES ON, THE GUARDIAN WILL EAT ALL OF THE VILLAGE'S FOOD!
BOW
I BEG YOU!

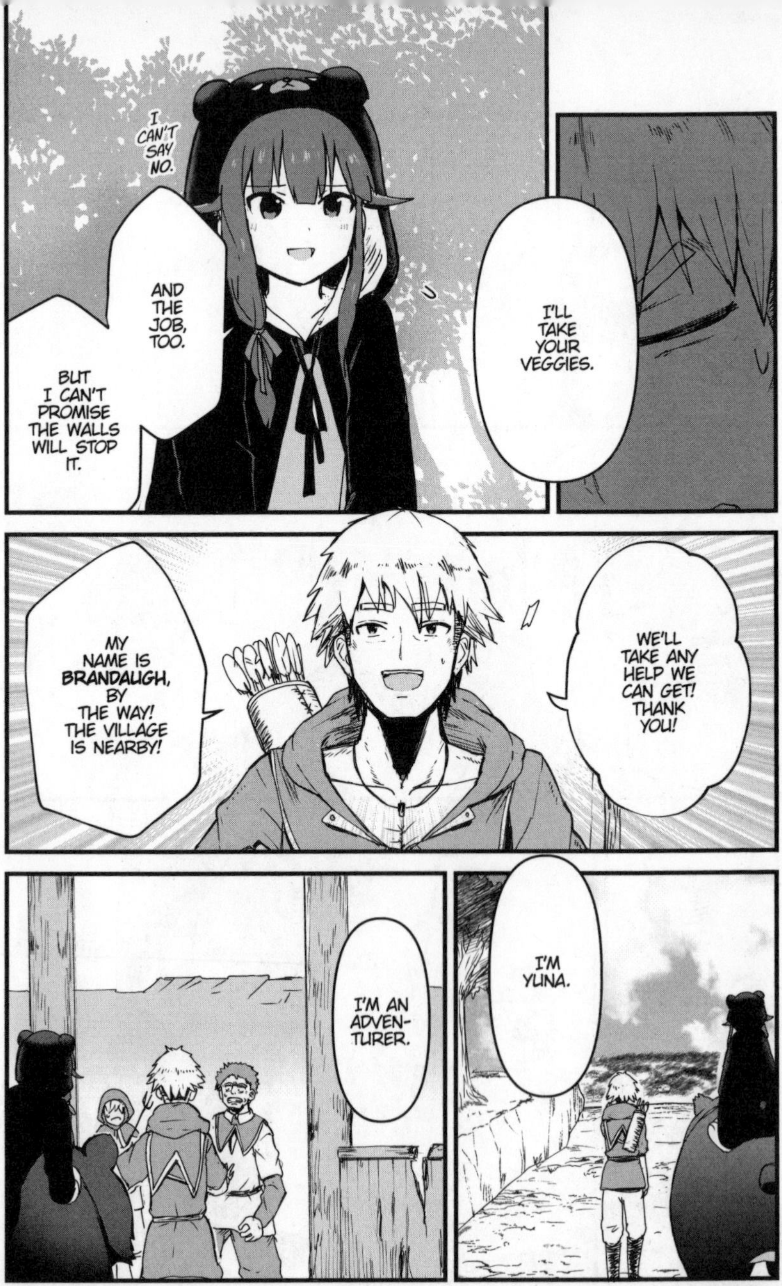
I CAN'T SAY NO.
I'LL TAKE YOUR VEGGIES.
AND THE JOB, TOO.
BUT I CAN'T PROMISE THE WALLS WILL STOP IT.
WE'LL TAKE ANY HELP WE CAN GET! THANK YOU!
MY NAME IS BRANDAUGH, BY THE WAY! THE VILLAGE IS NEARBY!
I'M YUNA.
I'M AN ADVENTURER.

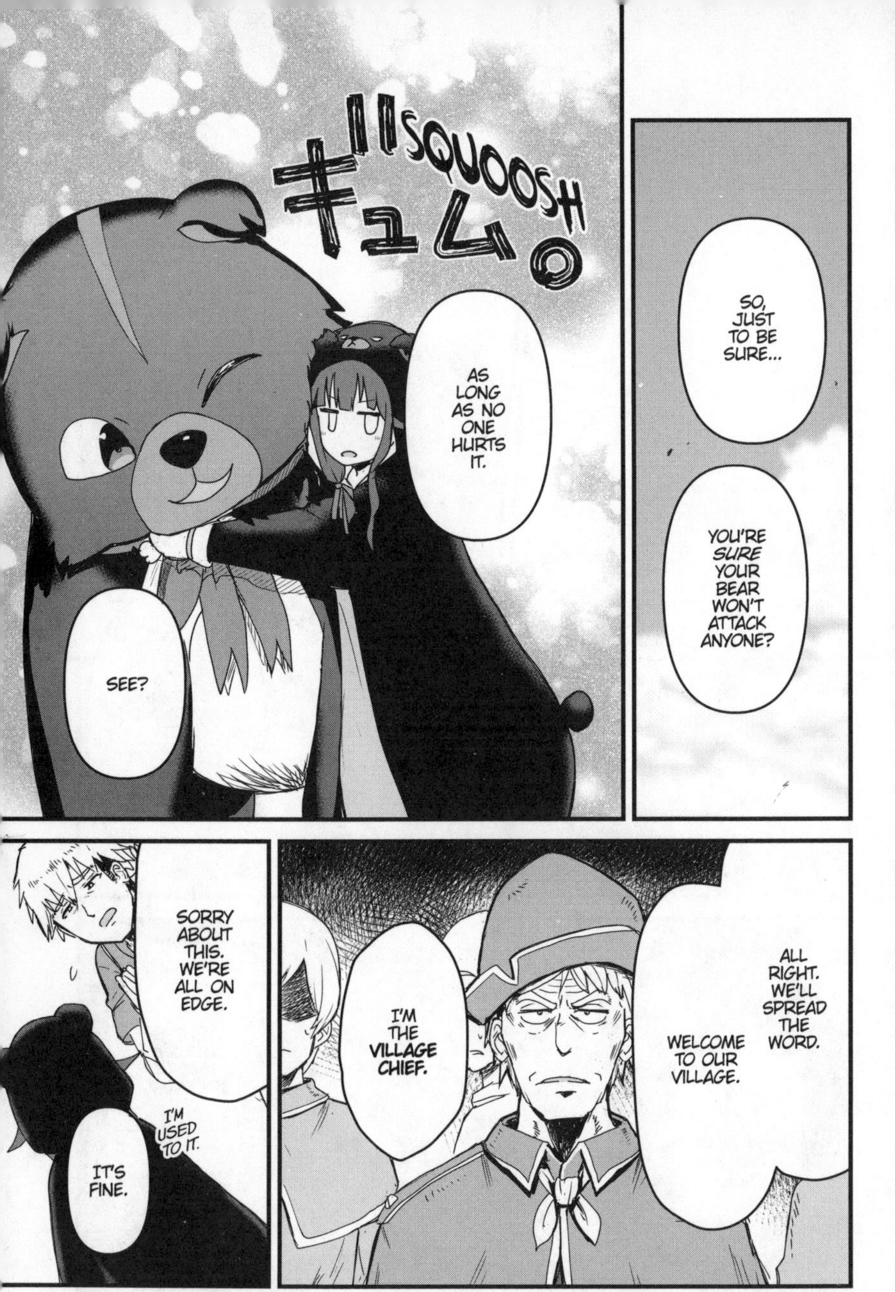

SO, JUST TO BE SURE...
YOU'RE *SURE* YOUR BEAR WON'T ATTACK ANYONE?
SQUOOSH
キュムっ
AS LONG AS NO ONE HURTS IT.
SEE?
ALL RIGHT. WE'LL SPREAD THE WORD.
WELCOME TO OUR VILLAGE.
I'M THE **VILLAGE CHIEF.**
SORRY ABOUT THIS. WE'RE ALL ON EDGE.
I'M USED TO IT.
IT'S FINE.

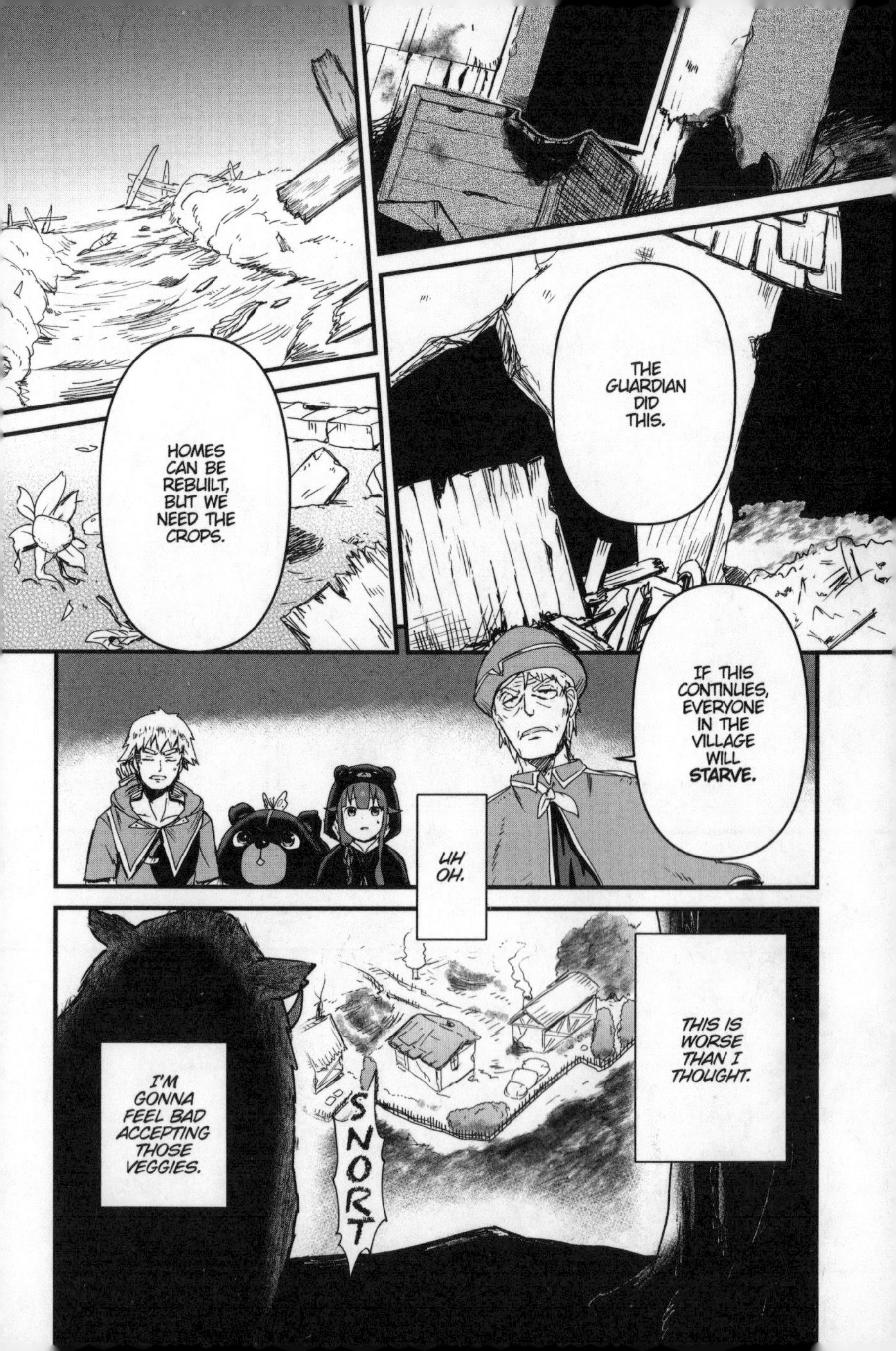
THE GUARDIAN DID THIS.
HOMES CAN BE REBUILT, BUT WE NEED THE CROPS.
IF THIS CONTINUES, EVERYONE IN THE VILLAGE WILL STARVE.
UH OH.
THIS IS WORSE THAN I THOUGHT.
SNORT
I'M GONNA FEEL BAD ACCEPTING THOSE VEGGIES.

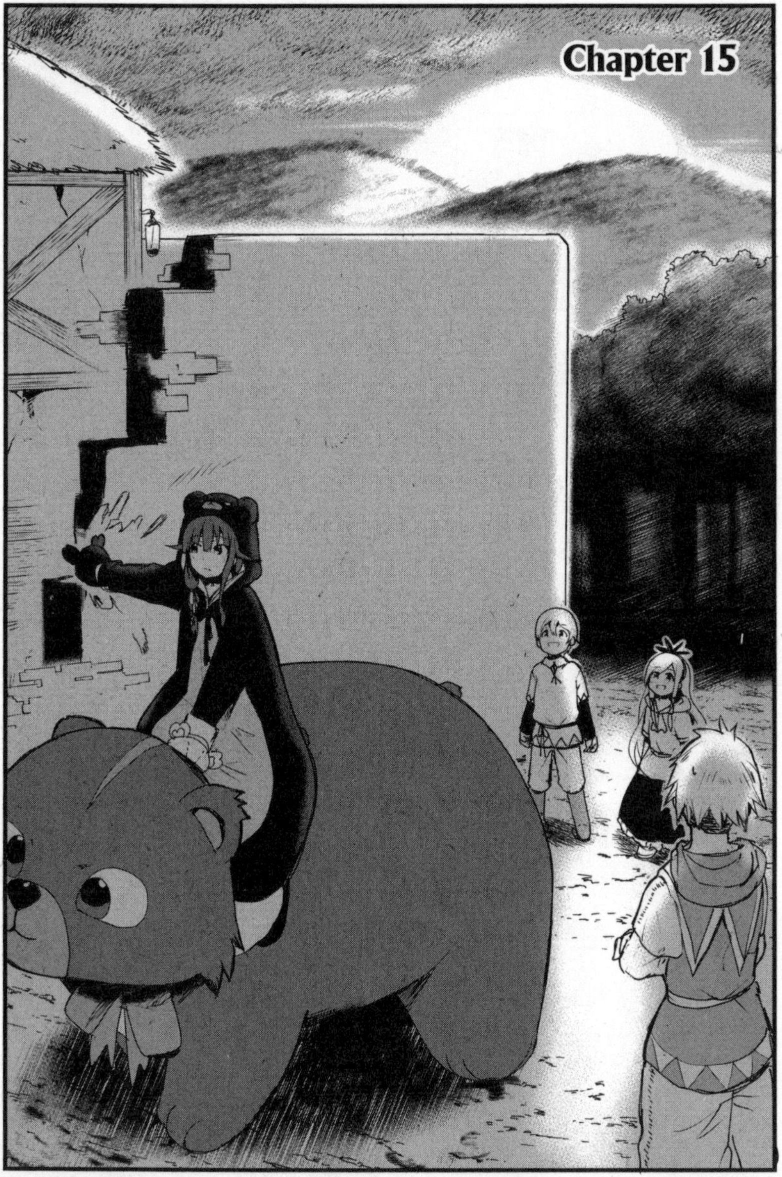
Chapter 15

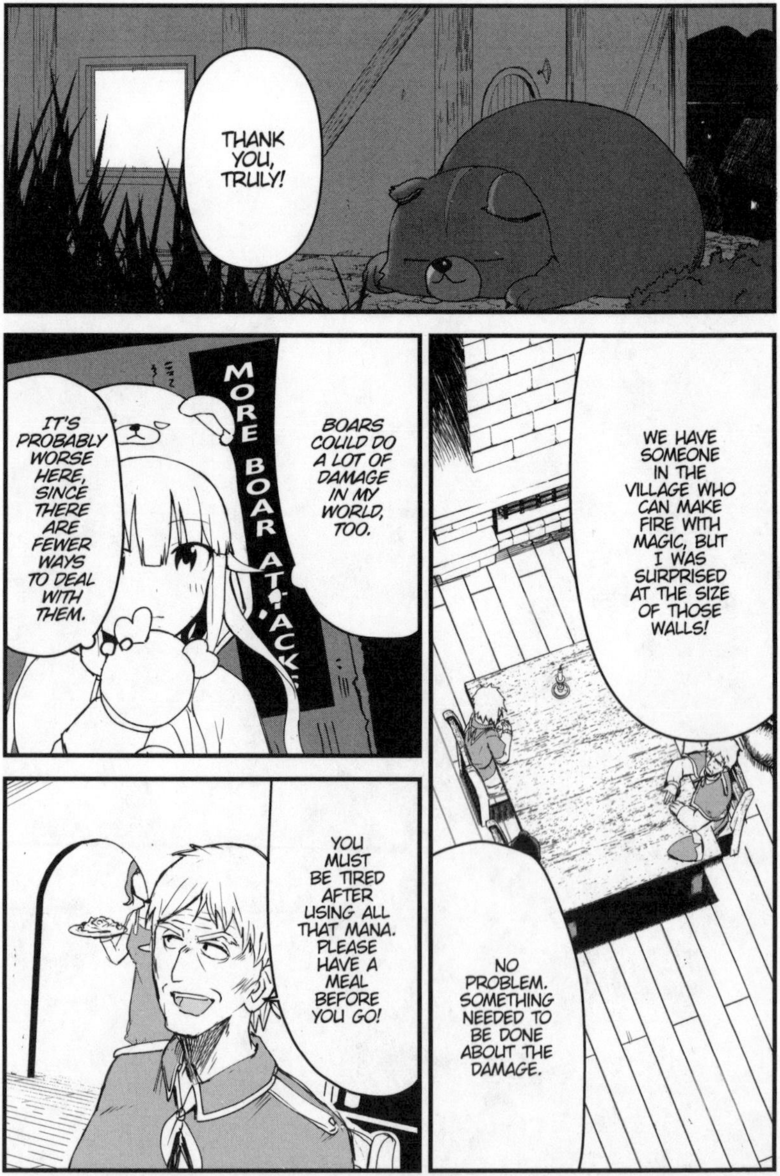
THANK YOU, TRULY!
WE HAVE SOMEONE IN THE VILLAGE WHO CAN MAKE FIRE WITH MAGIC, BUT I WAS SURPRISED AT THE SIZE OF THOSE WALLS!
NO PROBLEM. SOMETHING NEEDED TO BE DONE ABOUT THE DAMAGE.
BOARS COULD DO A LOT OF DAMAGE IN MY WORLD, TOO.
MORE BOAR ATTACKS
IT'S PROBABLY WORSE HERE, SINCE THERE ARE FEWER WAYS TO DEAL WITH THEM.
YOU MUST BE TIRED AFTER USING ALL THAT MANA. PLEASE HAVE A MEAL BEFORE YOU GO!

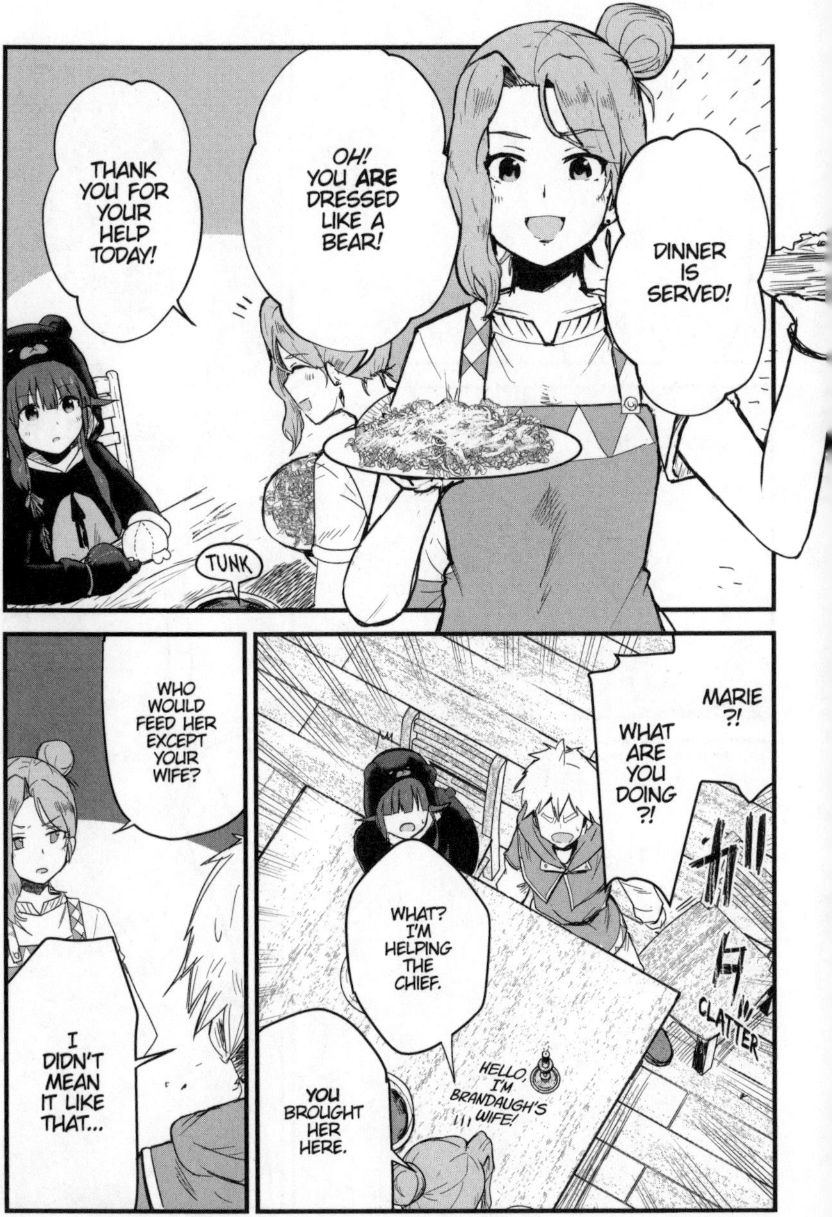
DINNER IS SERVED!
OH! YOU ARE DRESSED LIKE A BEAR!
THANK YOU FOR YOUR HELP TODAY!
TUNK
MARIE?!
WHAT ARE YOU DOING?!
CLATTER
WHAT? I'M HELPING THE CHIEF.
HELLO, I'M BRANDAUGH'S WIFE!
YOU BROUGHT HER HERE.
WHO WOULD FEED HER EXCEPT YOUR WIFE?
I DIDN'T MEAN IT LIKE THAT...

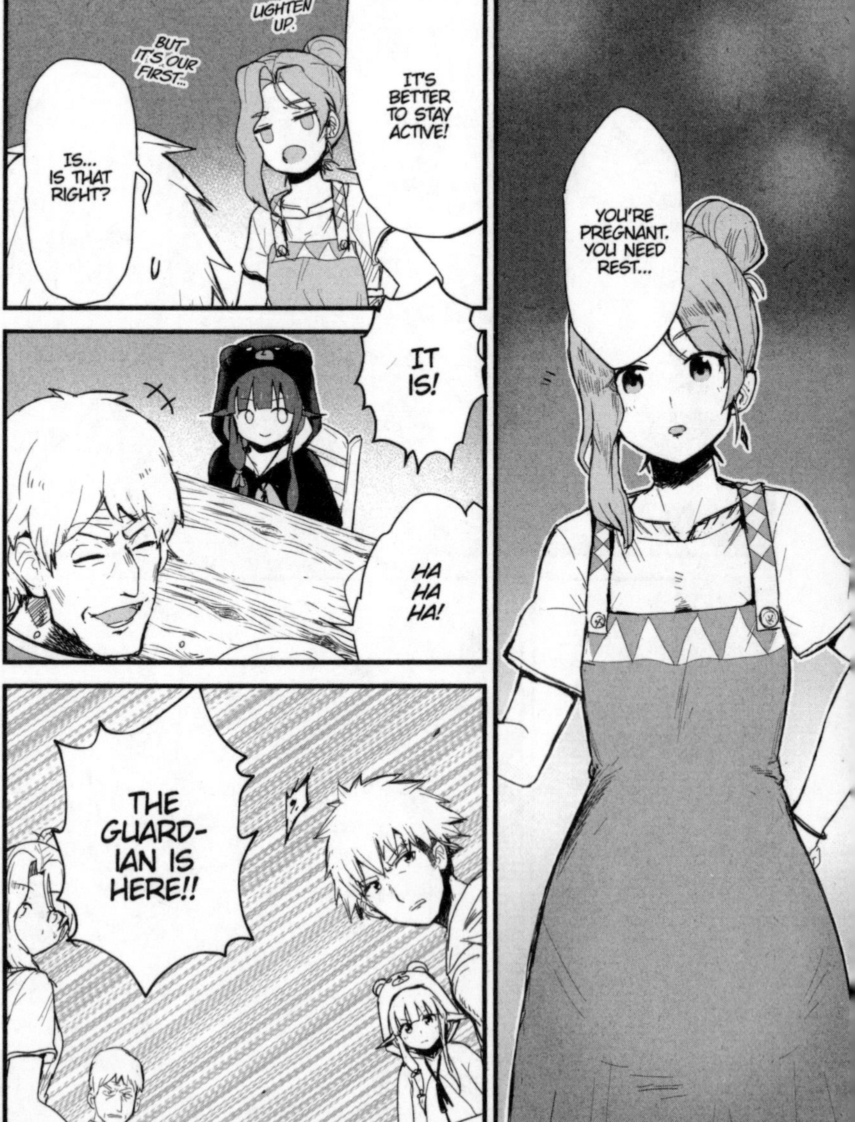
YOU'RE PREGNANT. YOU NEED REST...
IT'S BETTER TO STAY ACTIVE!
LIGHTEN UP.
BUT IT'S OUR FIRST...
IS... IS THAT RIGHT?
IT IS!
HA HA HA!
THE GUARDIAN IS HERE!!

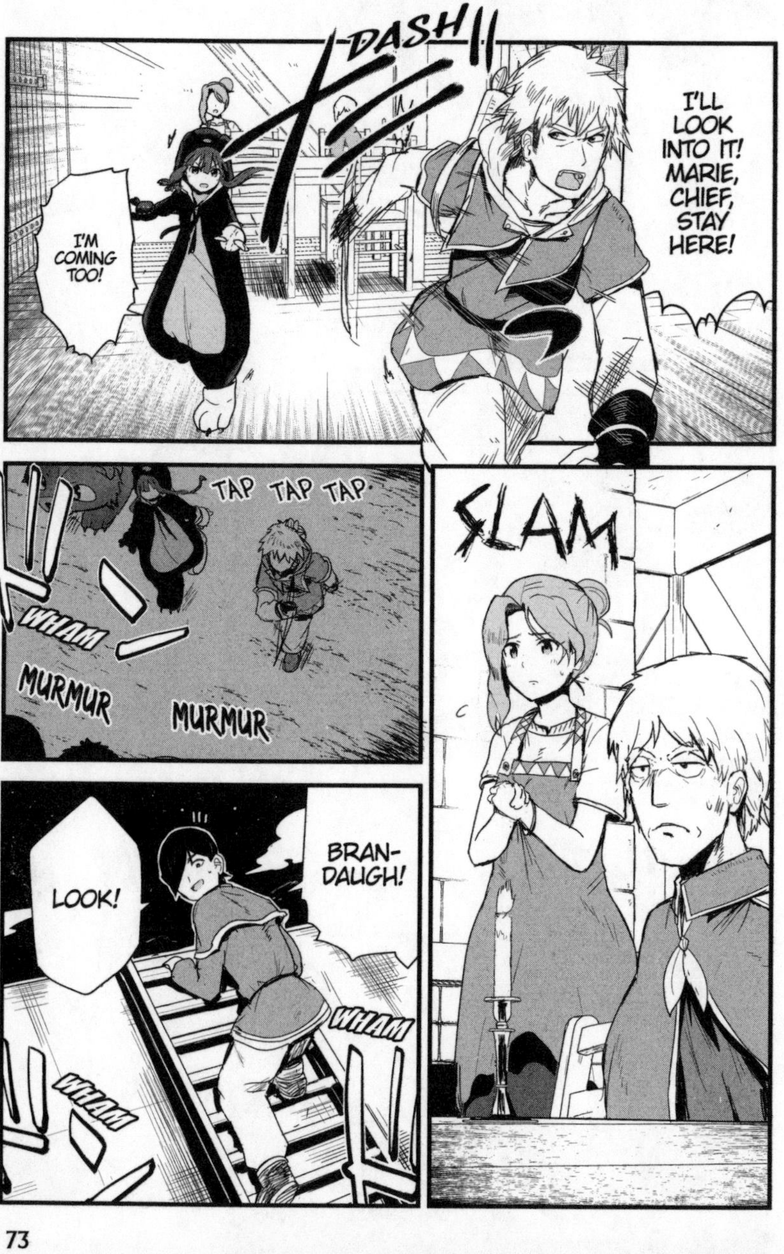
DASH
I'LL LOOK INTO IT! MARIE, CHIEF, STAY HERE!
I'M COMING TOO!
SLAM
TAP TAP TAP
WHAM
MURMUR
MURMUR
BRAN-DAUGH!
LOOK!
WHAM
WHAM

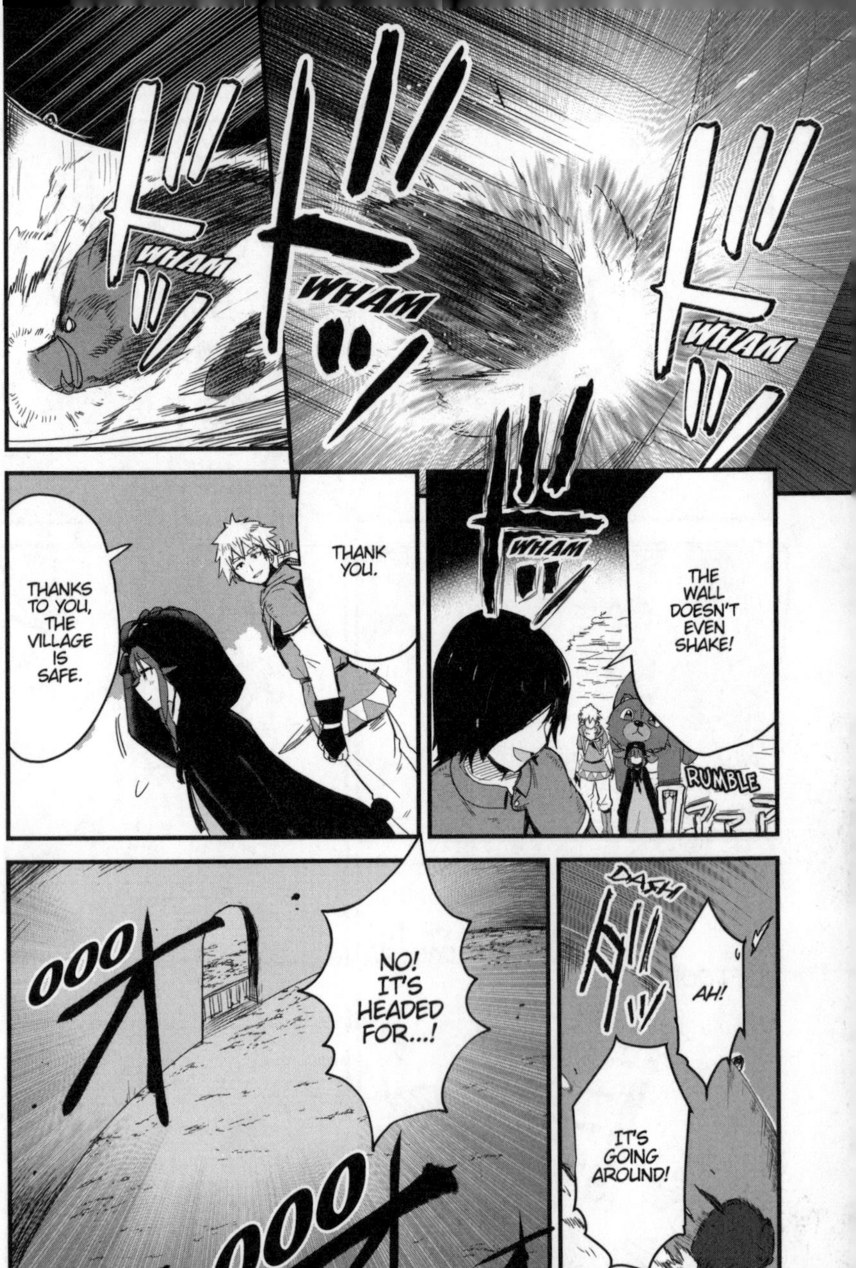
WHAM
WHAM
WHAM
WHAM
THE WALL DOESN'T EVEN SHAKE!
RUMBLE
THANK YOU.
THANKS TO YOU, THE VILLAGE IS SAFE.
DASH
AH!
IT'S GOING AROUND!
NO! IT'S HEADED FOR...!
OOO
OOO

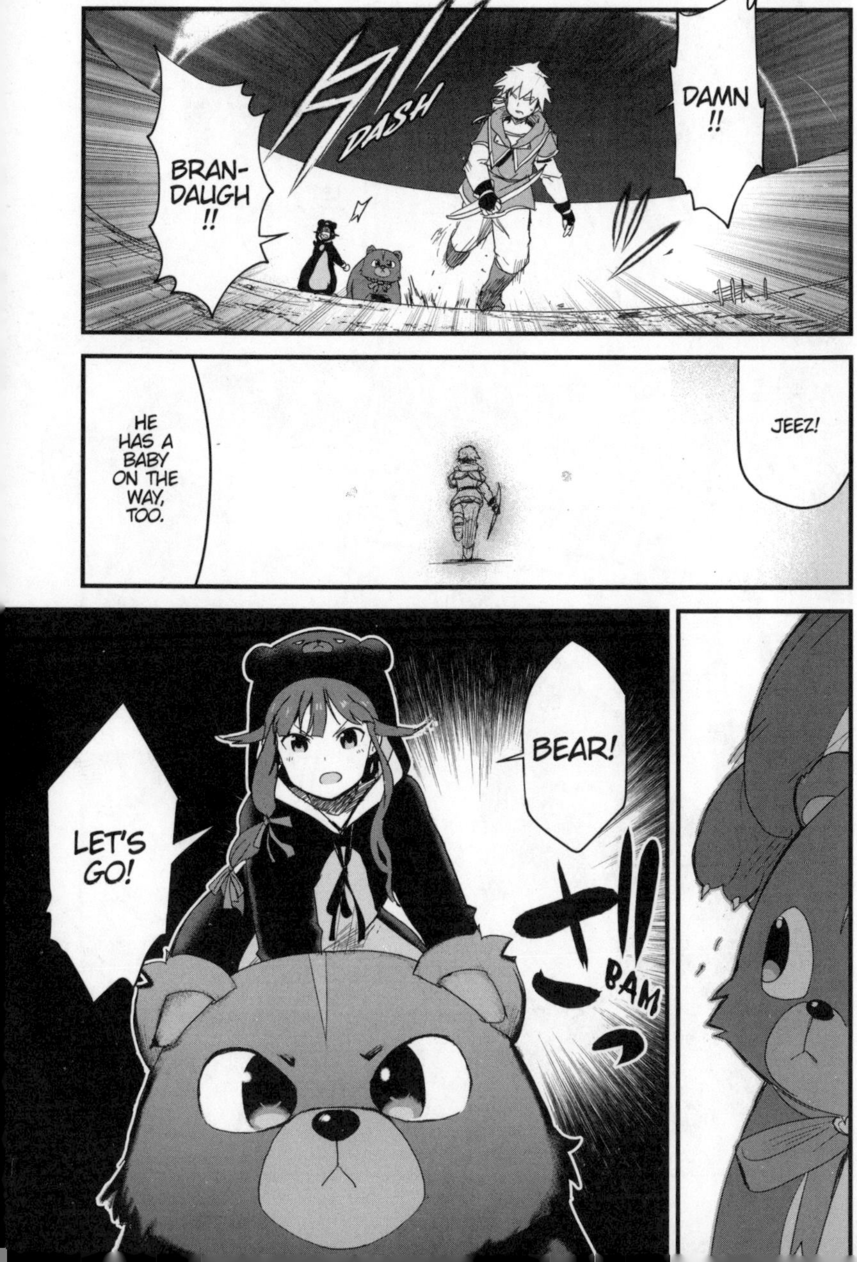
DAMN !!
DASH
BRAN-DAUGH !!
JEEZ!
HE HAS A BABY ON THE WAY, TOO.
BEAR!
BAM
LET'S GO!

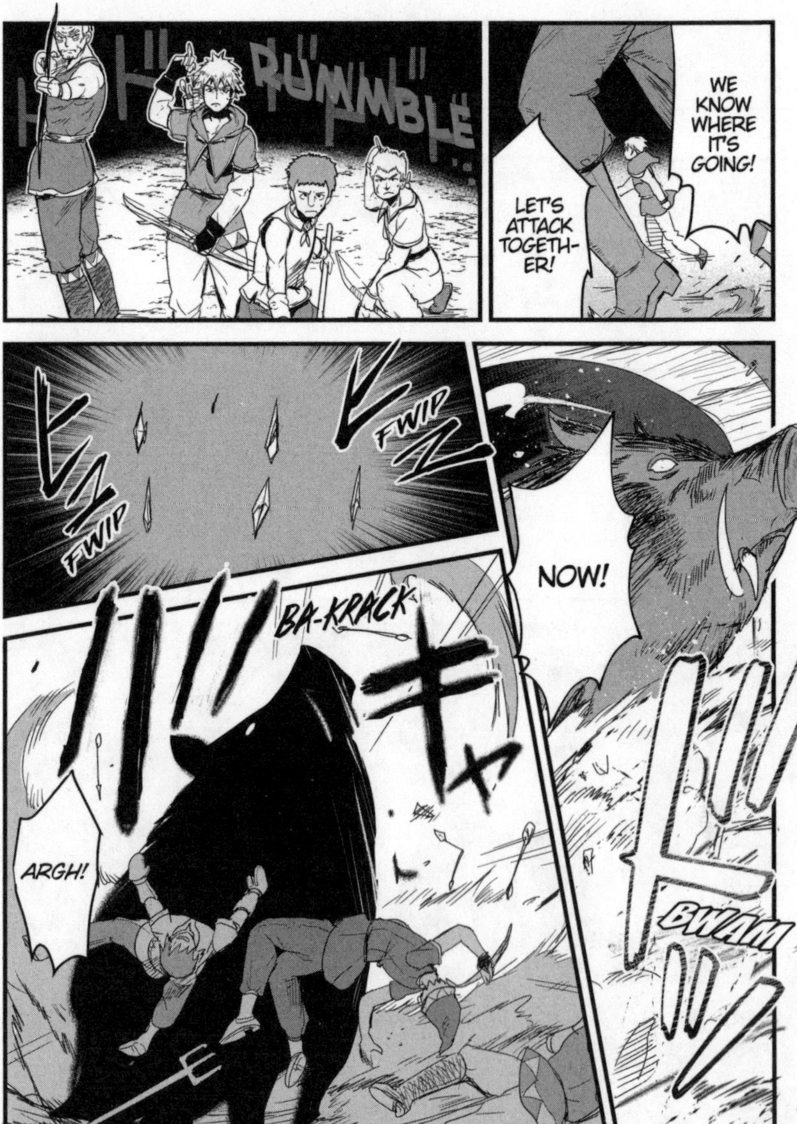

WE KNOW WHERE IT'S GOING!
LET'S ATTACK TOGETH-ER!
RUMMBLE
NOW!
BWAM
FWIP
FWIP
BA-KRACK
ARGH!

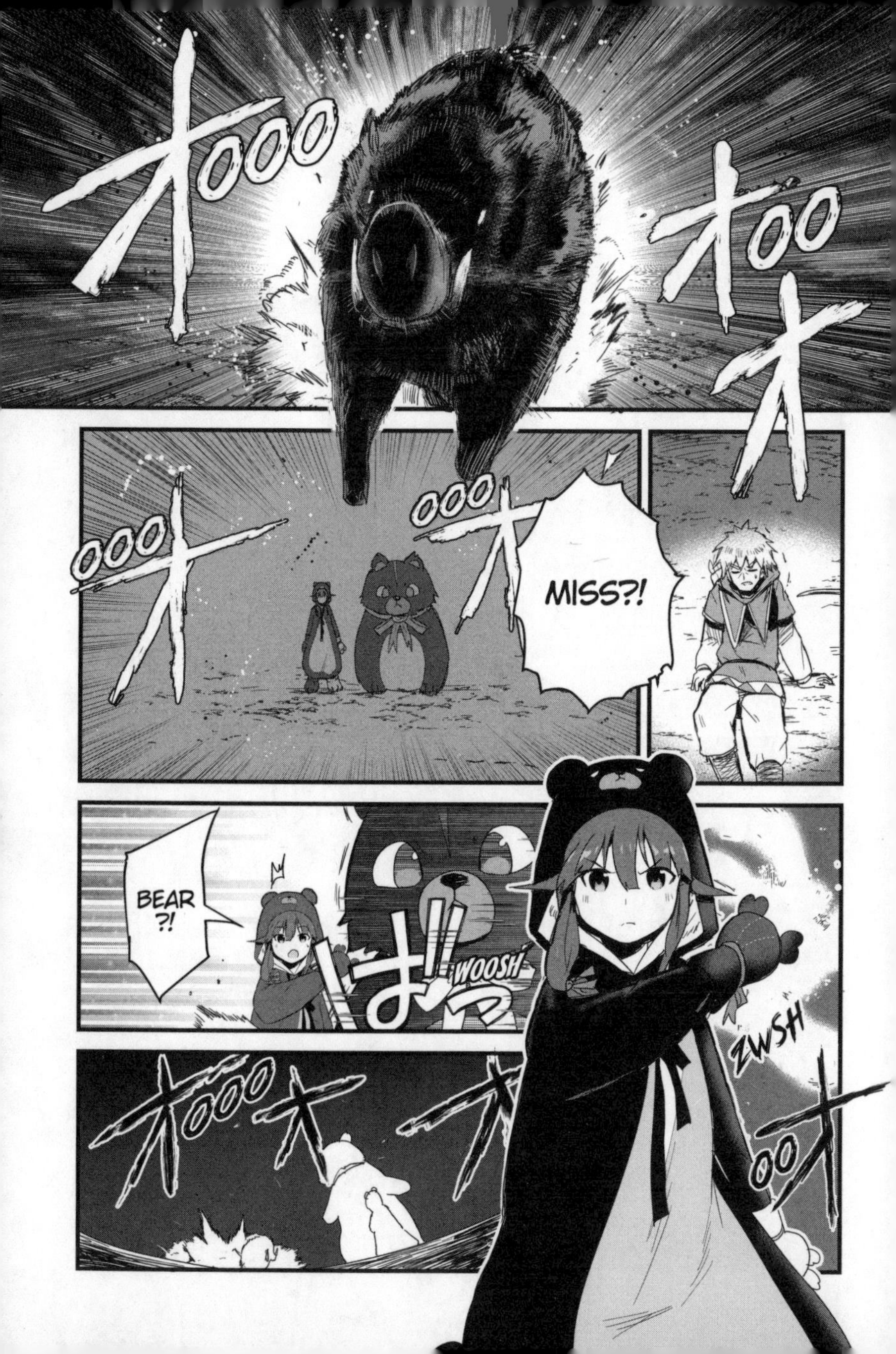

オOOオ
オOOO
MISS?!
OOOオ
OOOオ
ZWSH
BEAR ?!
WOOSH
OOオ
オOOOオ

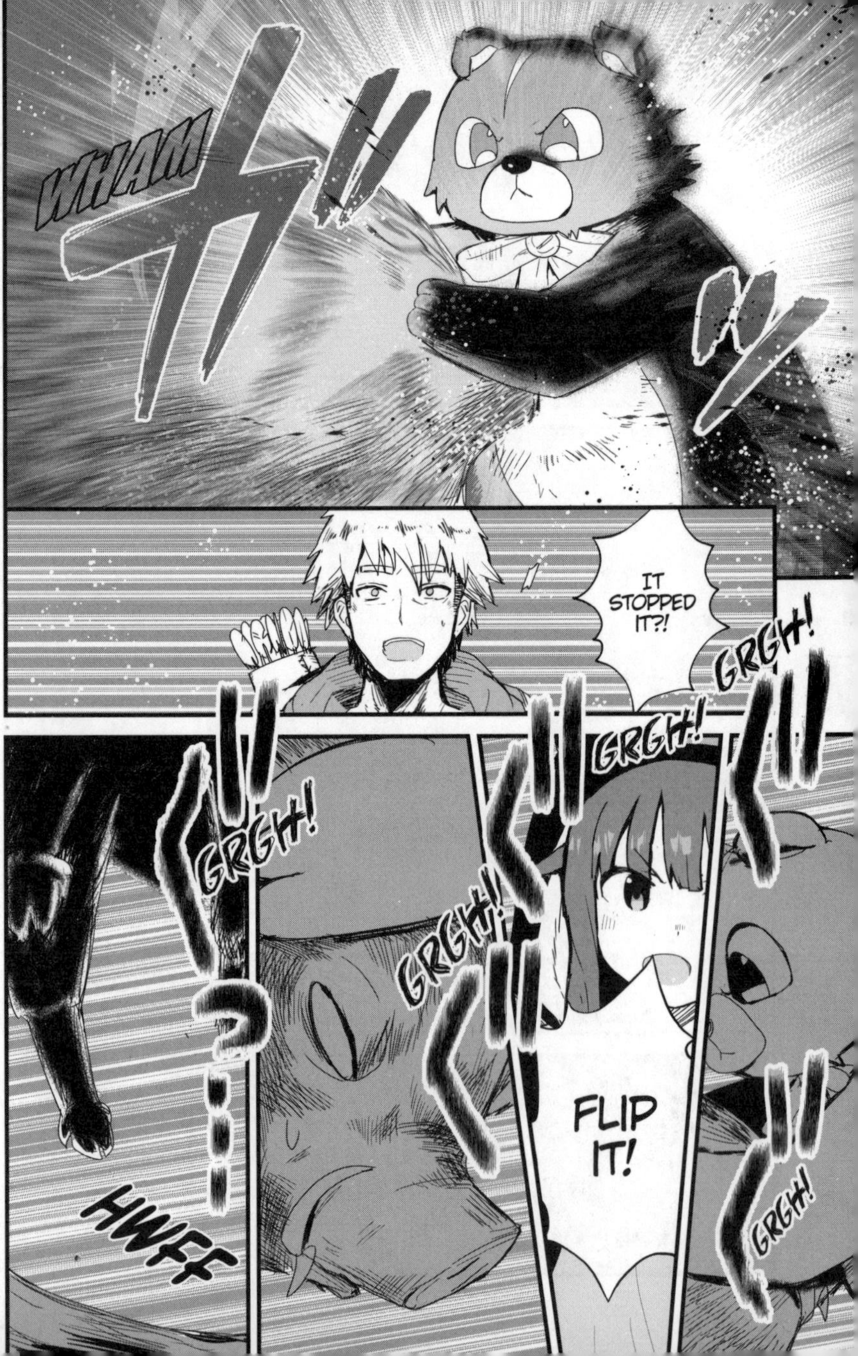
WHAM
IT STOPPED IT?!
GRGH!
GRGH!
FLIP IT!
GRGH!
GRGH!
GRGH!
GRGH!
HWFF

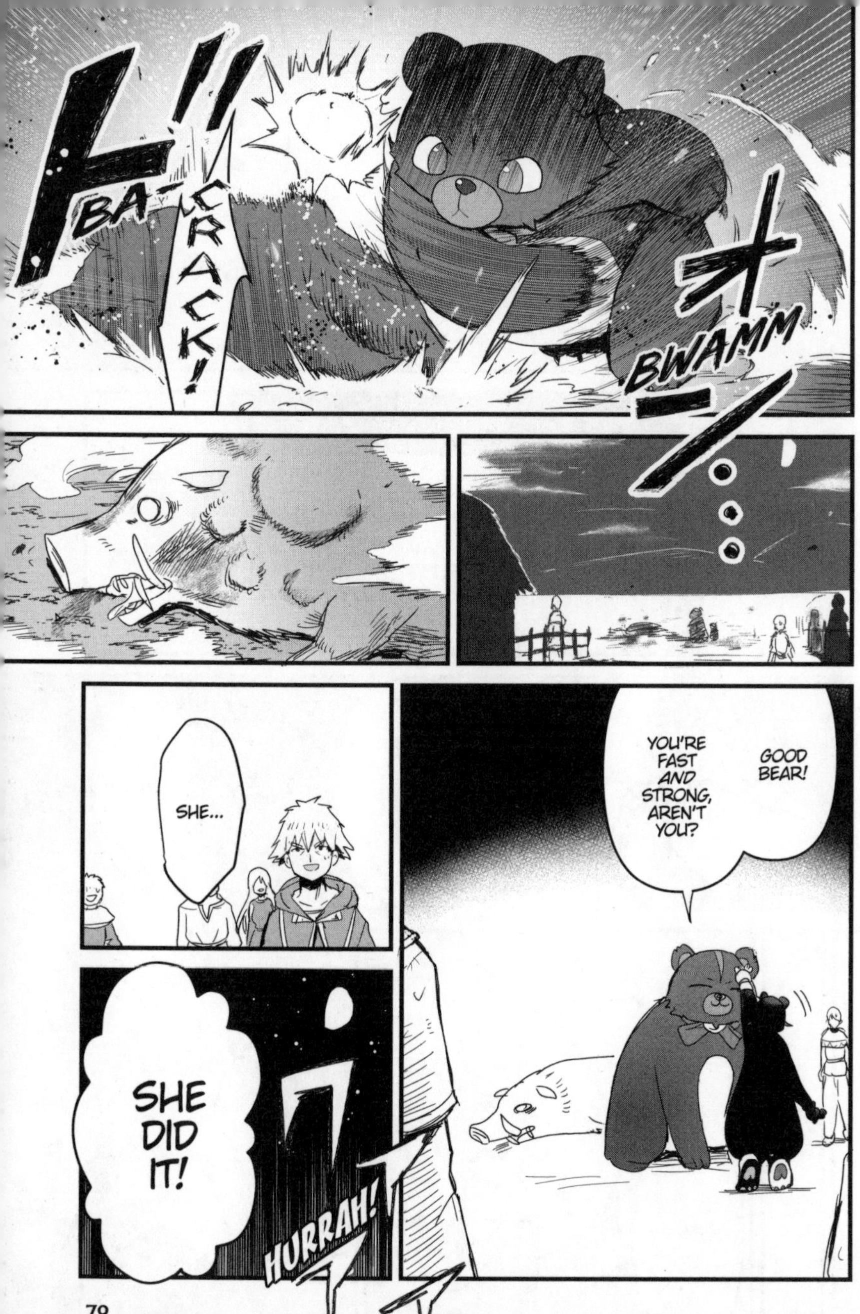
BA-CRACK!
BWAMM
...
GOOD BEAR!
YOU'RE FAST AND STRONG, AREN'T YOU?
SHE...
SHE DID IT!
HURRAH!

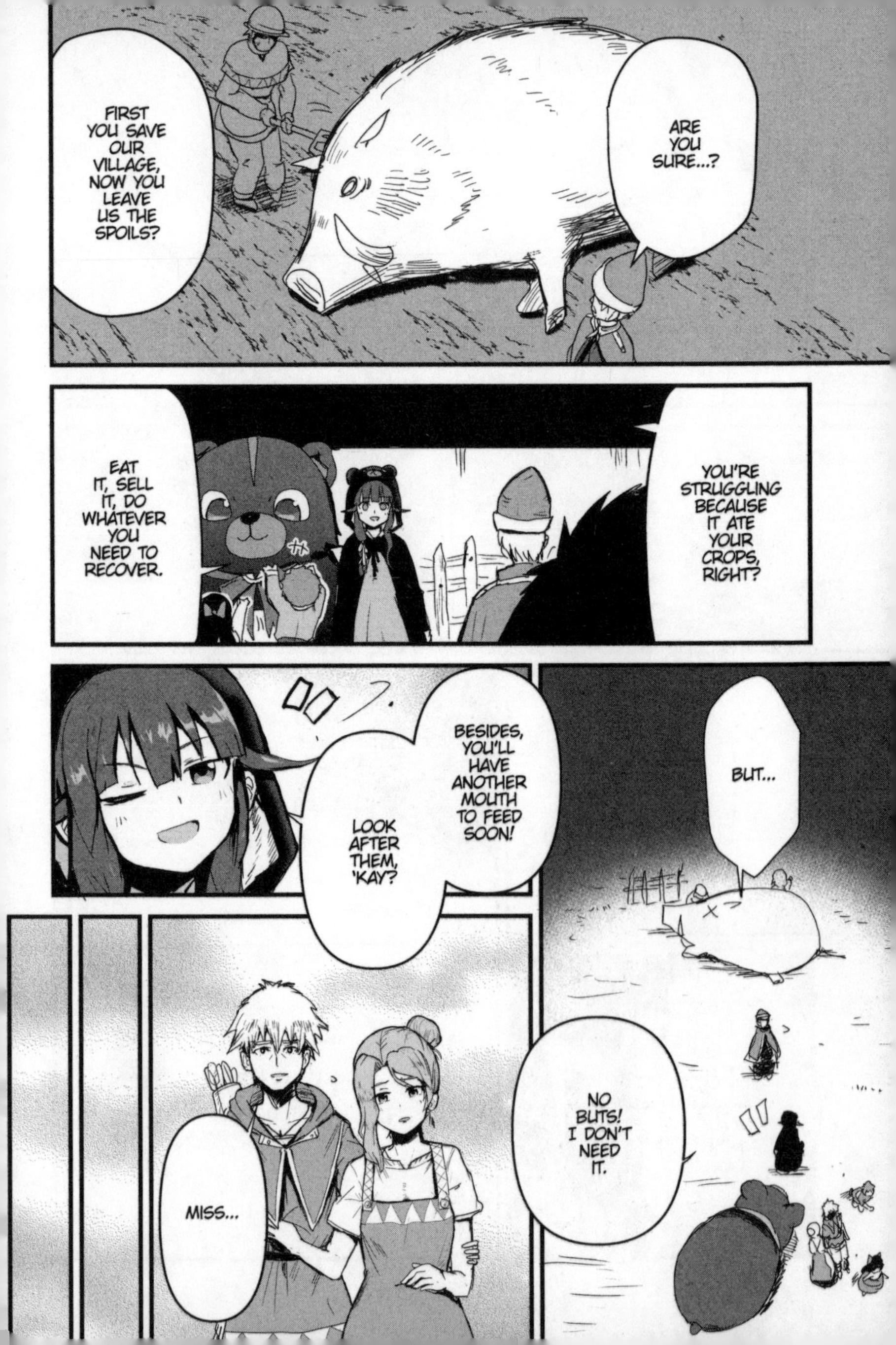
ARE YOU SURE...?
FIRST YOU SAVE OUR VILLAGE, NOW YOU LEAVE US THE SPOILS?
YOU'RE STRUGGLING BECAUSE IT ATE YOUR CROPS, RIGHT?
EAT IT, SELL IT, DO WHATEVER YOU NEED TO RECOVER.
BUT...
NO BUTS! I DON'T NEED IT.
BESIDES, YOU'LL HAVE ANOTHER MOUTH TO FEED SOON!
LOOK AFTER THEM, 'KAY?
MISS...

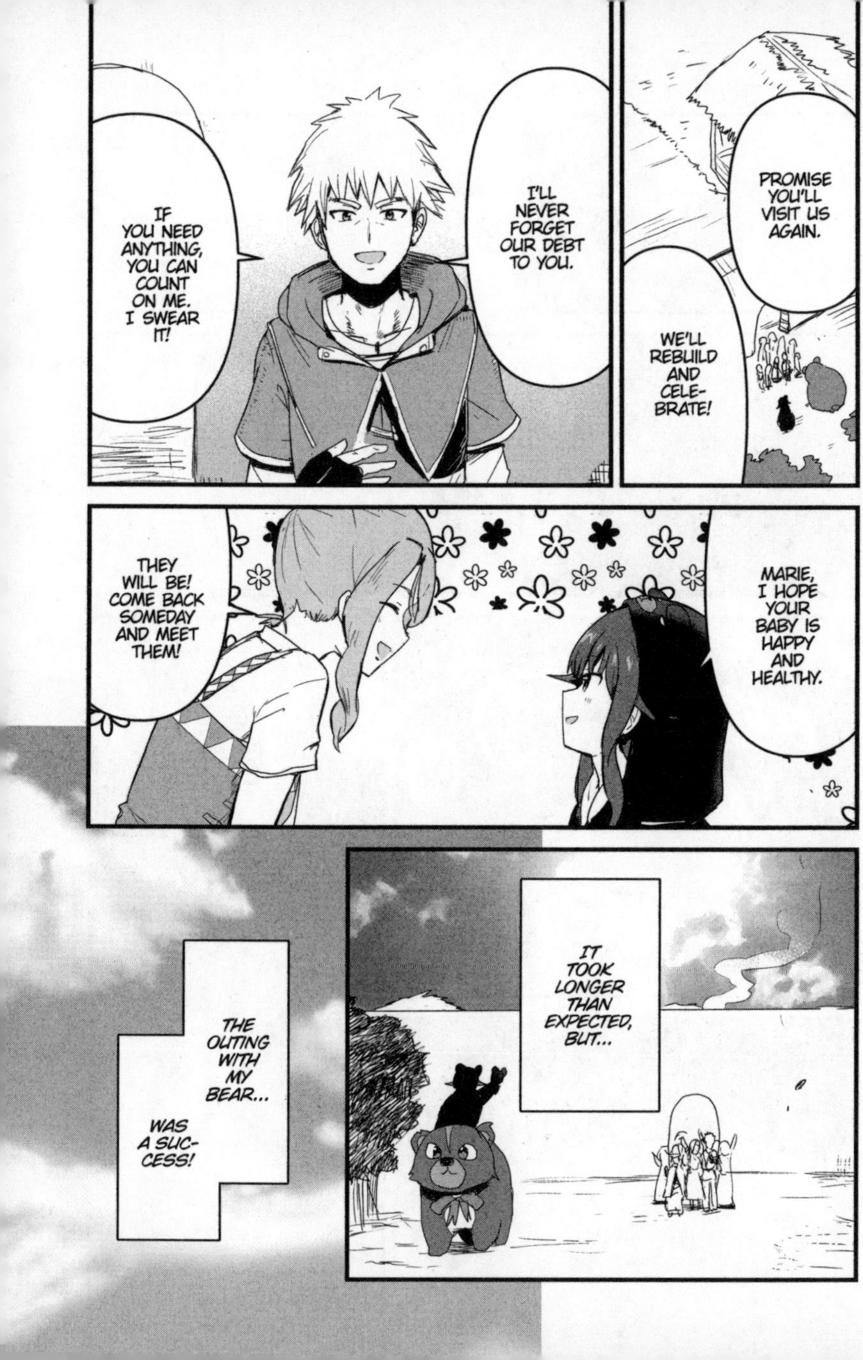
PROMISE YOU'LL VISIT US AGAIN.
WE'LL REBUILD AND CELE-BRATE!
I'LL NEVER FORGET OUR DEBT TO YOU.
IF YOU NEED ANYTHING, YOU CAN COUNT ON ME. I SWEAR IT!
MARIE, I HOPE YOUR BABY IS HAPPY AND HEALTHY.
THEY WILL BE! COME BACK SOMEDAY AND MEET THEM!
IT TOOK LONGER THAN EXPECTED, BUT...
THE OUTING WITH MY BEAR...
WAS A SUC-CESS!

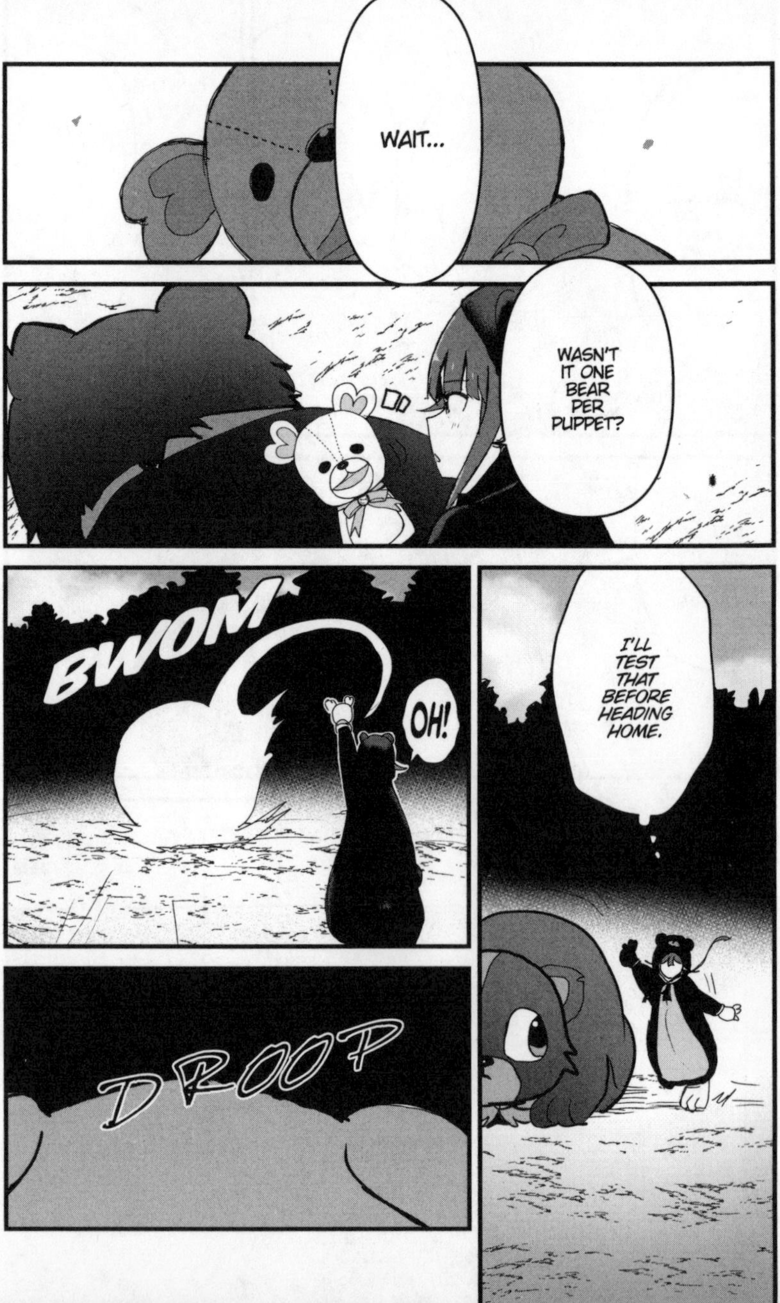
WAIT...
WASN'T IT ONE BEAR PER PUPPET?
I'LL TEST THAT BEFORE HEADING HOME.
OH!
BWOM
DROOP

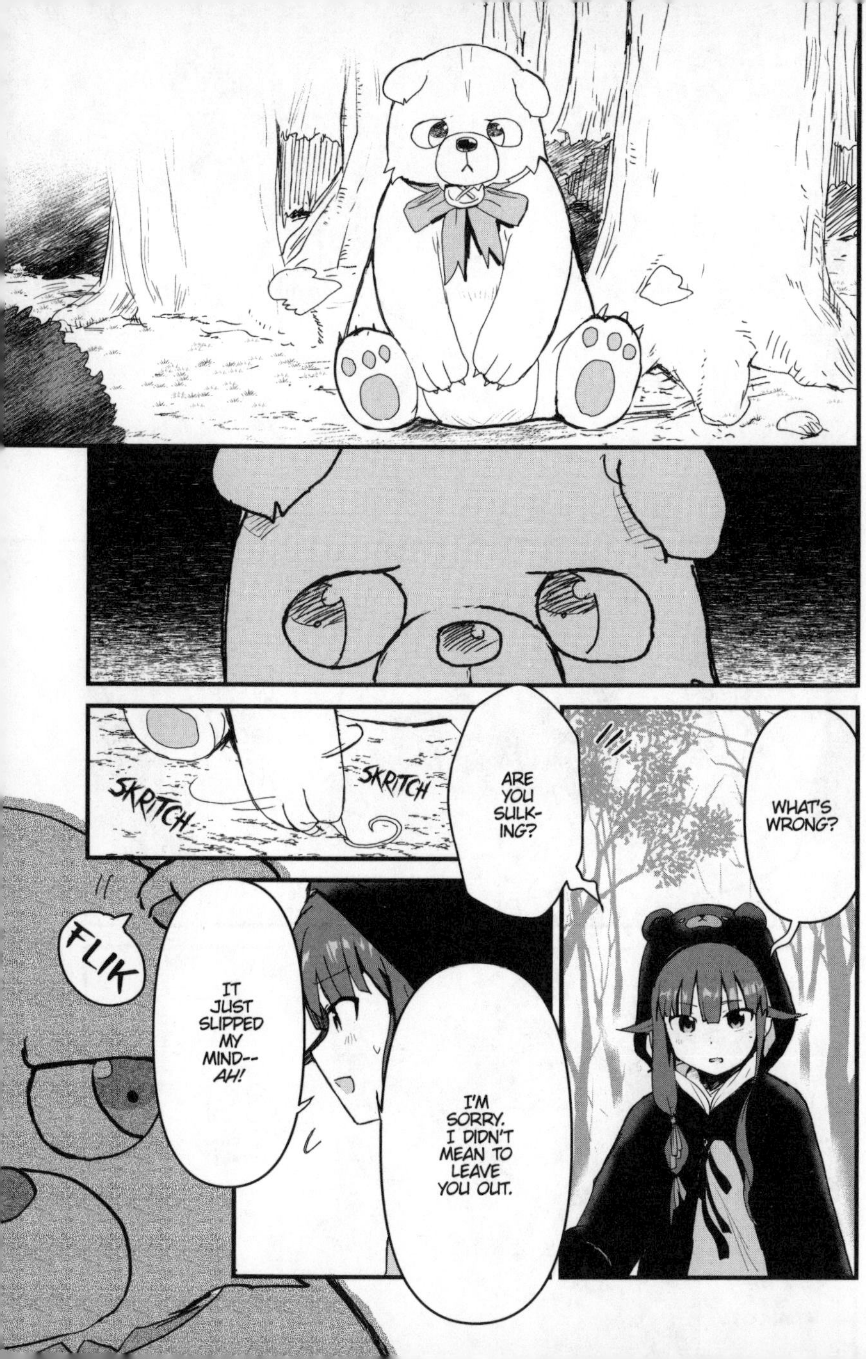
WHAT'S WRONG?
ARE YOU SULKING?
SKRITCH
SKRITCH
I'M SORRY. I DIDN'T MEAN TO LEAVE YOU OUT.
IT JUST SLIPPED MY MIND-- AH!
FLIK

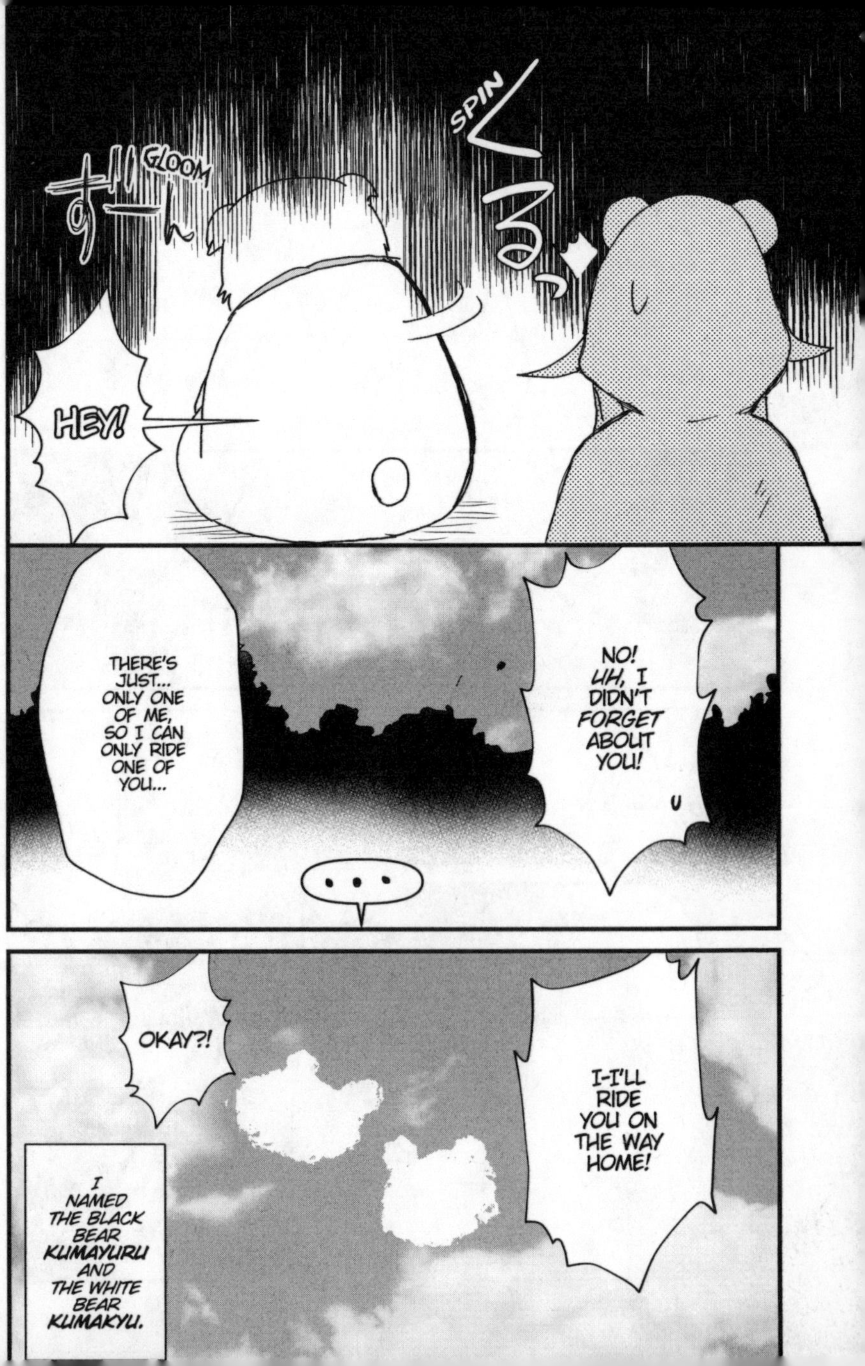
SPIN くるっ
GLOOM ず一ん
HEY!
NO! UH, I DIDN'T FORGET ABOUT YOU!
THERE'S JUST... ONLY ONE OF ME, SO I CAN ONLY RIDE ONE OF YOU...
...
I-I'LL RIDE YOU ON THE WAY HOME!
OKAY?!
I NAMED THE BLACK BEAR **KUMAYURU** AND THE WHITE BEAR **KUMAKYU**.

Chapter 16

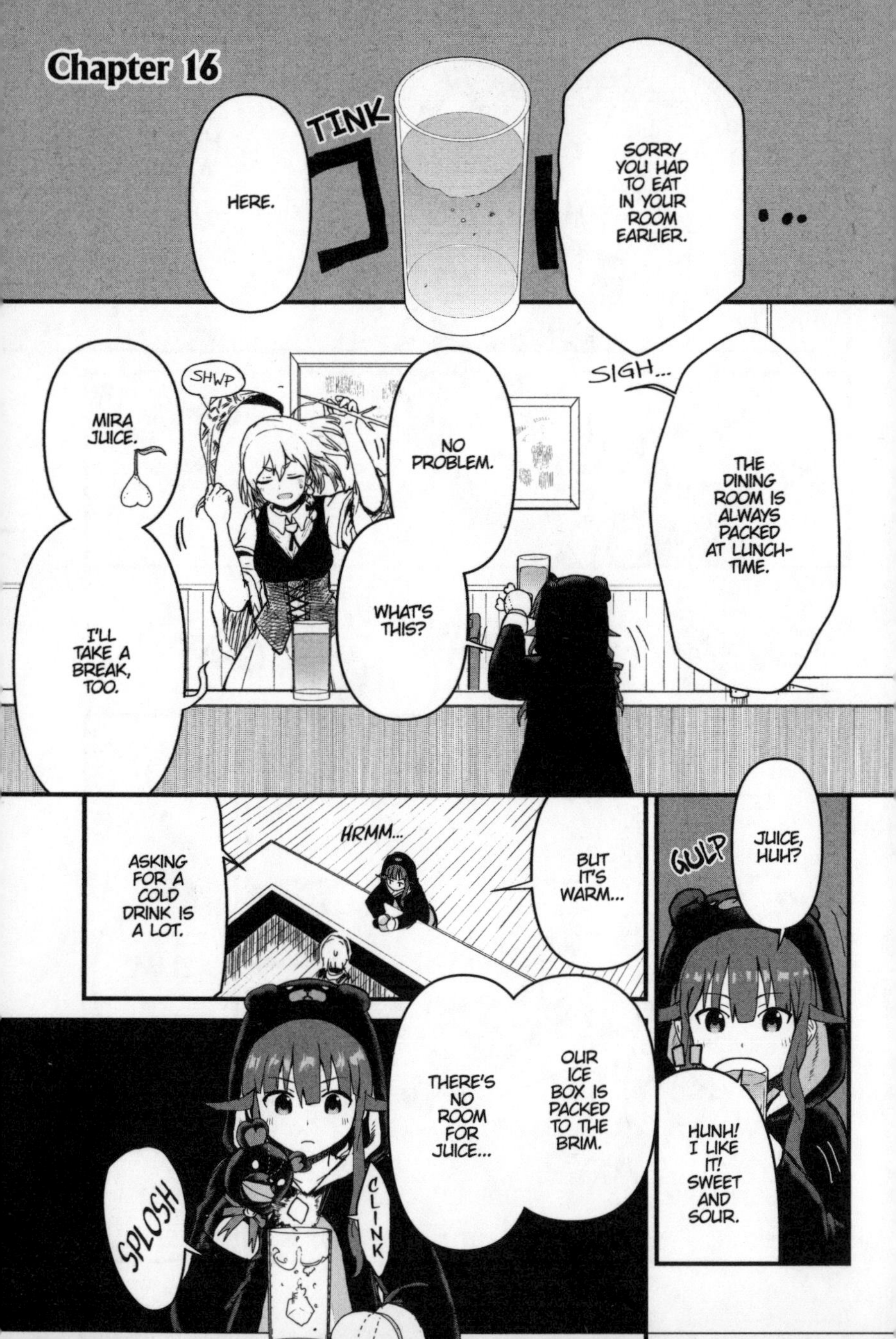
SORRY YOU HAD TO EAT IN YOUR ROOM EARLIER.
...
TINK
HERE.
SIGH...
THE DINING ROOM IS ALWAYS PACKED AT LUNCH-TIME.
NO PROBLEM.
WHAT'S THIS?
SHWP
MIRA JUICE.
I'LL TAKE A BREAK, TOO.
GULP
JUICE, HUH?
HUNH! I LIKE IT! SWEET AND SOUR.
BUT IT'S WARM...
HRMM...
ASKING FOR A COLD DRINK IS A LOT.
OUR ICE BOX IS PACKED TO THE BRIM.
THERE'S NO ROOM FOR JUICE...
CLINK
SPLOSH

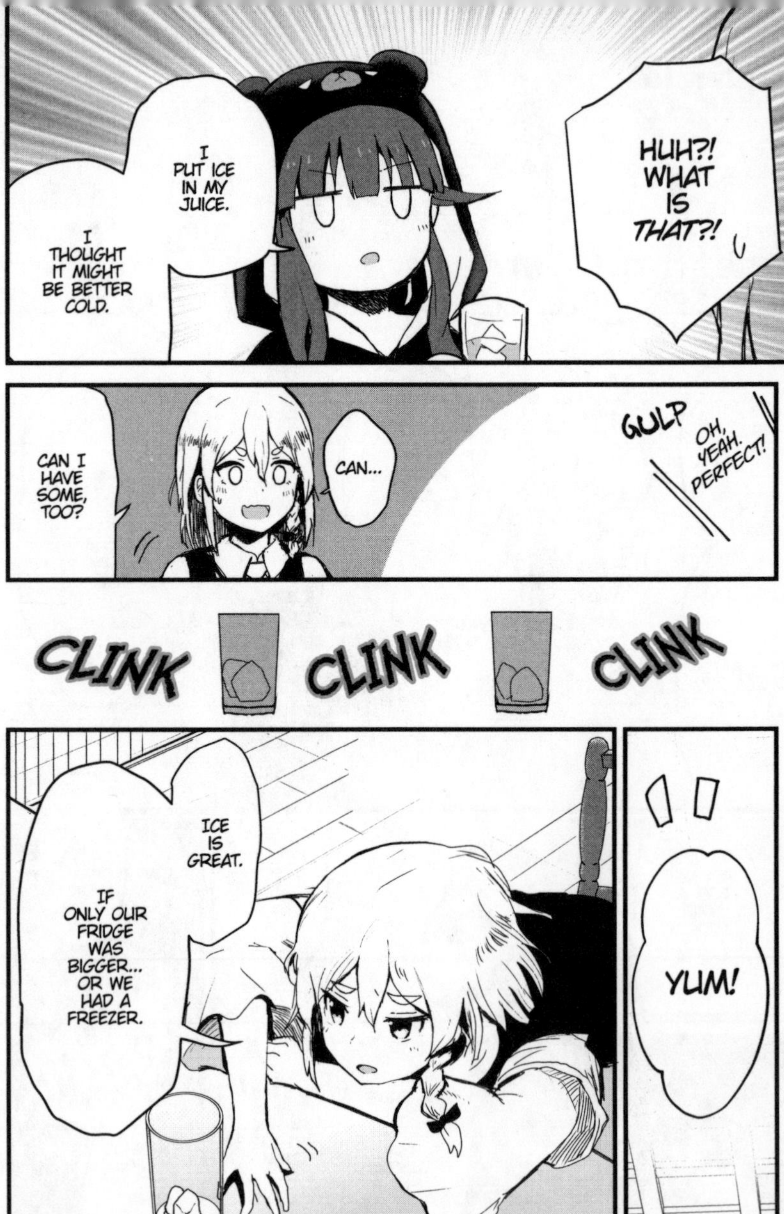
HUH?! WHAT IS THAT?!
I PUT ICE IN MY JUICE.
I THOUGHT IT MIGHT BE BETTER COLD.
GULP
OH, YEAH. PERFECT!
CAN...
CAN I HAVE SOME, TOO?
CLINK
CLINK
CLINK
YUM!
ICE IS GREAT.
IF ONLY OUR FRIDGE WAS BIGGER... OR WE HAD A FREEZER.

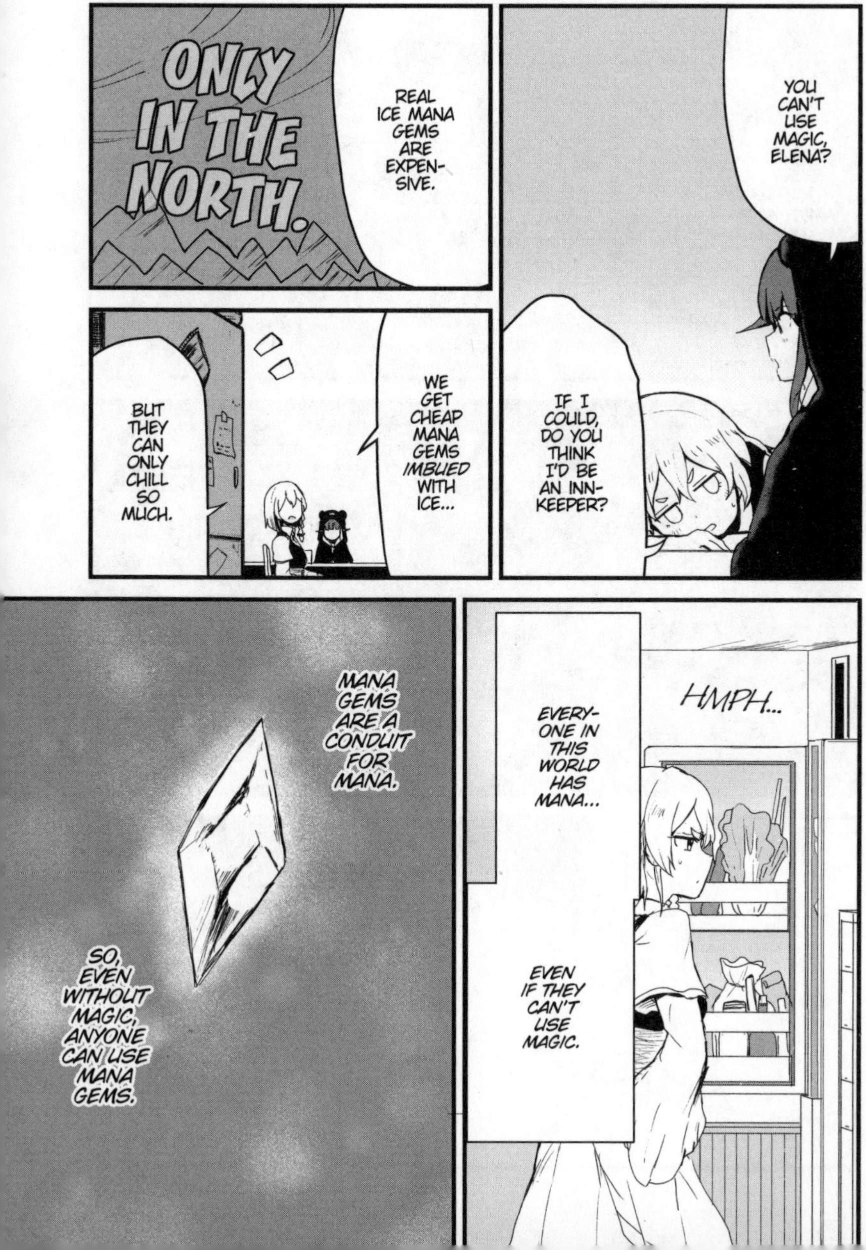
YOU CAN'T USE MAGIC, ELENA?
IF I COULD, DO YOU THINK I'D BE AN INNKEEPER?
REAL ICE MANA GEMS ARE EXPENSIVE.
ONLY IN THE NORTH.
WE GET CHEAP MANA GEMS *IMBUED* WITH ICE...
BUT THEY CAN ONLY CHILL SO MUCH.
HMPH...
EVERYONE IN THIS WORLD HAS MANA...
EVEN IF THEY CAN'T USE MAGIC.
MANA GEMS ARE A CONDUIT FOR MANA.
SO, EVEN WITHOUT MAGIC, ANYONE CAN USE MANA GEMS.

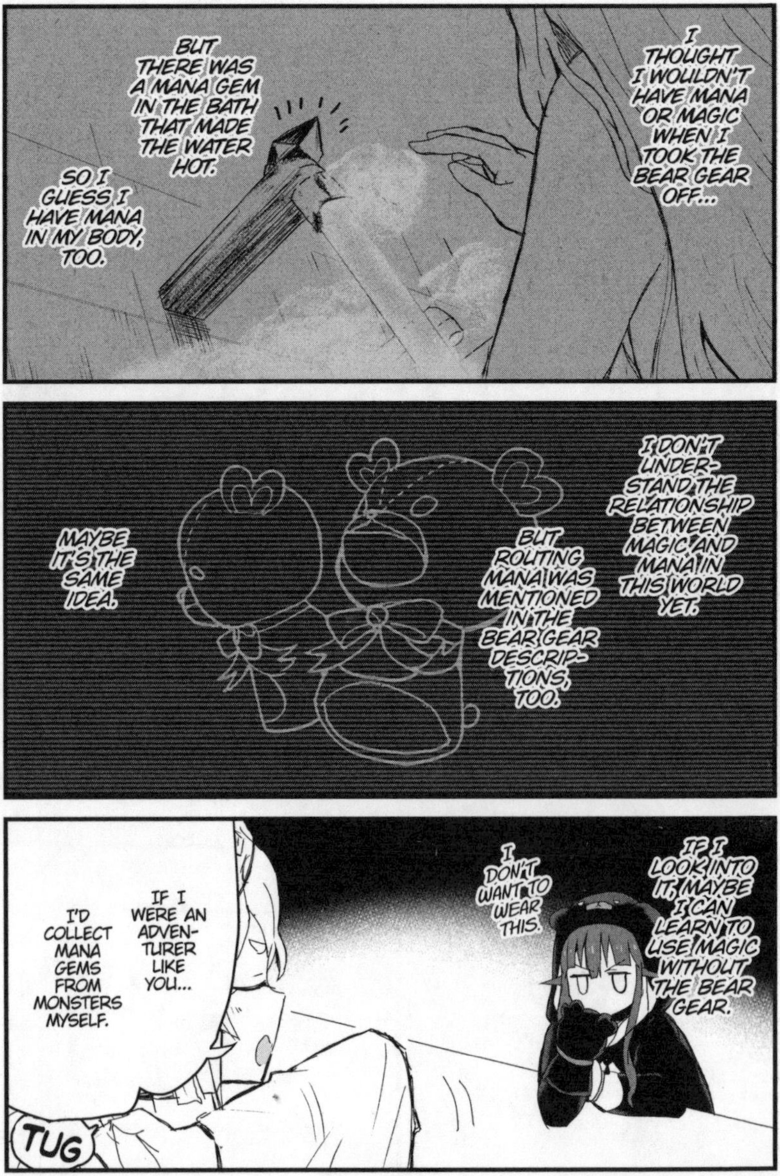
I THOUGHT I WOULDN'T HAVE MANA OR MAGIC WHEN I TOOK THE BEAR GEAR OFF...
BUT THERE WAS A MANA GEM IN THE BATH THAT MADE THE WATER HOT.
SO I GUESS I HAVE MANA IN MY BODY, TOO.
I DON'T UNDER-STAND THE RELATIONSHIP BETWEEN MAGIC AND MANA IN THIS WORLD YET.
BUT ROUTING MANA WAS MENTIONED IN THE BEAR GEAR DESCRIP-TIONS, TOO.
MAYBE IT'S THE SAME IDEA.
IF I LOOK INTO IT, MAYBE I CAN LEARN TO USE MAGIC WITHOUT THE BEAR GEAR.
I DON'T WANT TO WEAR THIS.
IF I WERE AN ADVEN-TURER LIKE YOU...
I'D COLLECT MANA GEMS FROM MONSTERS MYSELF.
TUG

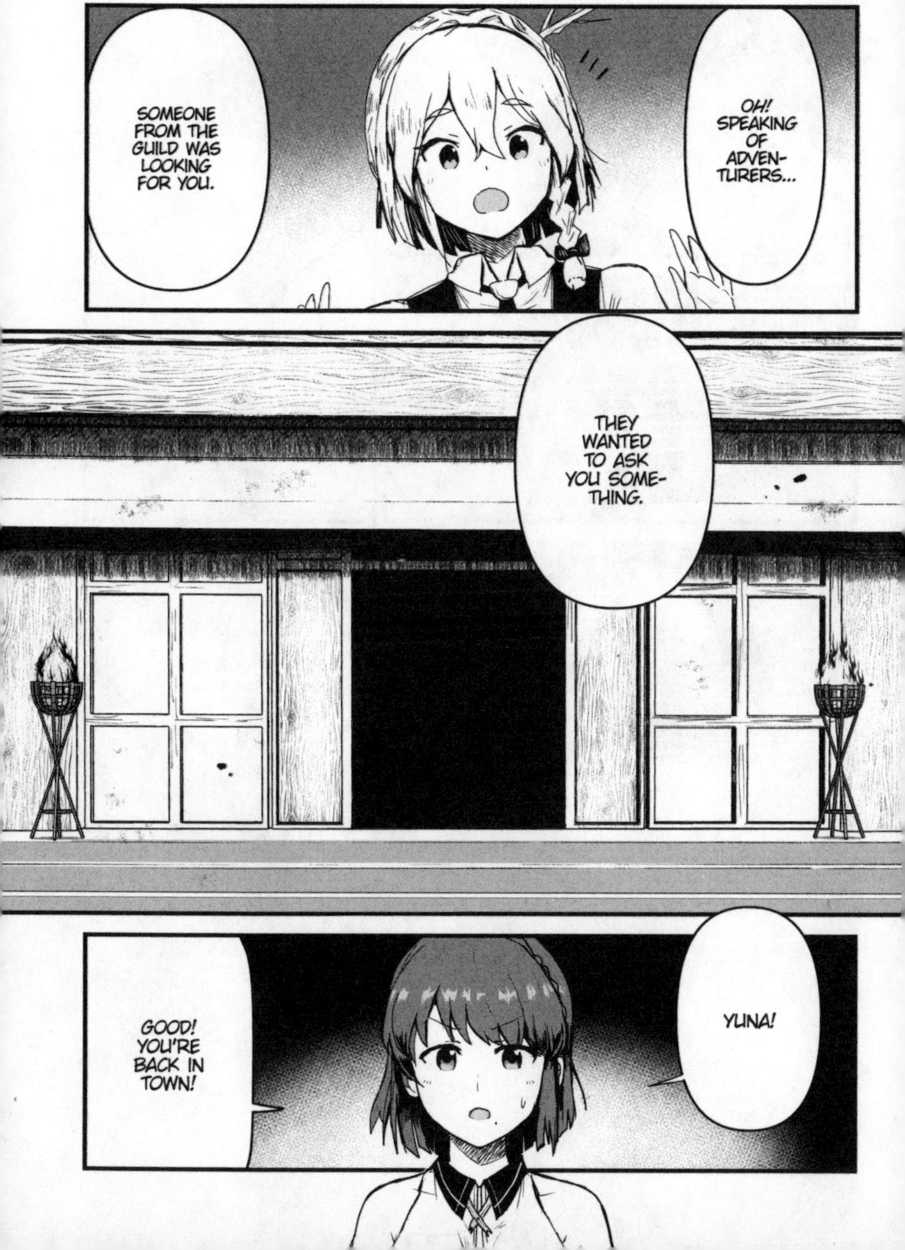
OH! SPEAKING OF ADVENTURERS...
SOMEONE FROM THE GUILD WAS LOOKING FOR YOU.
THEY WANTED TO ASK YOU SOMETHING.
YUNA!
GOOD! YOU'RE BACK IN TOWN!

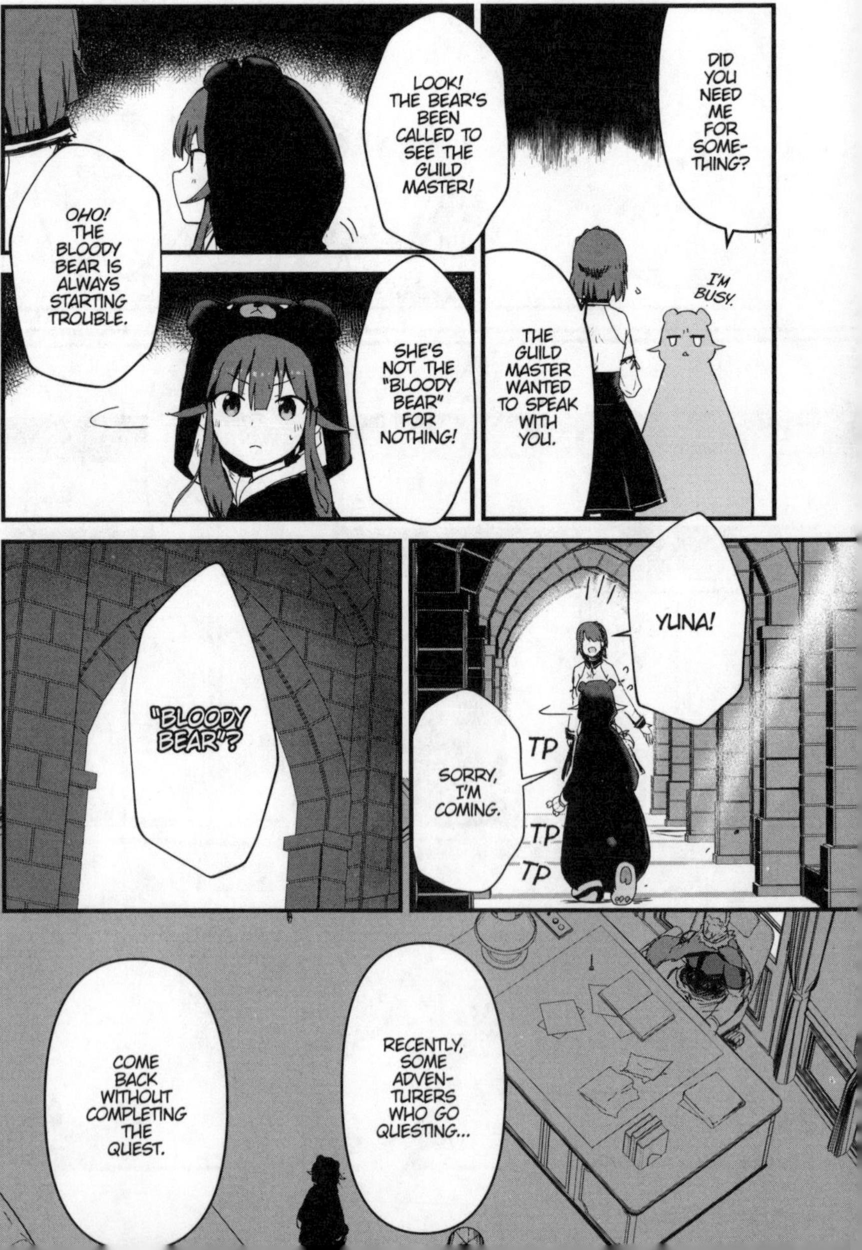
DID YOU NEED ME FOR SOMETHING?
I'M BUSY.
THE GUILD MASTER WANTED TO SPEAK WITH YOU.
LOOK! THE BEAR'S BEEN CALLED TO SEE THE GUILD MASTER!
OHO! THE BLOODY BEAR IS ALWAYS STARTING TROUBLE.
SHE'S NOT THE "BLOODY BEAR" FOR NOTHING!
YUNA!
SORRY, I'M COMING.
TP
TP
TP
"BLOODY BEAR"?
RECENTLY, SOME ADVENTURERS WHO GO QUESTING...
COME BACK WITHOUT COMPLETING THE QUEST.

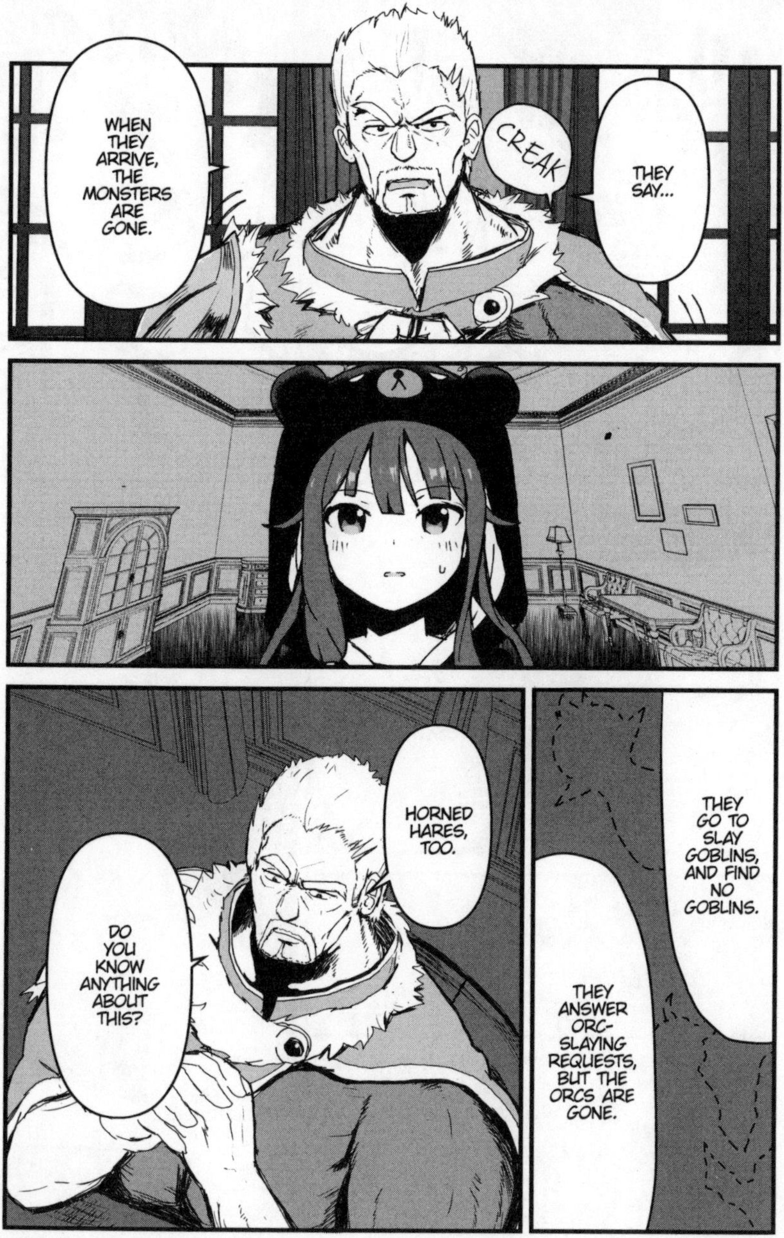
THEY SAY...
CREAK
WHEN THEY ARRIVE, THE MONSTERS ARE GONE.
THEY GO TO SLAY GOBLINS, AND FIND NO GOBLINS.
THEY ANSWER ORC-SLAYING REQUESTS, BUT THE ORCS ARE GONE.
HORNED HARES, TOO.
DO YOU KNOW ANYTHING ABOUT THIS?

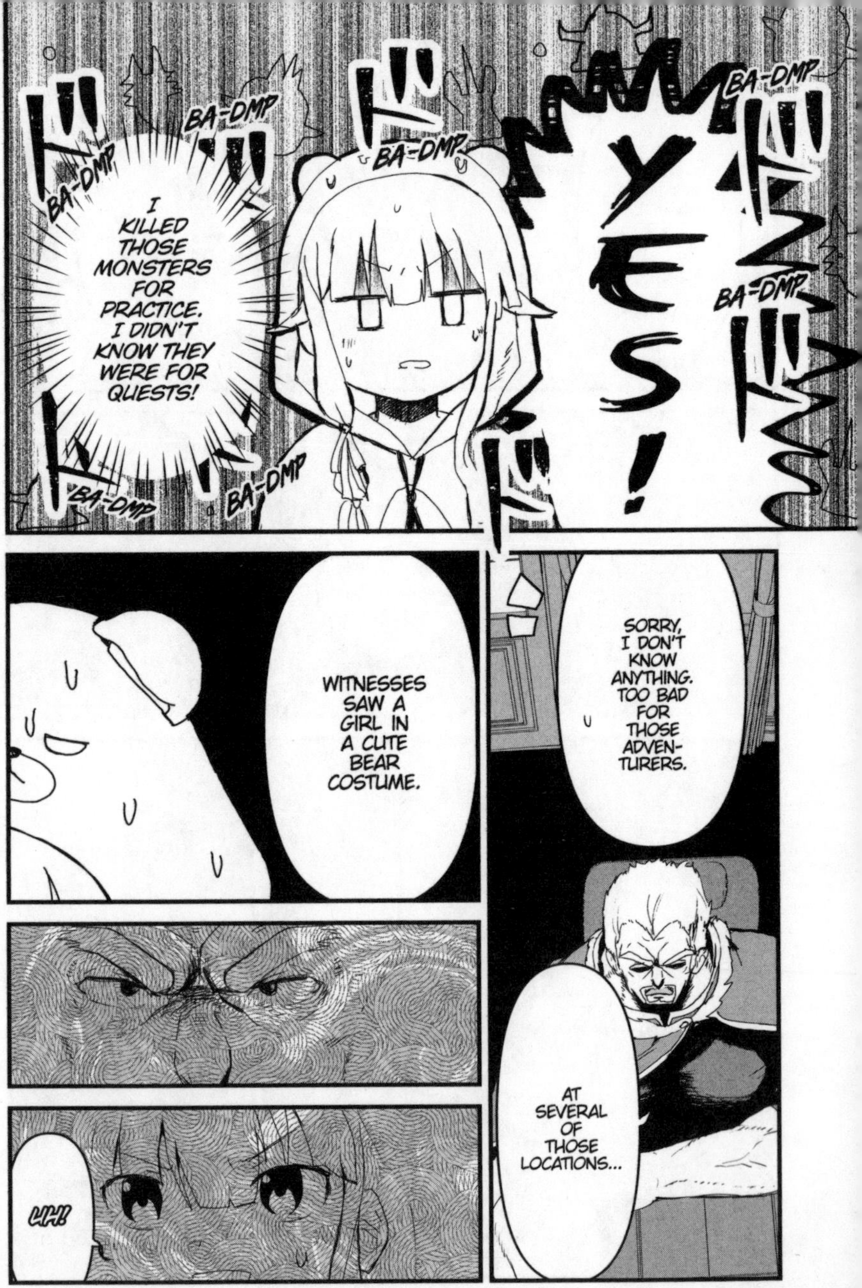
BA-DMP
YES!
BA-DMP
BA-DMP
BA-DMP
BA-DMP
I KILLED THOSE MONSTERS FOR PRACTICE. I DIDN'T KNOW THEY WERE FOR QUESTS!
BA-DMP
BA-DMP
BA-DMP
SORRY, I DON'T KNOW ANYTHING. TOO BAD FOR THOSE ADVEN-TURERS.
AT SEVERAL OF THOSE LOCATIONS...
WITNESSES SAW A GIRL IN A CUTE BEAR COSTUME.
UH!

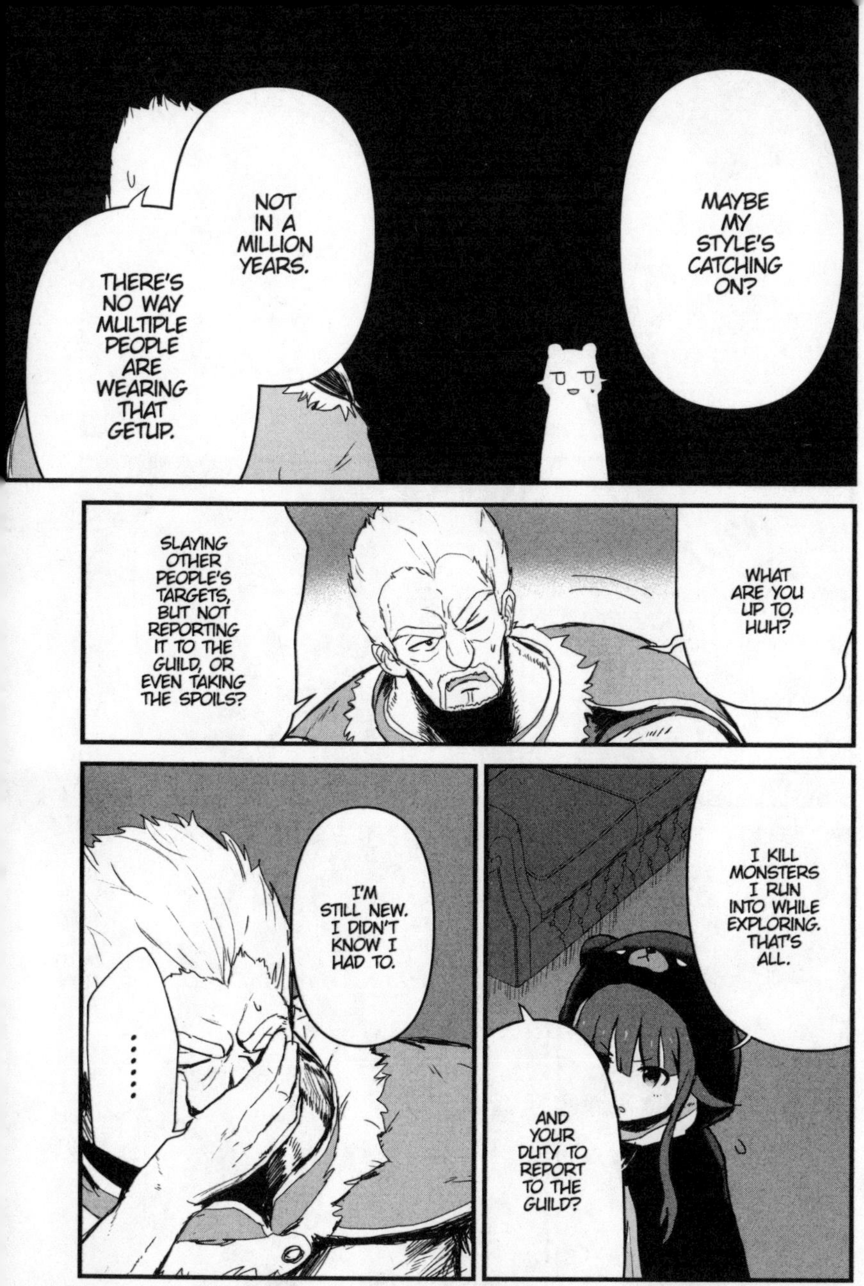
MAYBE MY STYLE'S CATCHING ON?
NOT IN A MILLION YEARS.
THERE'S NO WAY MULTIPLE PEOPLE ARE WEARING THAT GETUP.
WHAT ARE YOU UP TO, HUH?
SLAYING OTHER PEOPLE'S TARGETS, BUT NOT REPORTING IT TO THE GUILD, OR EVEN TAKING THE SPOILS?
I KILL MONSTERS I RUN INTO WHILE EXPLORING. THAT'S ALL.
AND YOUR DUTY TO REPORT TO THE GUILD?
I'M STILL NEW. I DIDN'T KNOW I HAD TO.
......

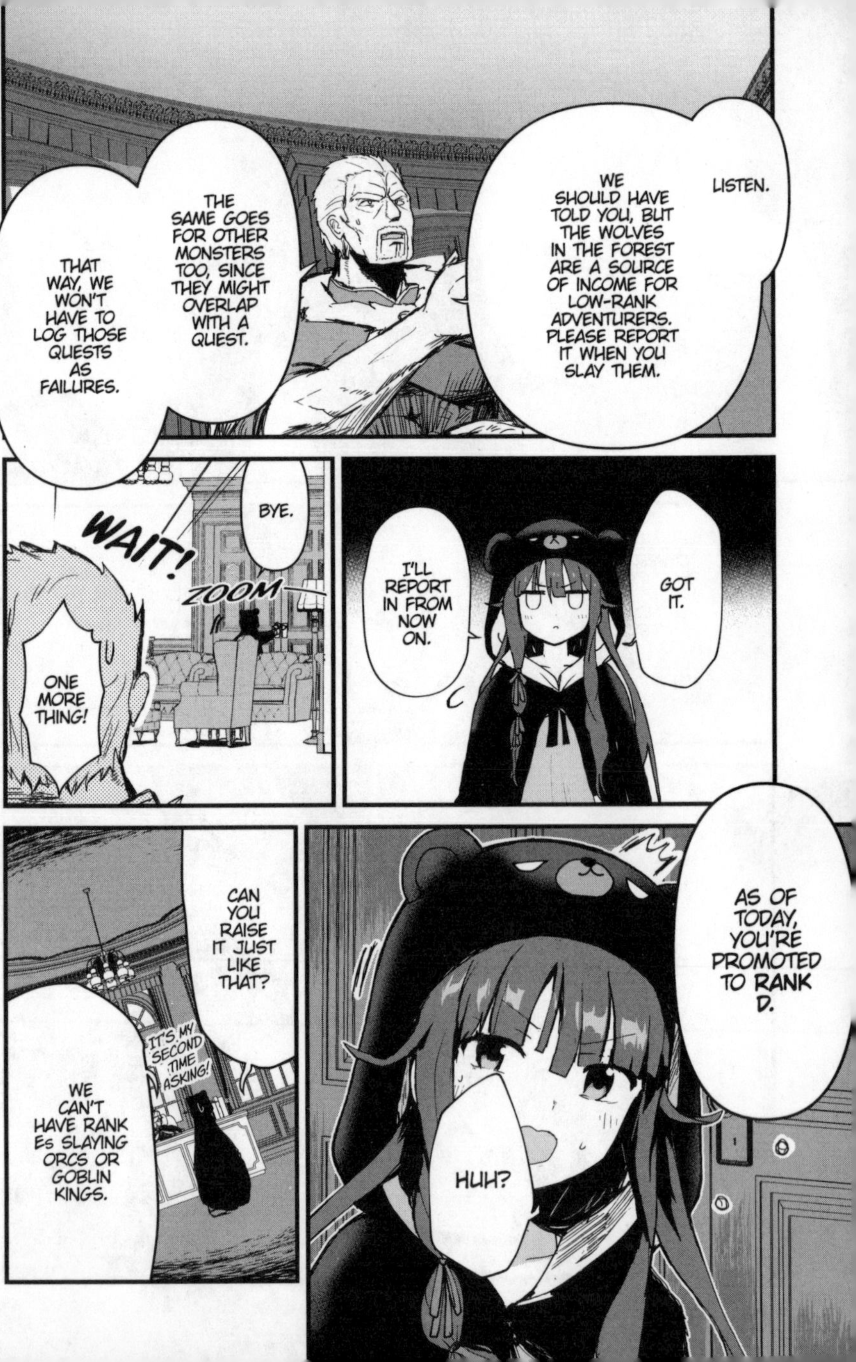
LISTEN.
WE SHOULD HAVE TOLD YOU, BUT THE WOLVES IN THE FOREST ARE A SOURCE OF INCOME FOR LOW-RANK ADVENTURERS. PLEASE REPORT IT WHEN YOU SLAY THEM.
THE SAME GOES FOR OTHER MONSTERS TOO, SINCE THEY MIGHT OVERLAP WITH A QUEST.
THAT WAY, WE WON'T HAVE TO LOG THOSE QUESTS AS FAILURES.
GOT IT.
I'LL REPORT IN FROM NOW ON.
BYE.
ZOOM
WAIT!
ONE MORE THING!
AS OF TODAY, YOU'RE PROMOTED TO RANK D.
HUH?
CAN YOU RAISE IT JUST LIKE THAT?
IT'S MY SECOND TIME ASKING!
WE CAN'T HAVE RANK Es SLAYING ORCS OR GOBLIN KINGS.

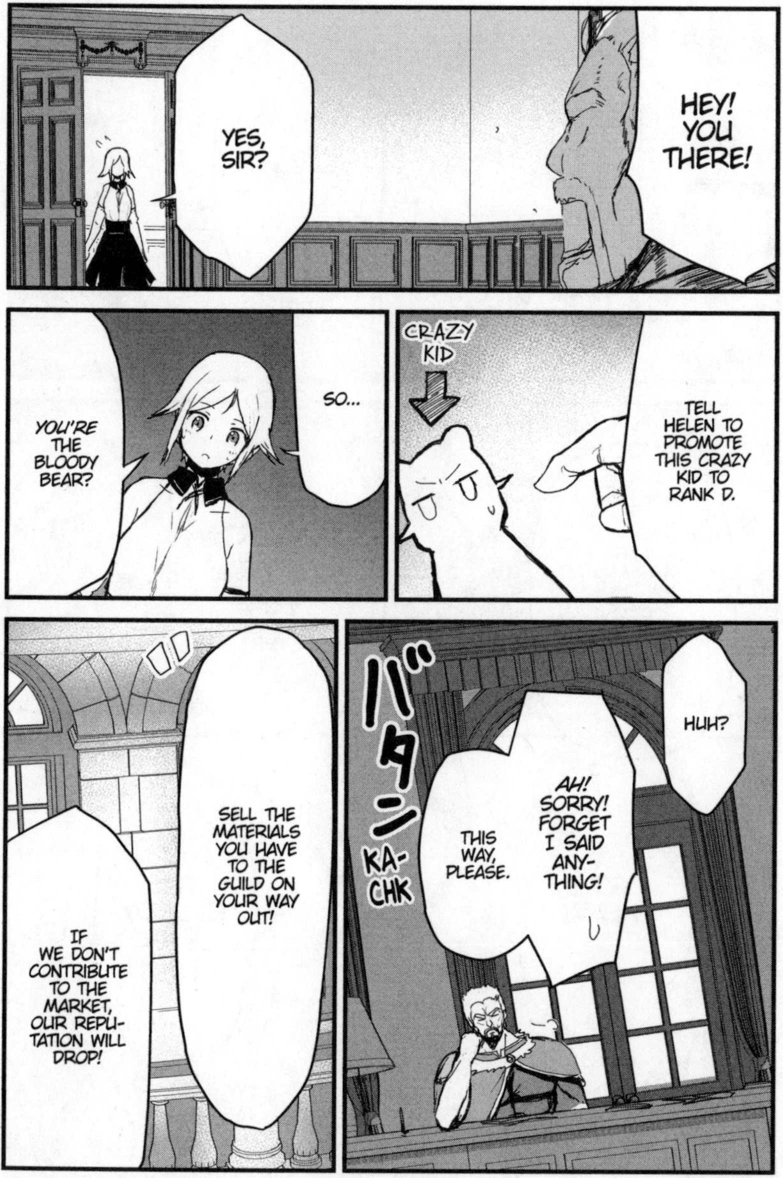
HEY! YOU THERE!
YES, SIR?
TELL HELEN TO PROMOTE THIS CRAZY KID TO RANK D.
CRAZY KID
SO...
YOU'RE THE BLOODY BEAR?
HUH?
AH! SORRY! FORGET I SAID ANYTHING!
THIS WAY, PLEASE.
バタン
KA-CHK
SELL THE MATERIALS YOU HAVE TO THE GUILD ON YOUR WAY OUT!
IF WE DON'T CONTRIBUTE TO THE MARKET, OUR REPUTATION WILL DROP!

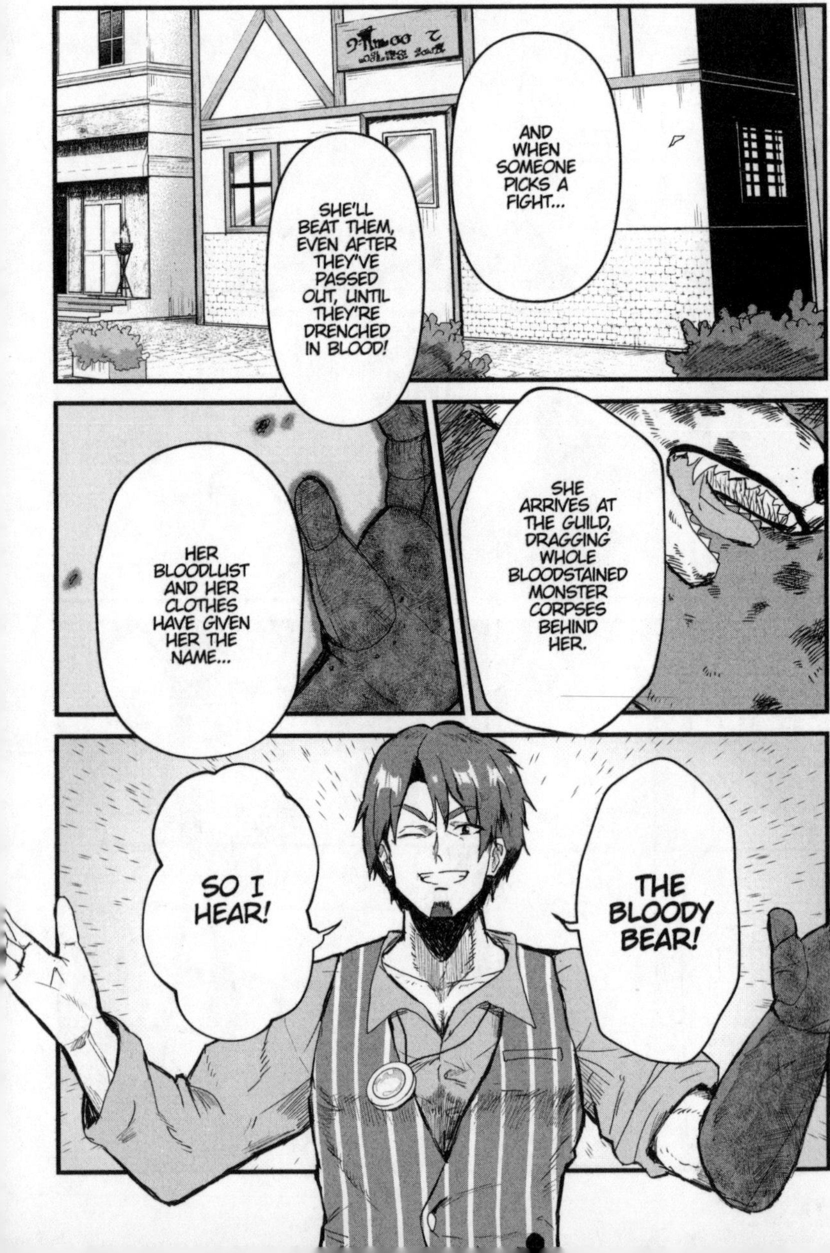
AND WHEN SOMEONE PICKS A FIGHT...
SHE'LL BEAT THEM, EVEN AFTER THEY'VE PASSED OUT, UNTIL THEY'RE DRENCHED IN BLOOD!
SHE ARRIVES AT THE GUILD, DRAGGING WHOLE BLOODSTAINED MONSTER CORPSES BEHIND HER.
HER BLOODLUST AND HER CLOTHES HAVE GIVEN HER THE NAME...
THE BLOODY BEAR!
SO I HEAR!

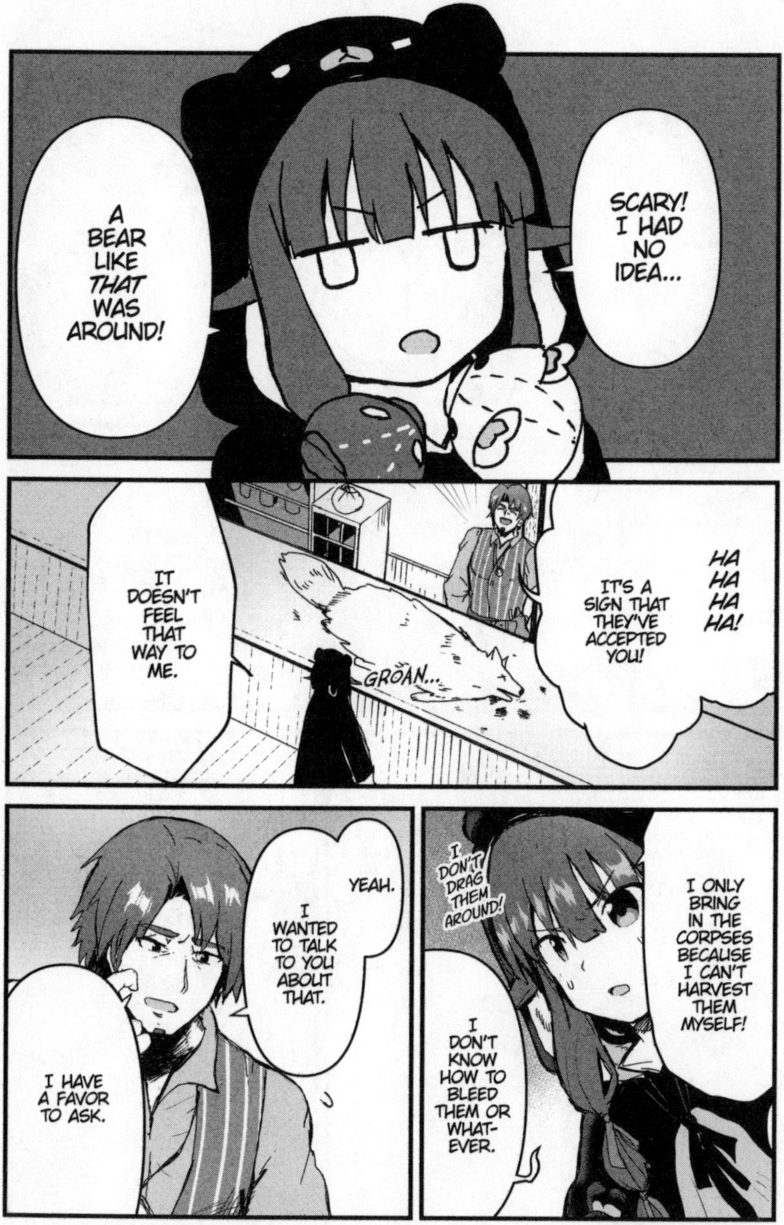
SCARY! I HAD NO IDEA...
A BEAR LIKE *THAT* WAS AROUND!
HA HA HA HA!
IT'S A SIGN THAT THEY'VE ACCEPTED YOU!
GROAN...
IT DOESN'T FEEL THAT WAY TO ME.
I ONLY BRING IN THE CORPSES BECAUSE I CAN'T HARVEST THEM MYSELF!
I DON'T DRAG THEM AROUND!
I DON'T KNOW HOW TO BLEED THEM OR WHATEVER.
YEAH.
I WANTED TO TALK TO YOU ABOUT THAT.
I HAVE A FAVOR TO ASK.

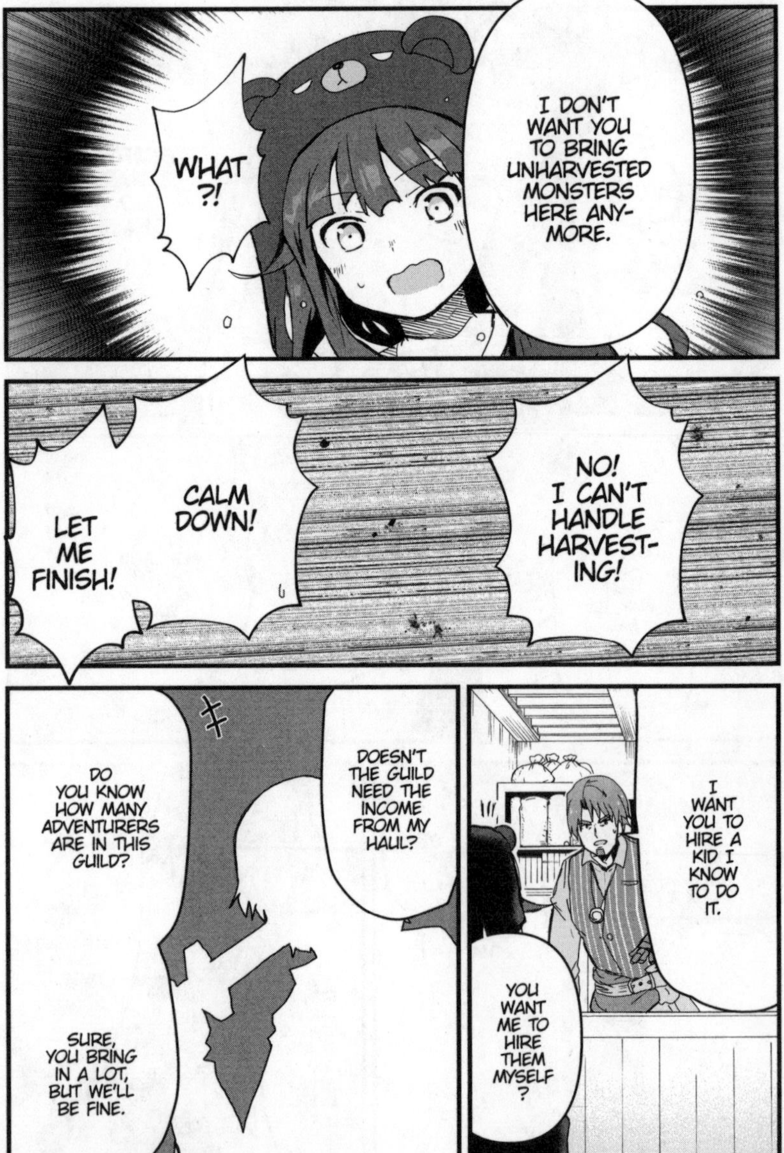
I DON'T WANT YOU TO BRING UNHARVESTED MONSTERS HERE ANYMORE.
WHAT?!
NO! I CAN'T HANDLE HARVESTING!
CALM DOWN!
LET ME FINISH!
I WANT YOU TO HIRE A KID I KNOW TO DO IT.
YOU WANT ME TO HIRE THEM MYSELF?
DOESN'T THE GUILD NEED THE INCOME FROM MY HAUL?
DO YOU KNOW HOW MANY ADVENTURERS ARE IN THIS GUILD?
SURE, YOU BRING IN A LOT, BUT WE'LL BE FINE.

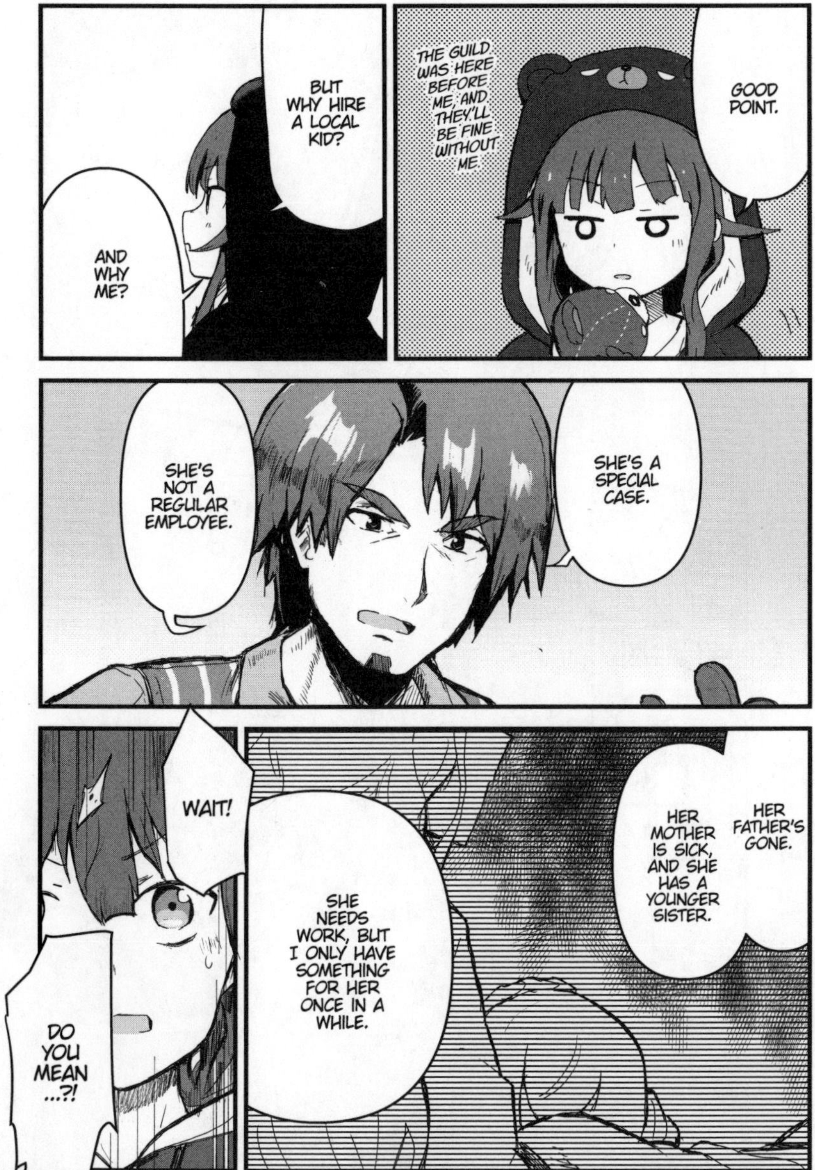
GOOD POINT.
THE GUILD WAS HERE BEFORE ME, AND THEY'LL BE FINE WITHOUT ME.
BUT WHY HIRE A LOCAL KID?
AND WHY ME?
SHE'S A SPECIAL CASE.
SHE'S NOT A REGULAR EMPLOYEE.
HER FATHER'S GONE.
HER MOTHER IS SICK, AND SHE HAS A YOUNGER SISTER.
SHE NEEDS WORK, BUT I ONLY HAVE SOMETHING FOR HER ONCE IN A WHILE.
WAIT!
DO YOU MEAN ...?!

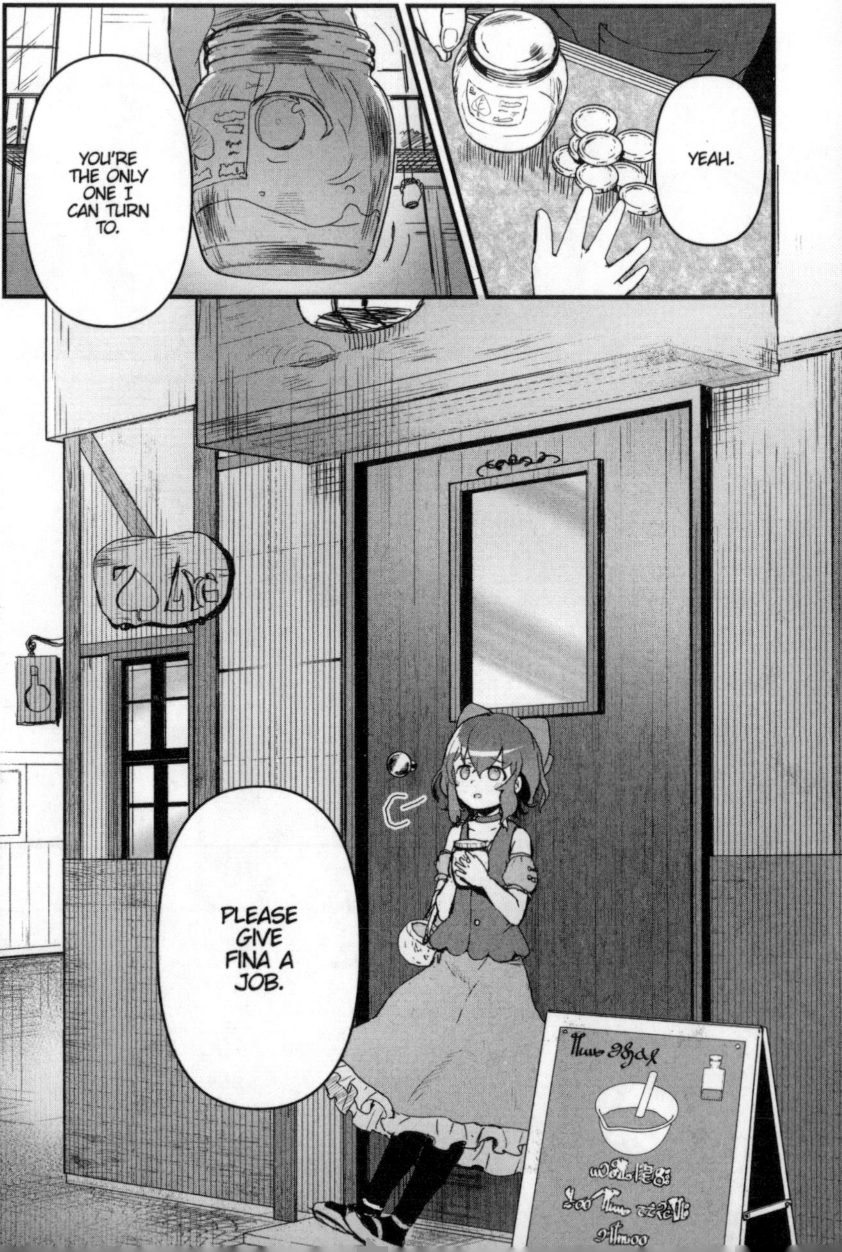
YEAH.
YOU'RE THE ONLY ONE I CAN TURN TO.
PLEASE GIVE FINA A JOB.

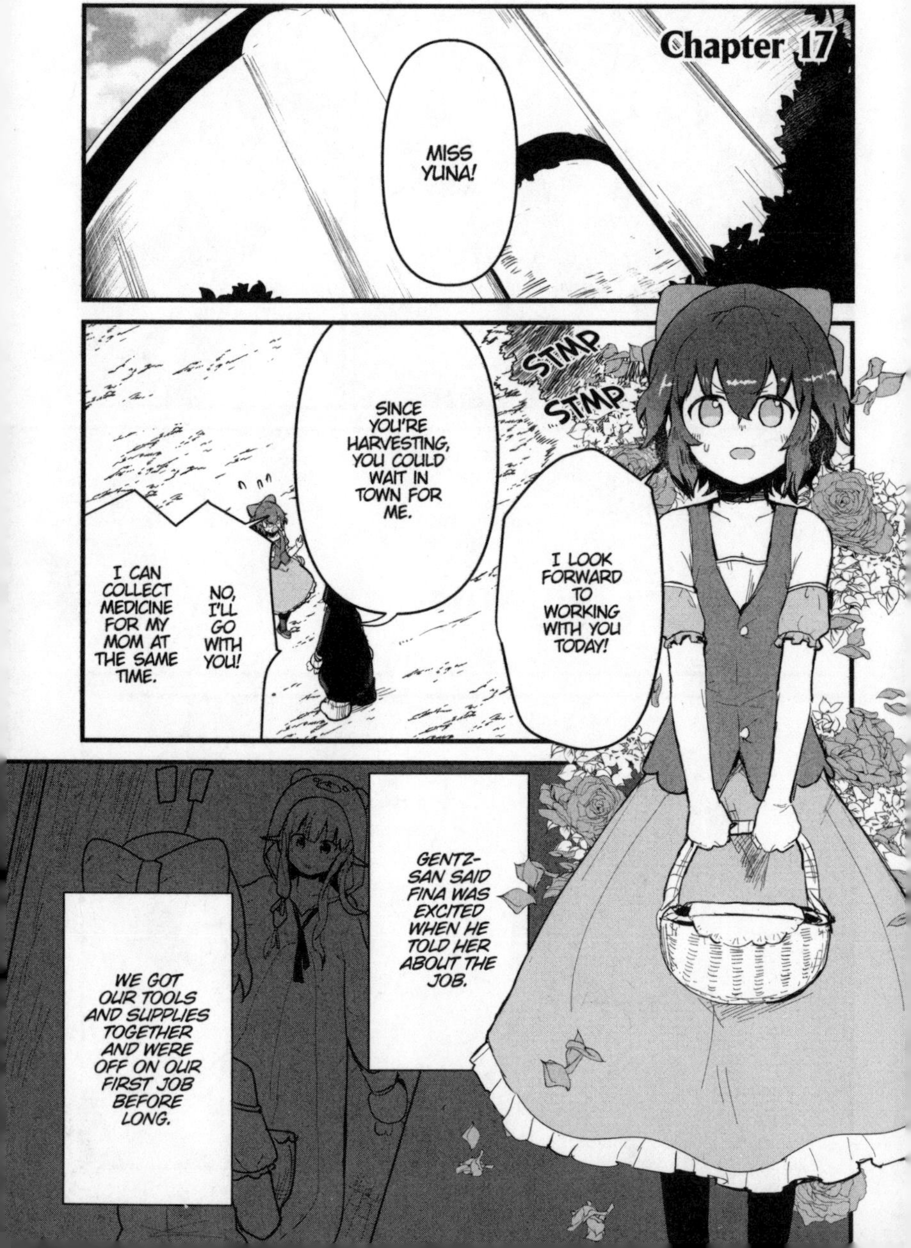
Chapter 17
MISS YUNA!
I LOOK FORWARD TO WORKING WITH YOU TODAY!
STMP STMP
SINCE YOU'RE HARVESTING, YOU COULD WAIT IN TOWN FOR ME.
NO, I'LL GO WITH YOU!
I CAN COLLECT MEDICINE FOR MY MOM AT THE SAME TIME.
GENTZ-SAN SAID FINA WAS EXCITED WHEN HE TOLD HER ABOUT THE JOB.
WE GOT OUR TOOLS AND SUPPLIES TOGETHER AND WERE OFF ON OUR FIRST JOB BEFORE LONG.

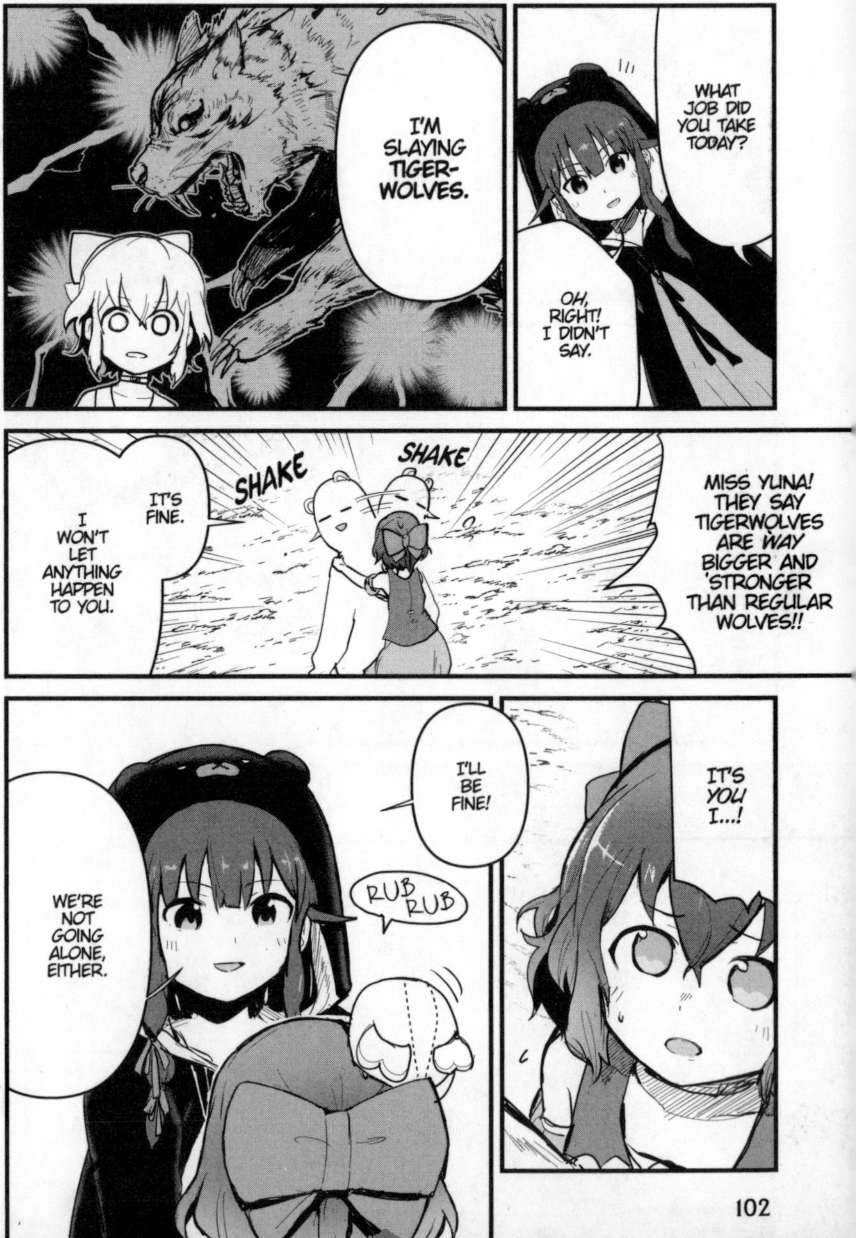
WHAT JOB DID YOU TAKE TODAY?
OH, RIGHT! I DIDN'T SAY.
I'M SLAYING TIGER-WOLVES.
MISS YUNA! THEY SAY TIGERWOLVES ARE WAY BIGGER AND STRONGER THAN REGULAR WOLVES!!
SHAKE
SHAKE
IT'S FINE.
I WON'T LET ANYTHING HAPPEN TO YOU.
IT'S YOU I...!
I'LL BE FINE!
RUB RUB
WE'RE NOT GOING ALONE, EITHER.

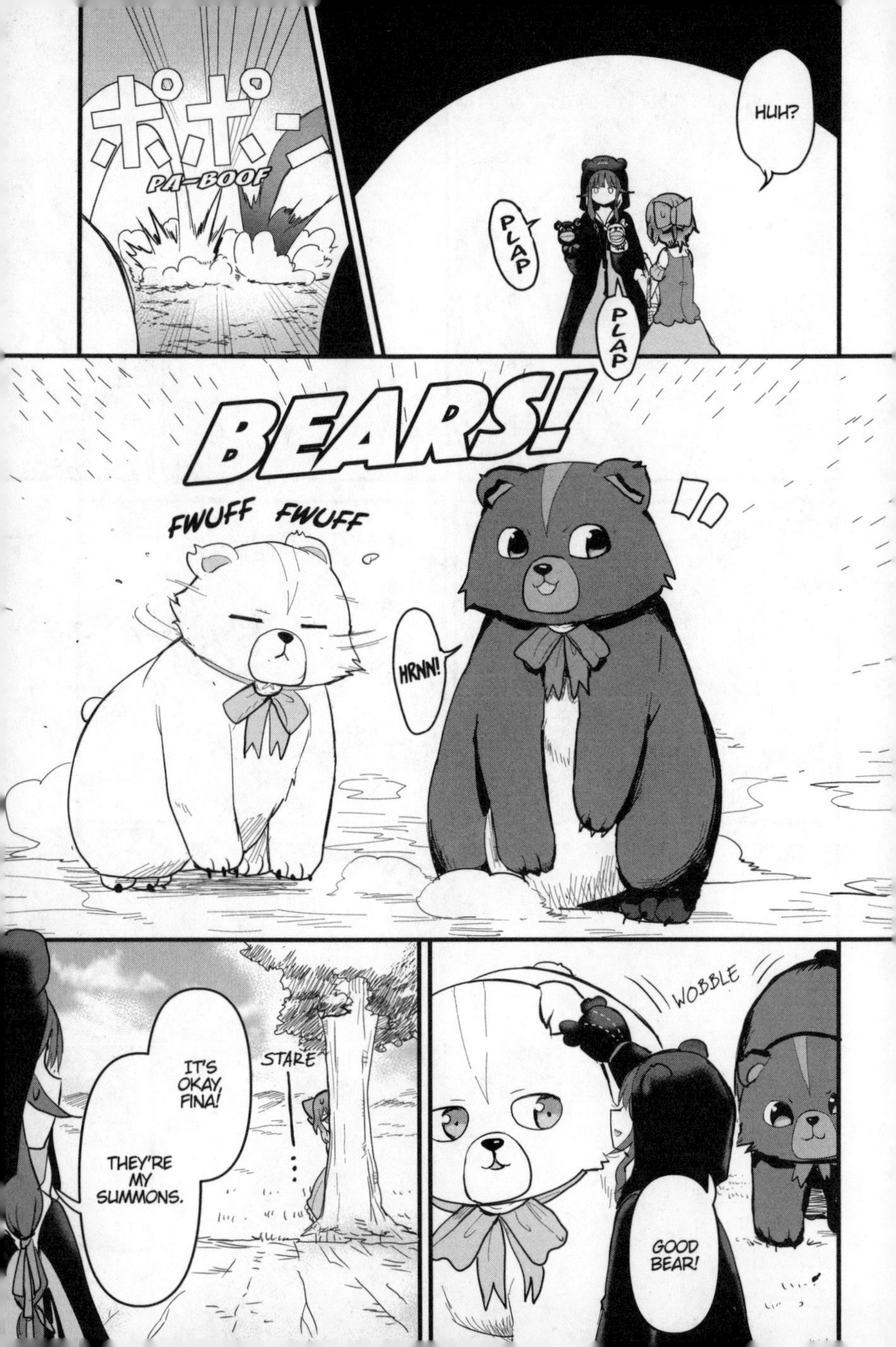
HUH?
PLAP
PLAP
PA-BOOF
BEARS!
HRNN!
FWUFF FWUFF
WOBBLE
GOOD BEAR!
STARE
...
IT'S OKAY, FINA!
THEY'RE MY SUMMONS.

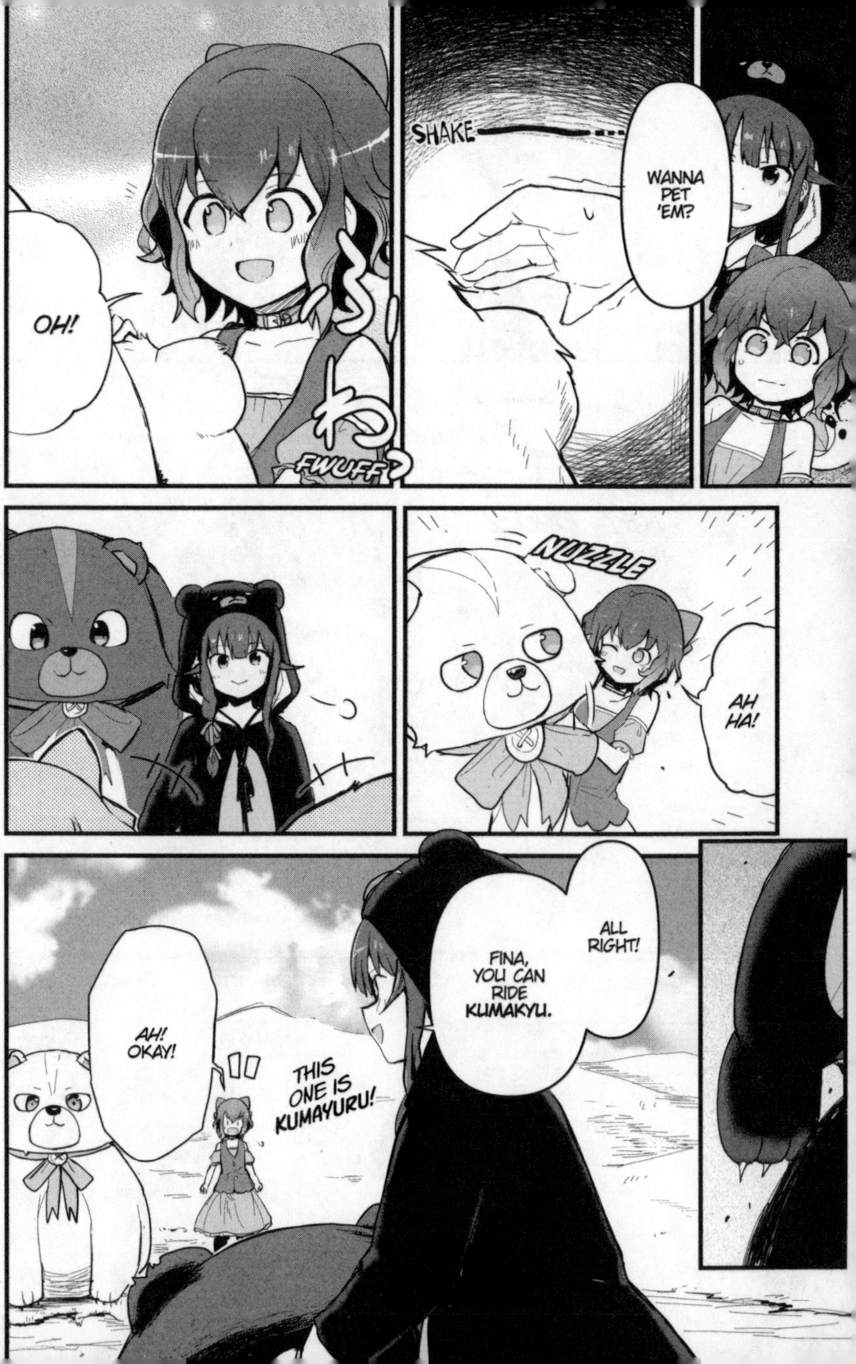
WANNA PET 'EM?
SHAKE
OH!
FWUFF
NUZZLE
AH HA!
ALL RIGHT!
FINA, YOU CAN RIDE KUMAKYU.
THIS ONE IS KUMAYURU!
AH! OKAY!

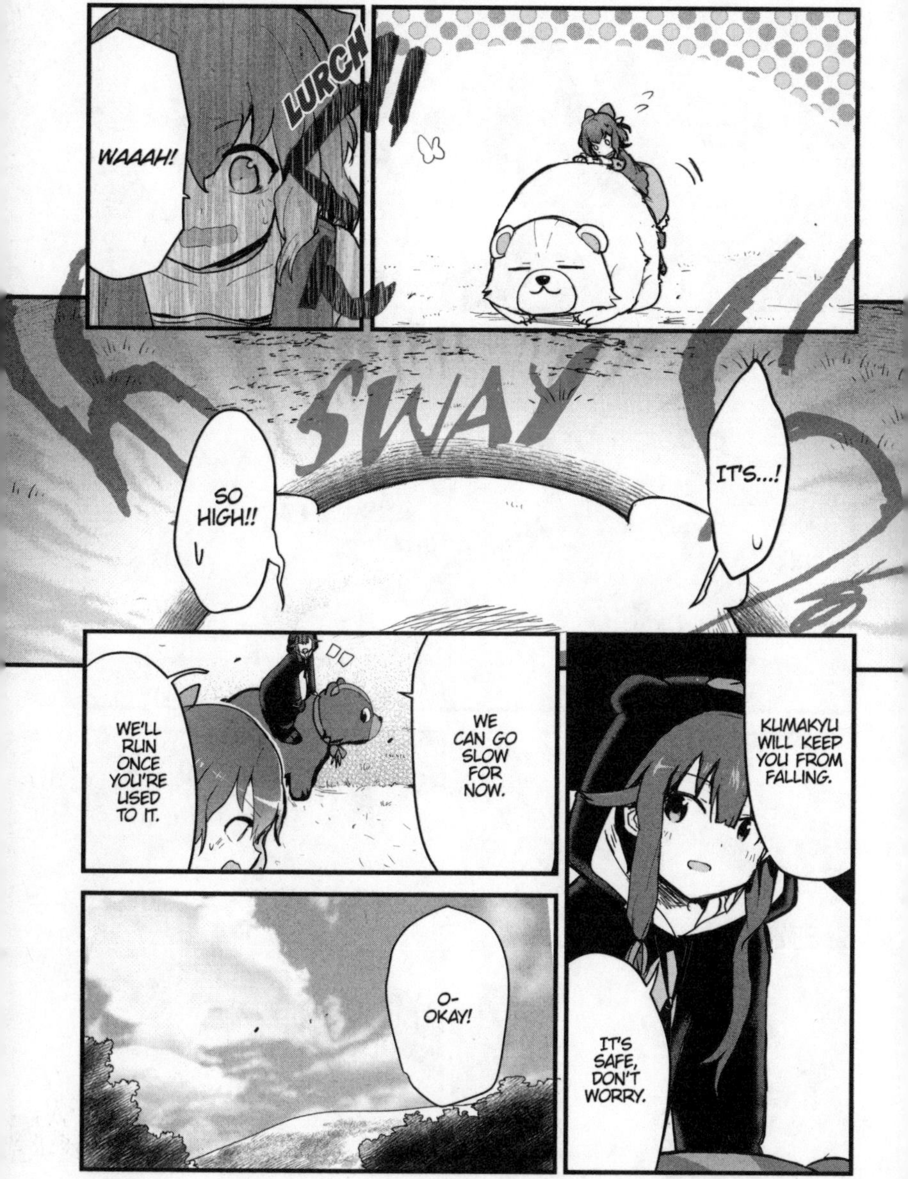
LURCH
WAAAH!
SWAY
IT'S...!
SO HIGH!!
KUMAKYU WILL KEEP YOU FROM FALLING.
IT'S SAFE, DON'T WORRY.
WE CAN GO SLOW FOR NOW.
WE'LL RUN ONCE YOU'RE USED TO IT.
O-OKAY!

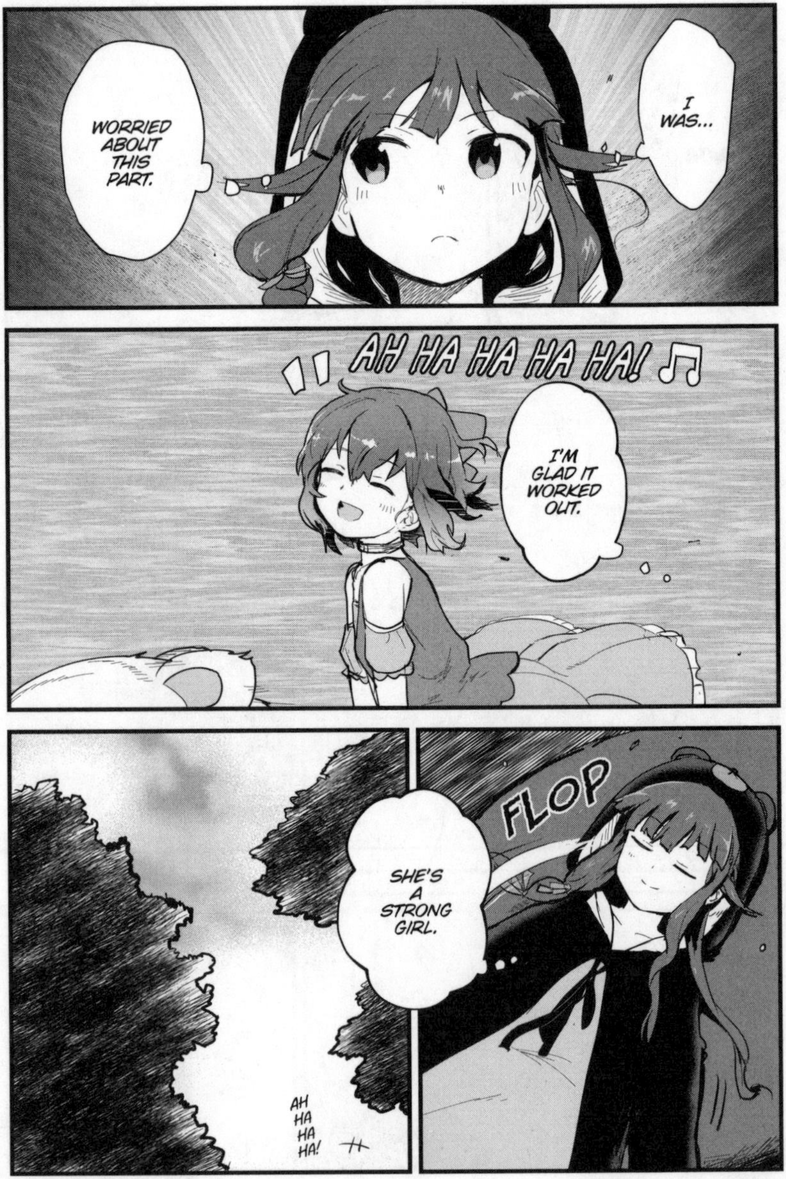
I WAS...
WORRIED ABOUT THIS PART.
AH HA HA HA HA! ♫
I'M GLAD IT WORKED OUT.
FLOP
SHE'S A STRONG GIRL.
AH HA HA HA!

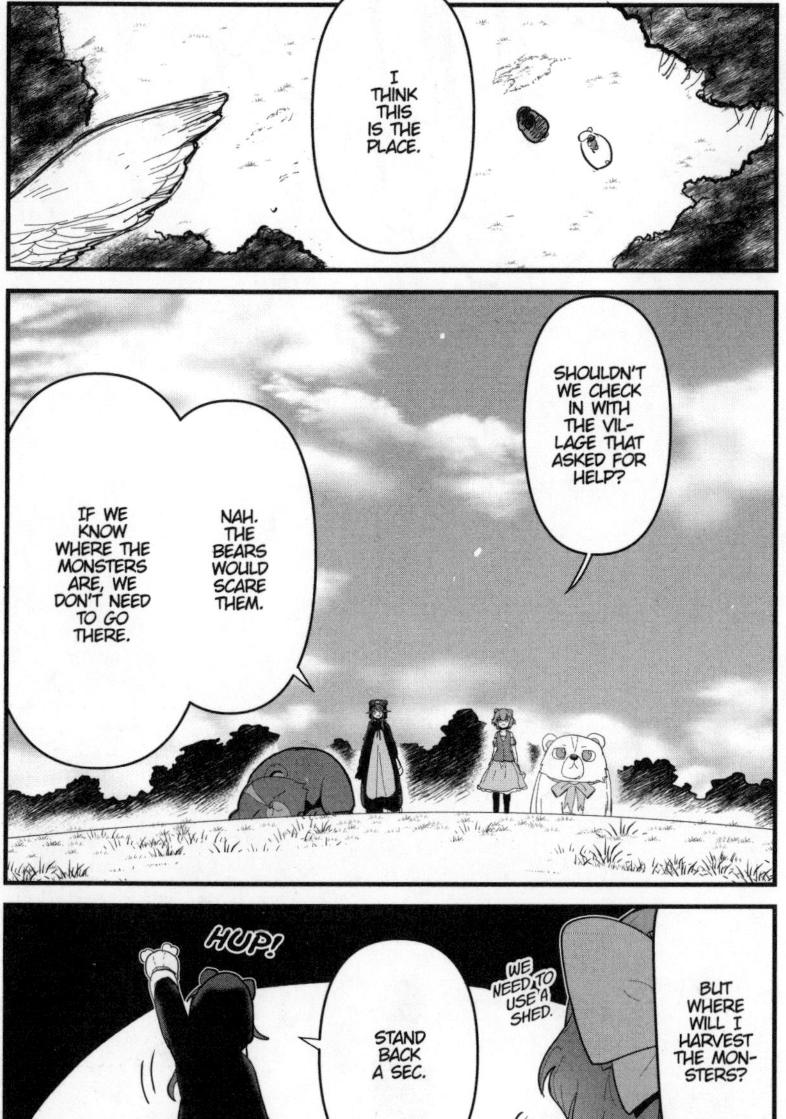
I THINK THIS IS THE PLACE.
SHOULDN'T WE CHECK IN WITH THE VIL-LAGE THAT ASKED FOR HELP?
NAH. THE BEARS WOULD SCARE THEM.
IF WE KNOW WHERE THE MONSTERS ARE, WE DON'T NEED TO GO THERE.
BUT WHERE WILL I HARVEST THE MON-STERS?
WE NEED TO USE A SHED.
STAND BACK A SEC.
HUP!

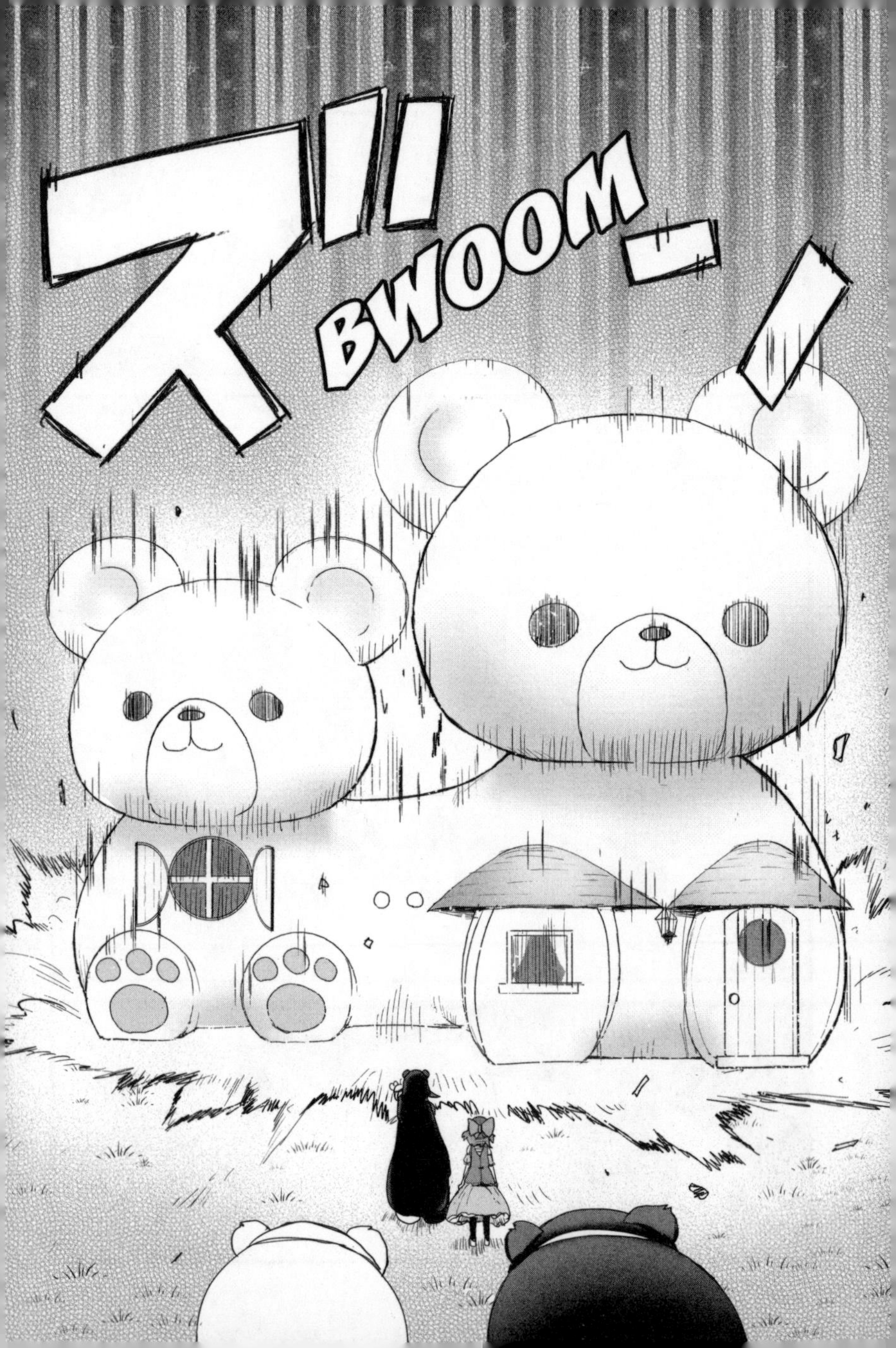
ズー
BWOOM

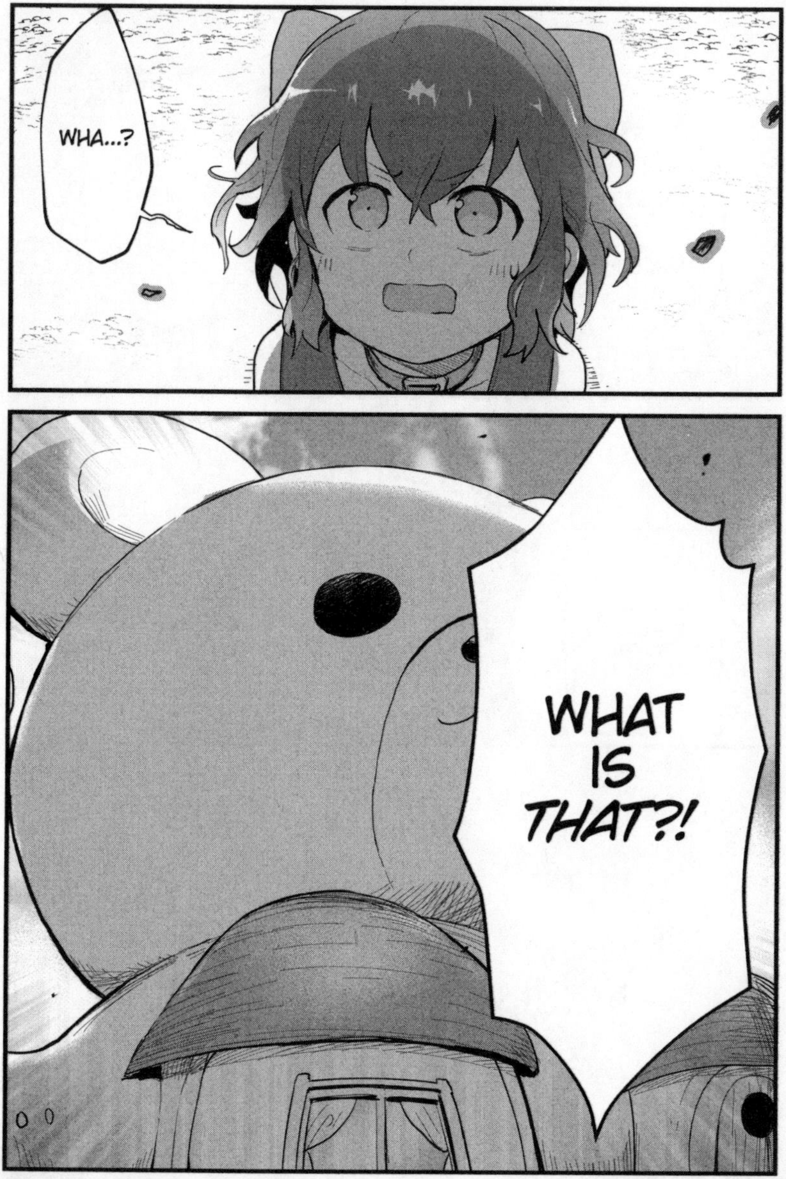
WHA...?
WHAT IS THAT?!

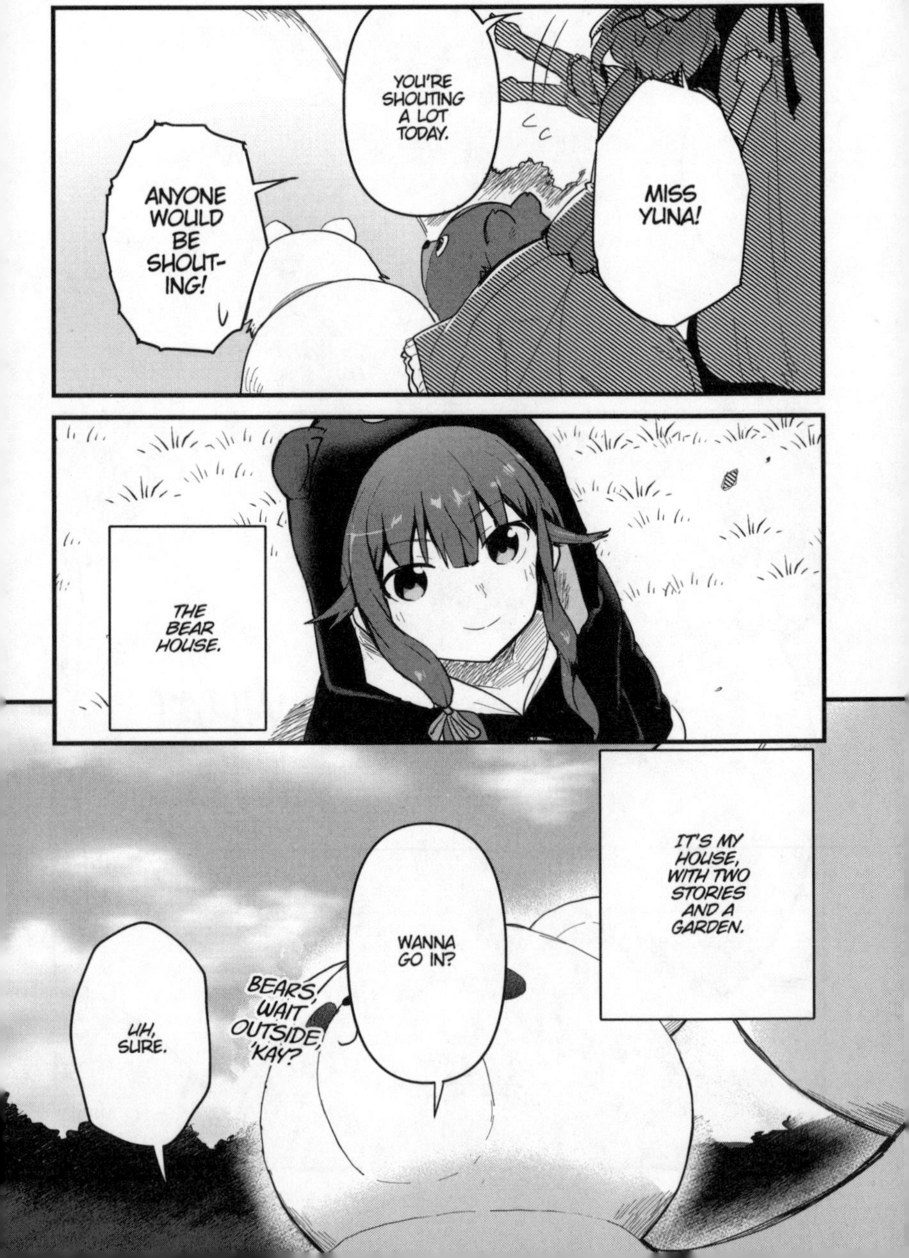
MISS YUNA!
YOU'RE SHOUTING A LOT TODAY.
ANYONE WOULD BE SHOUT-ING!
THE BEAR HOUSE.
IT'S MY HOUSE, WITH TWO STORIES AND A GARDEN.
WANNA GO IN?
BEARS, WAIT OUTSIDE, 'KAY?
UH, SURE.

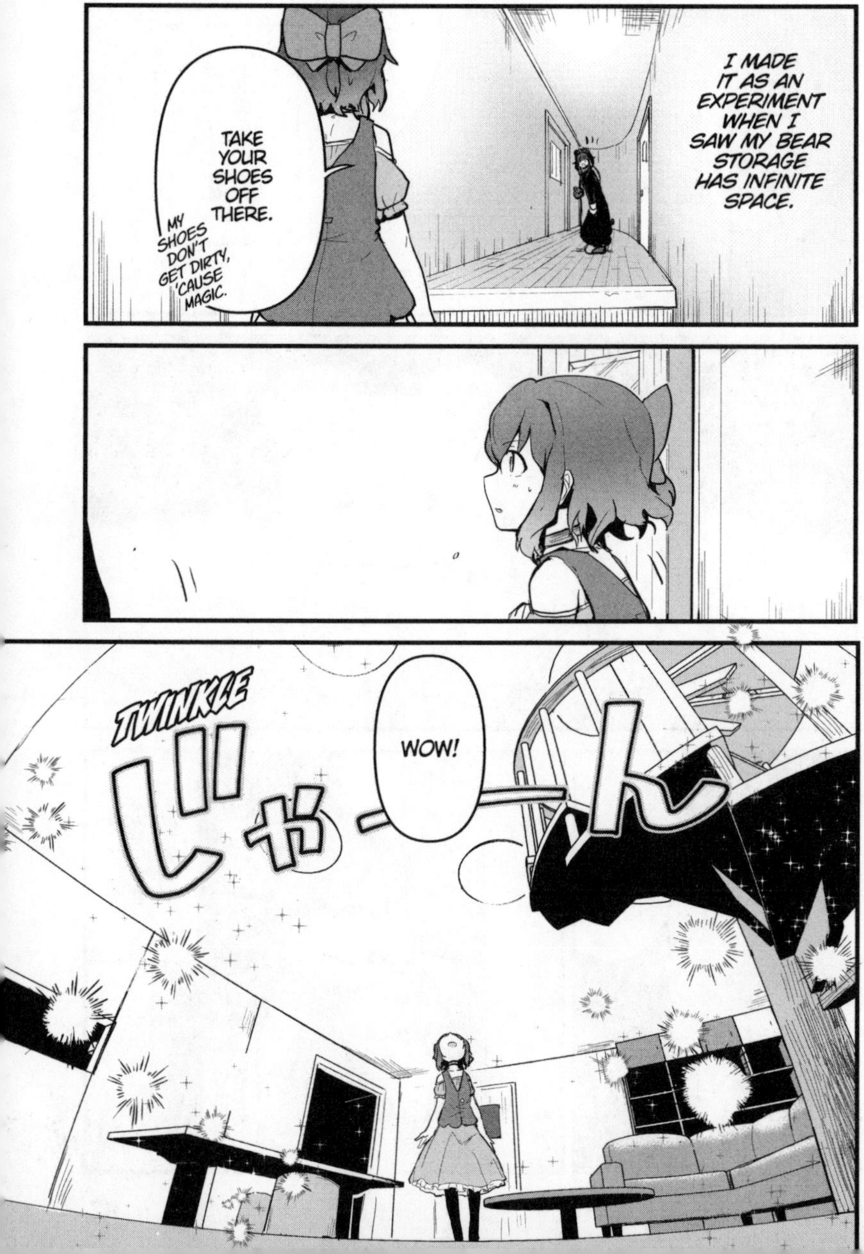
I MADE IT AS AN EXPERIMENT WHEN I SAW MY BEAR STORAGE HAS INFINITE SPACE.
TAKE YOUR SHOES OFF THERE.
MY SHOES DON'T GET DIRTY, 'CAUSE MAGIC.
TWINKLE
じゃーん
WOW!

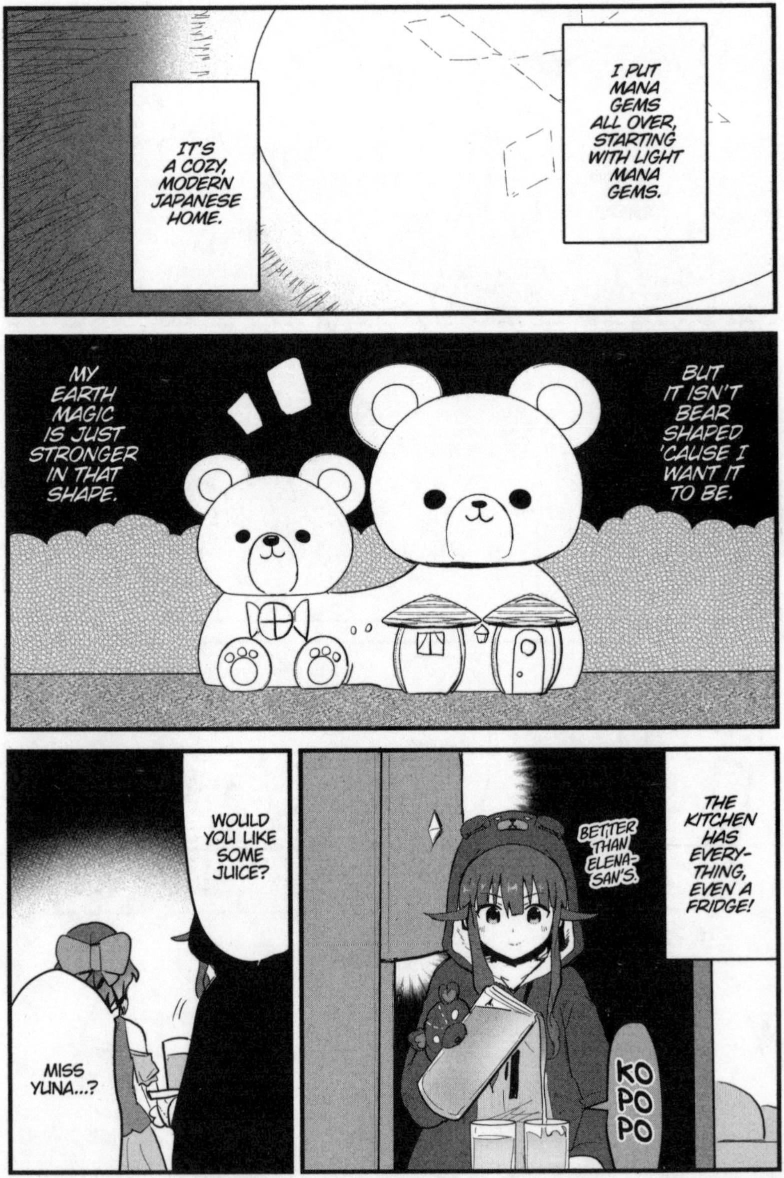
I PUT MANA GEMS ALL OVER, STARTING WITH LIGHT MANA GEMS.
IT'S A COZY, MODERN JAPANESE HOME.
BUT IT ISN'T BEAR SHAPED 'CAUSE I WANT IT TO BE.
MY EARTH MAGIC IS JUST STRONGER IN THAT SHAPE.
THE KITCHEN HAS EVERY-THING, EVEN A FRIDGE!
BETTER THAN ELENA-SAN'S.
KOPOPO
WOULD YOU LIKE SOME JUICE?
MISS YUNA...?

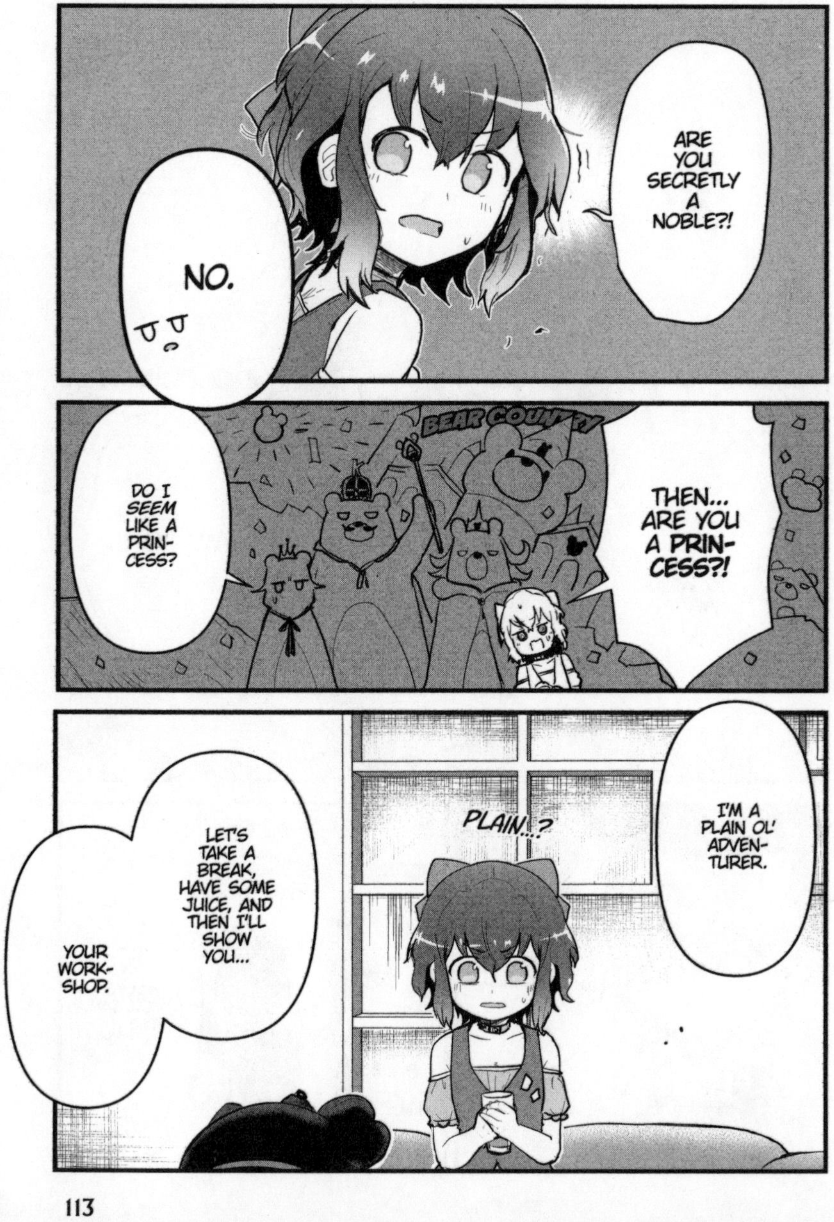
ARE YOU SECRETLY A NOBLE?!
NO.
BEAR COUNTRY
THEN... ARE YOU A PRINCESS?!
DO I SEEM LIKE A PRINCESS?
I'M A PLAIN OL' ADVENTURER.
PLAIN...?
LET'S TAKE A BREAK, HAVE SOME JUICE, AND THEN I'LL SHOW YOU...
YOUR WORKSHOP.

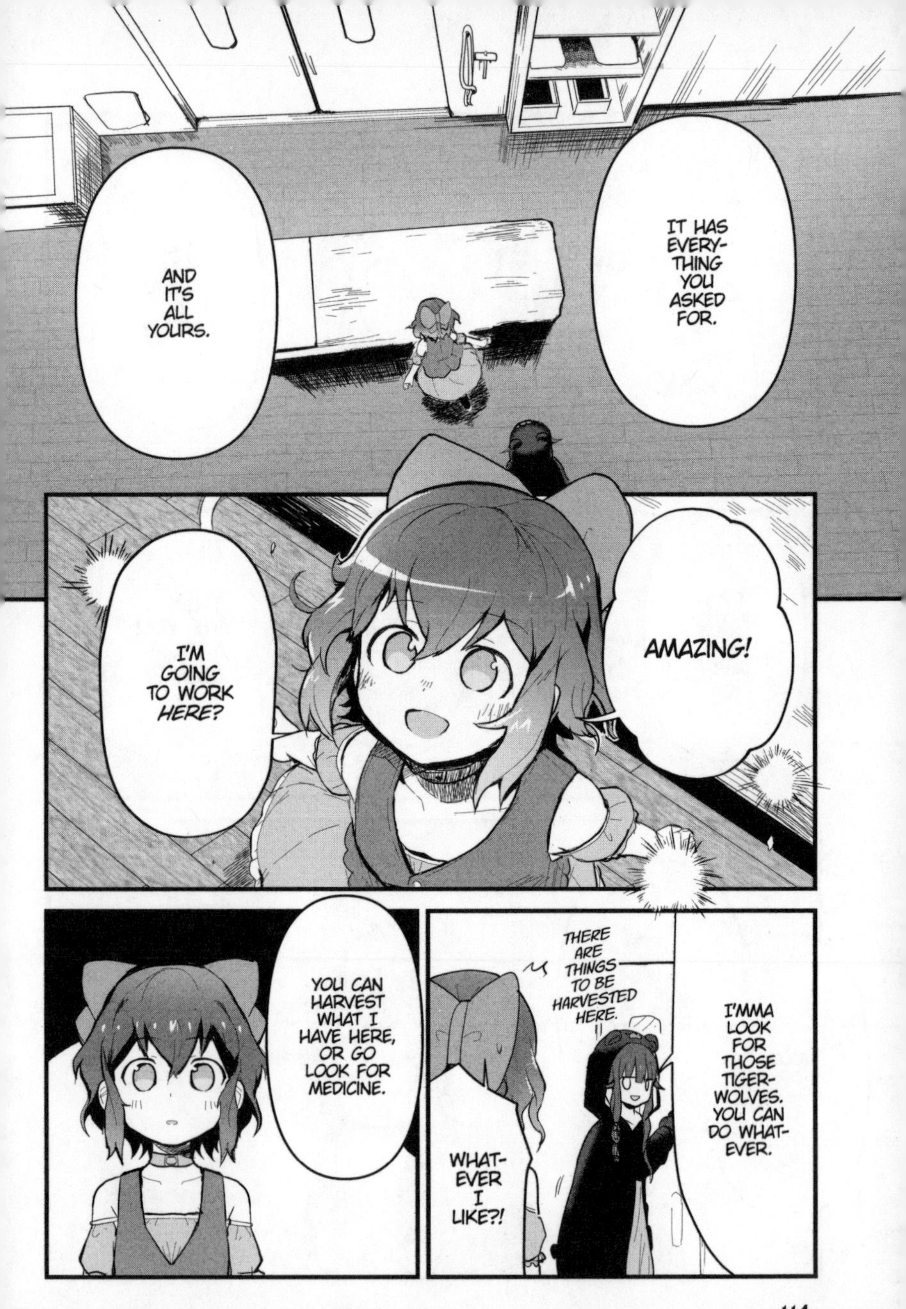
IT HAS EVERYTHING YOU ASKED FOR.
AND IT'S ALL YOURS.
AMAZING!
I'M GOING TO WORK HERE?
I'MMA LOOK FOR THOSE TIGER-WOLVES. YOU CAN DO WHATEVER.
THERE ARE THINGS TO BE HARVESTED HERE.
WHATEVER I LIKE?!
YOU CAN HARVEST WHAT I HAVE HERE, OR GO LOOK FOR MEDICINE.

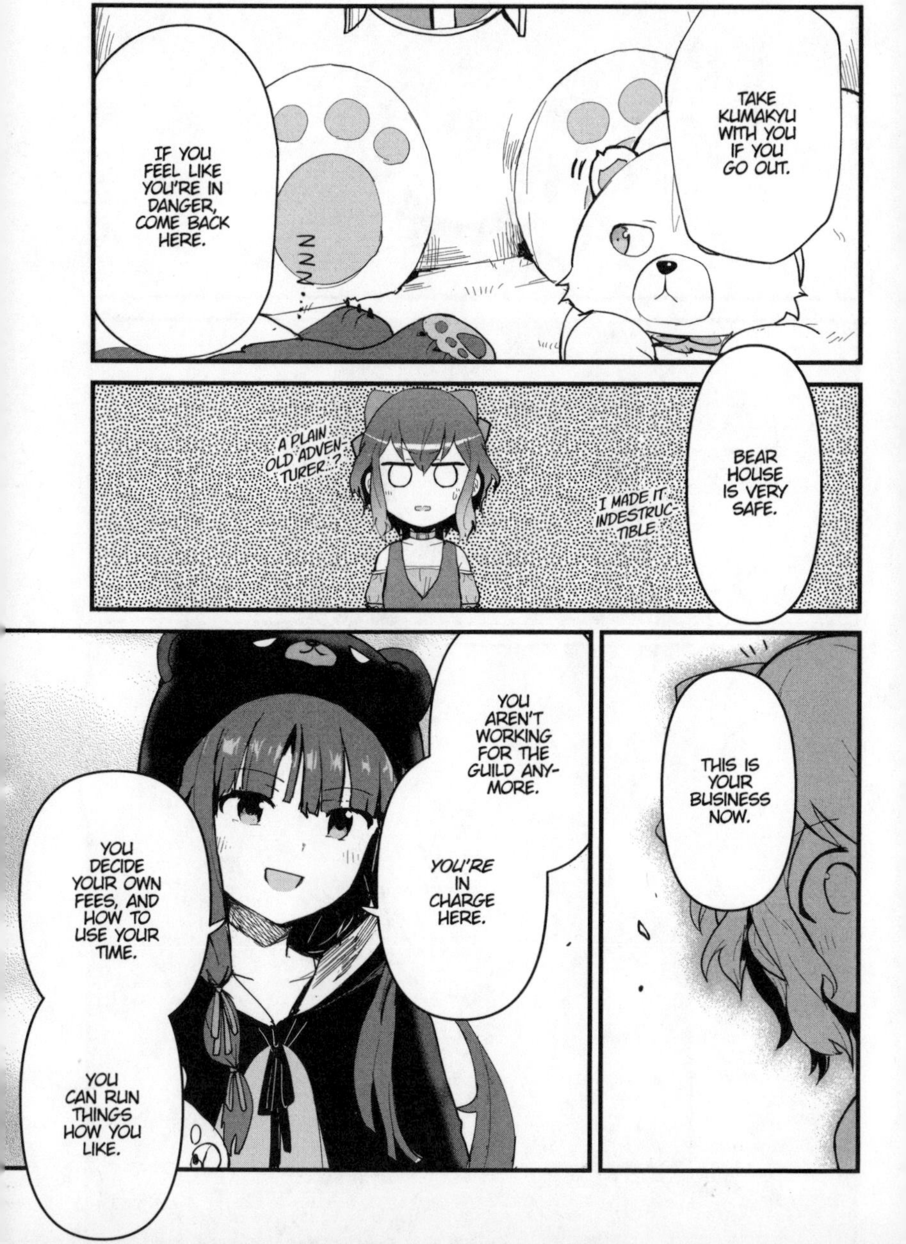
TAKE KUMAKYU WITH YOU IF YOU GO OUT.
IF YOU FEEL LIKE YOU'RE IN DANGER, COME BACK HERE.
ZZZ...
BEAR HOUSE IS VERY SAFE.
I MADE IT INDESTRUCTIBLE.
A PLAIN OLD ADVENTURER...?
THIS IS YOUR BUSINESS NOW.
YOU AREN'T WORKING FOR THE GUILD ANYMORE.
YOU'RE IN CHARGE HERE.
YOU DECIDE YOUR OWN FEES, AND HOW TO USE YOUR TIME.
YOU CAN RUN THINGS HOW YOU LIKE.

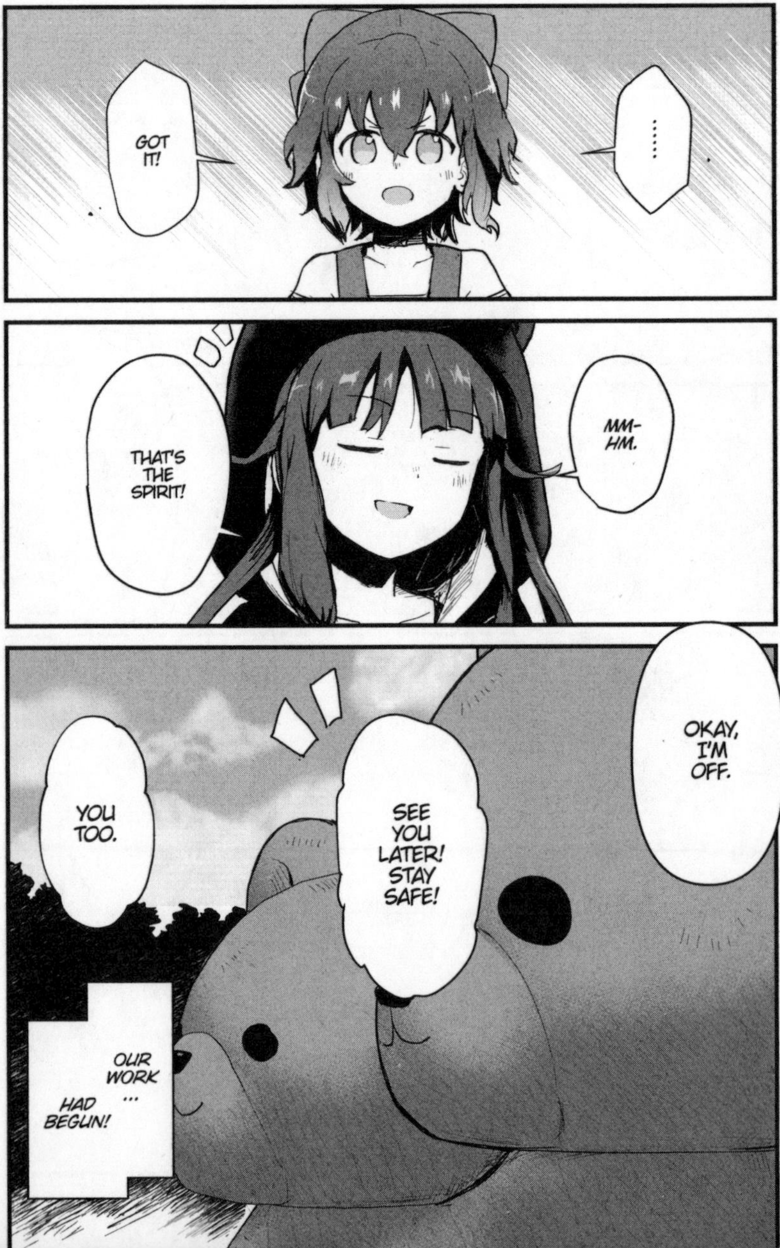
......
GOT IT!
MM-HM.
THAT'S THE SPIRIT!
OKAY, I'M OFF.
SEE YOU LATER! STAY SAFE!
YOU TOO.
OUR WORK ... HAD BEGUN!

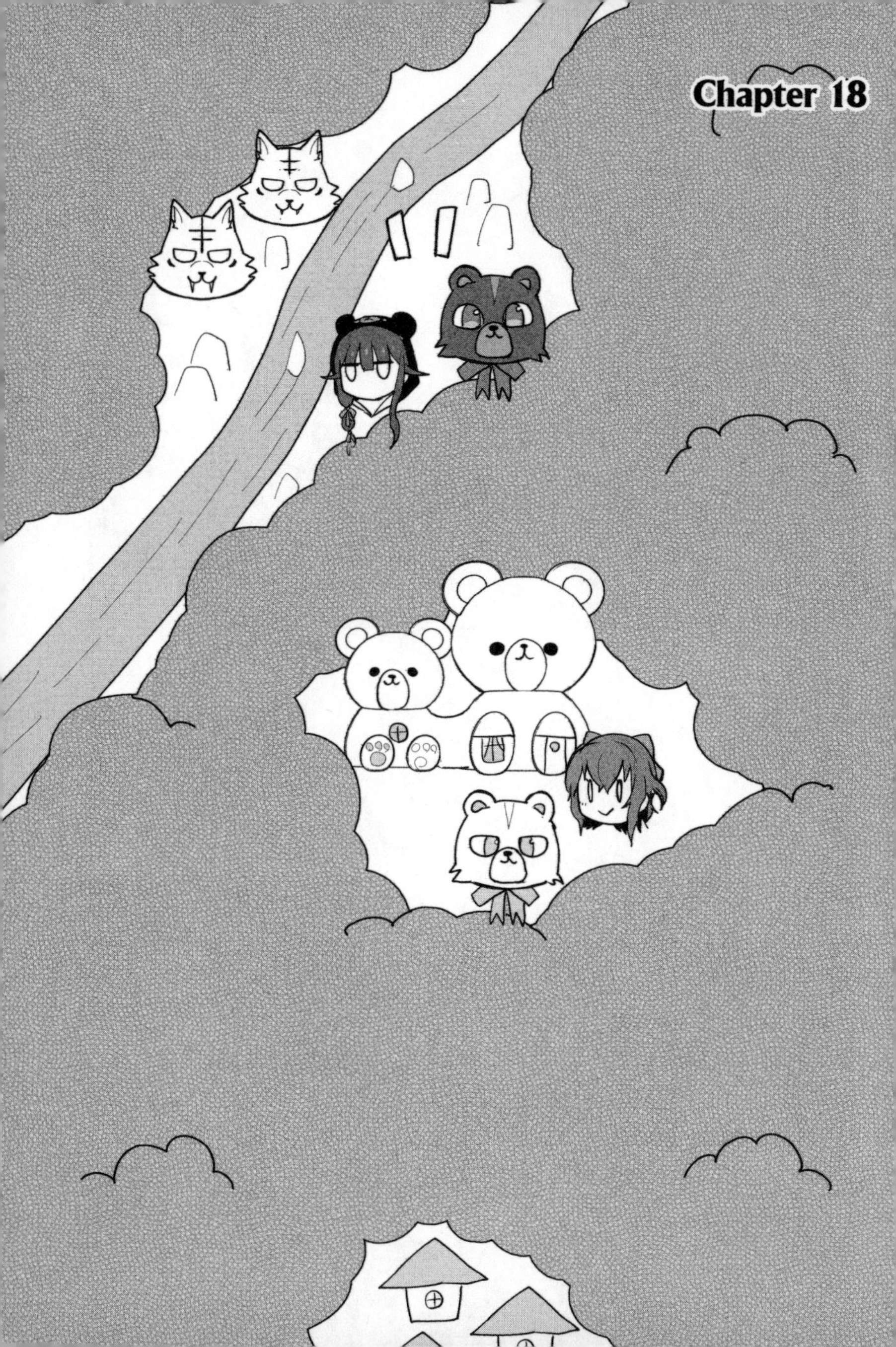
Chapter 18

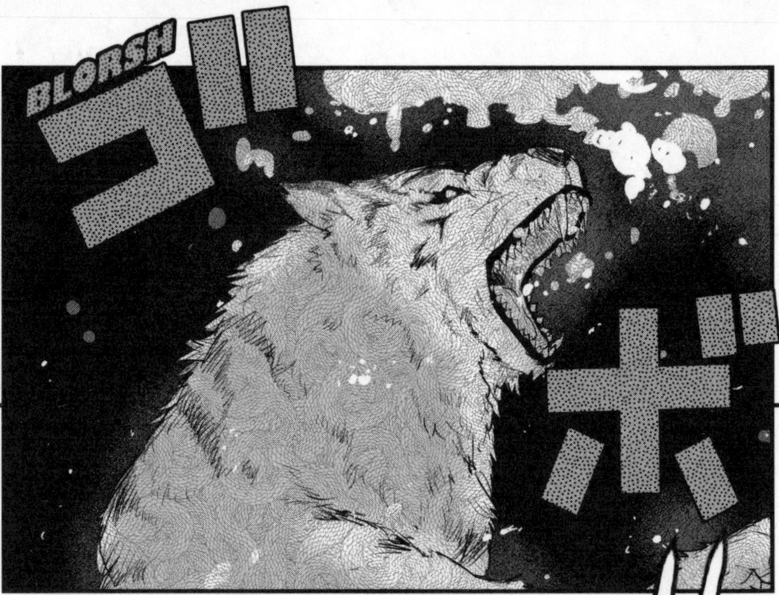
BLORSH
ゴボ

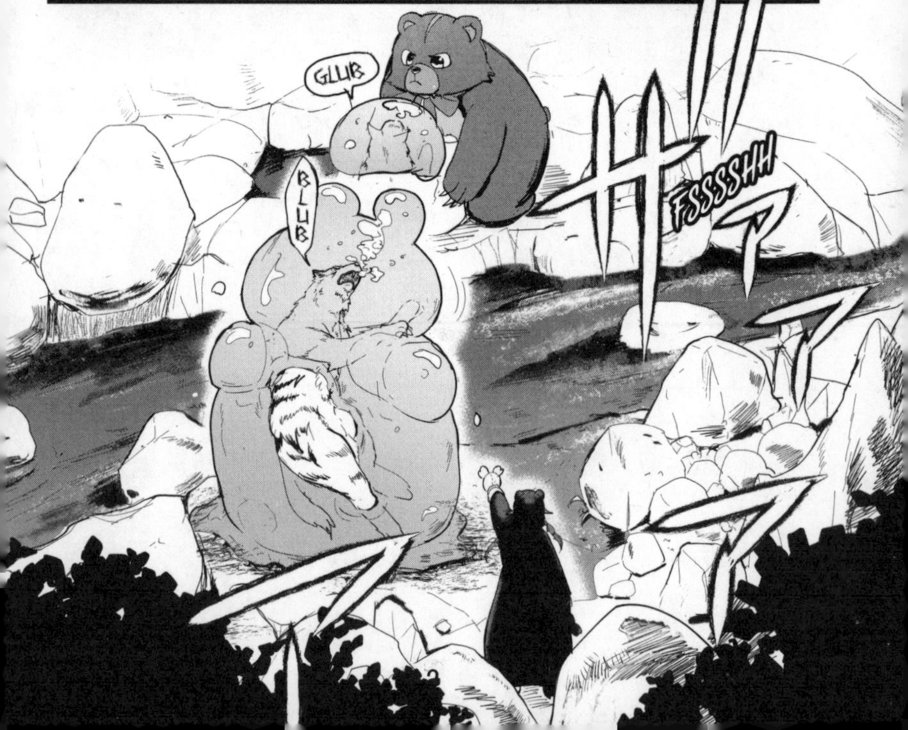
GLUB
BLUB
FSSSSHH

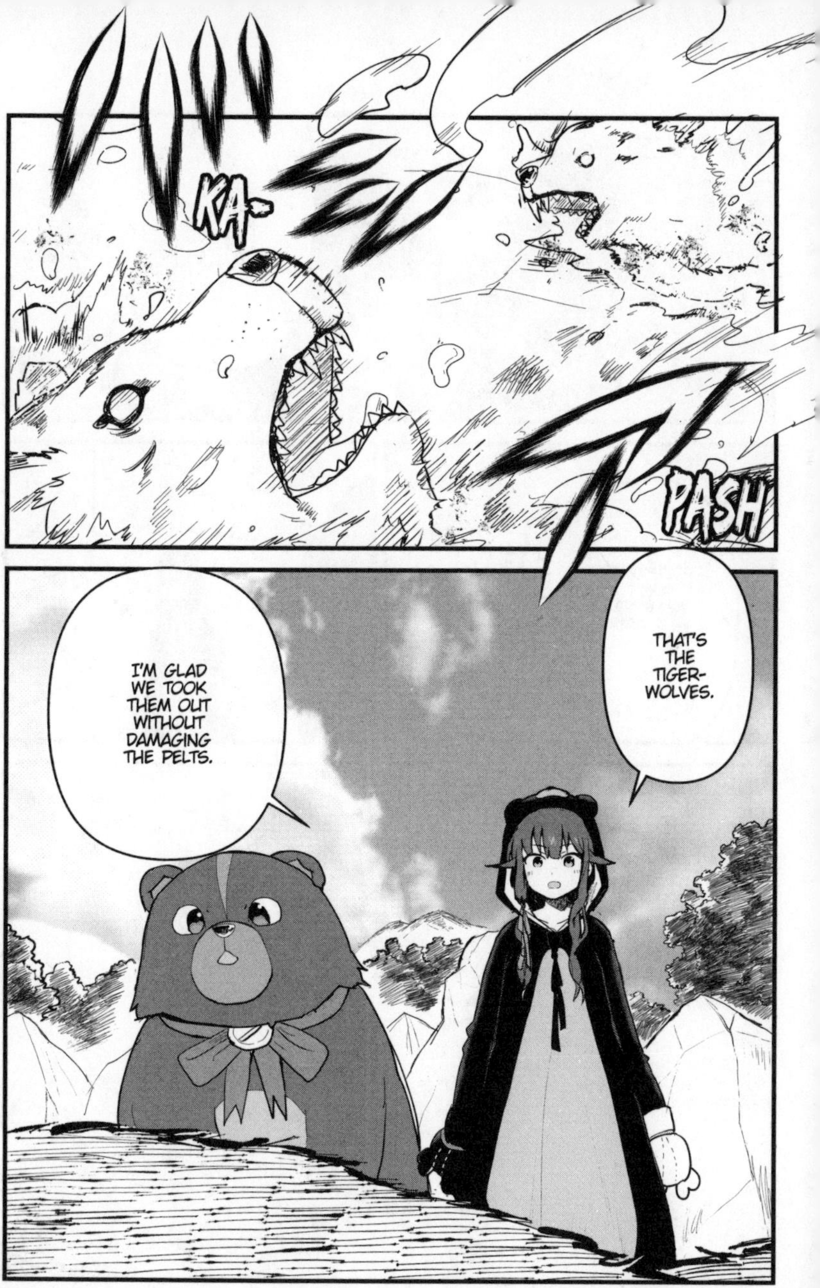
KA-
PASH
THAT'S THE TIGER-WOLVES.
I'M GLAD WE TOOK THEM OUT WITHOUT DAMAGING THE PELTS.

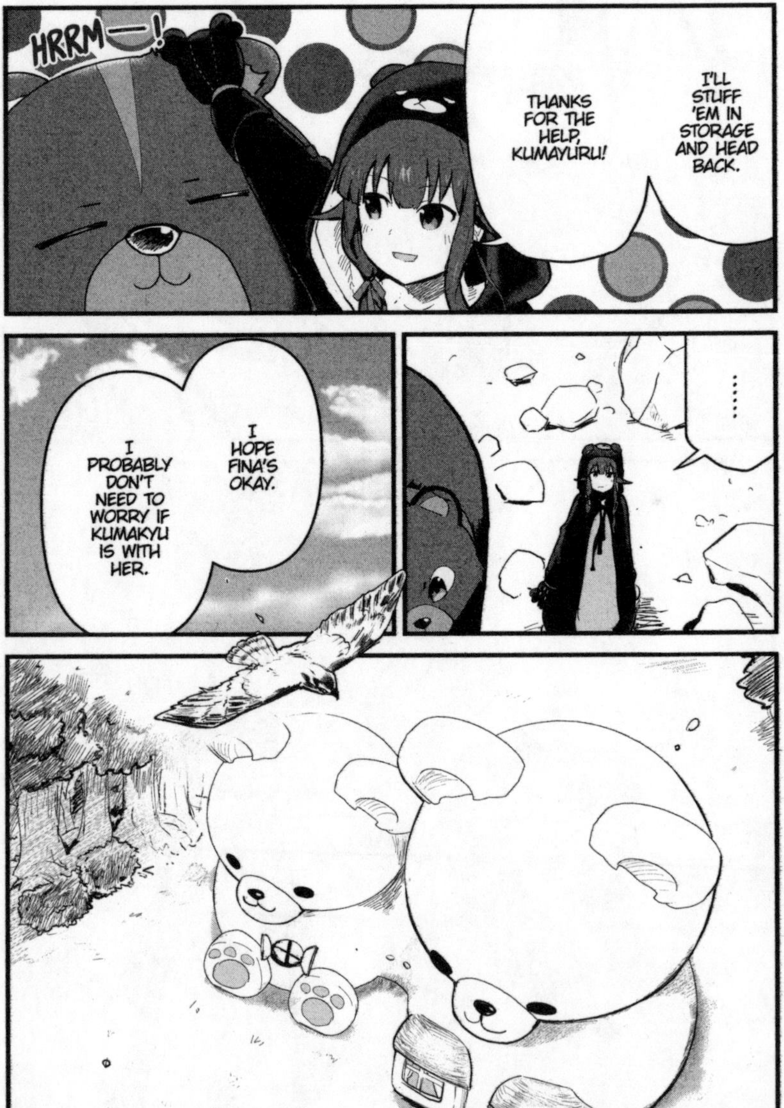
THANKS FOR THE HELP, KUMAYURU!
I'LL STUFF 'EM IN STORAGE AND HEAD BACK.
HRRM—!
......
I HOPE FINA'S OKAY.
I PROBABLY DON'T NEED TO WORRY IF KUMAKYU IS WITH HER.

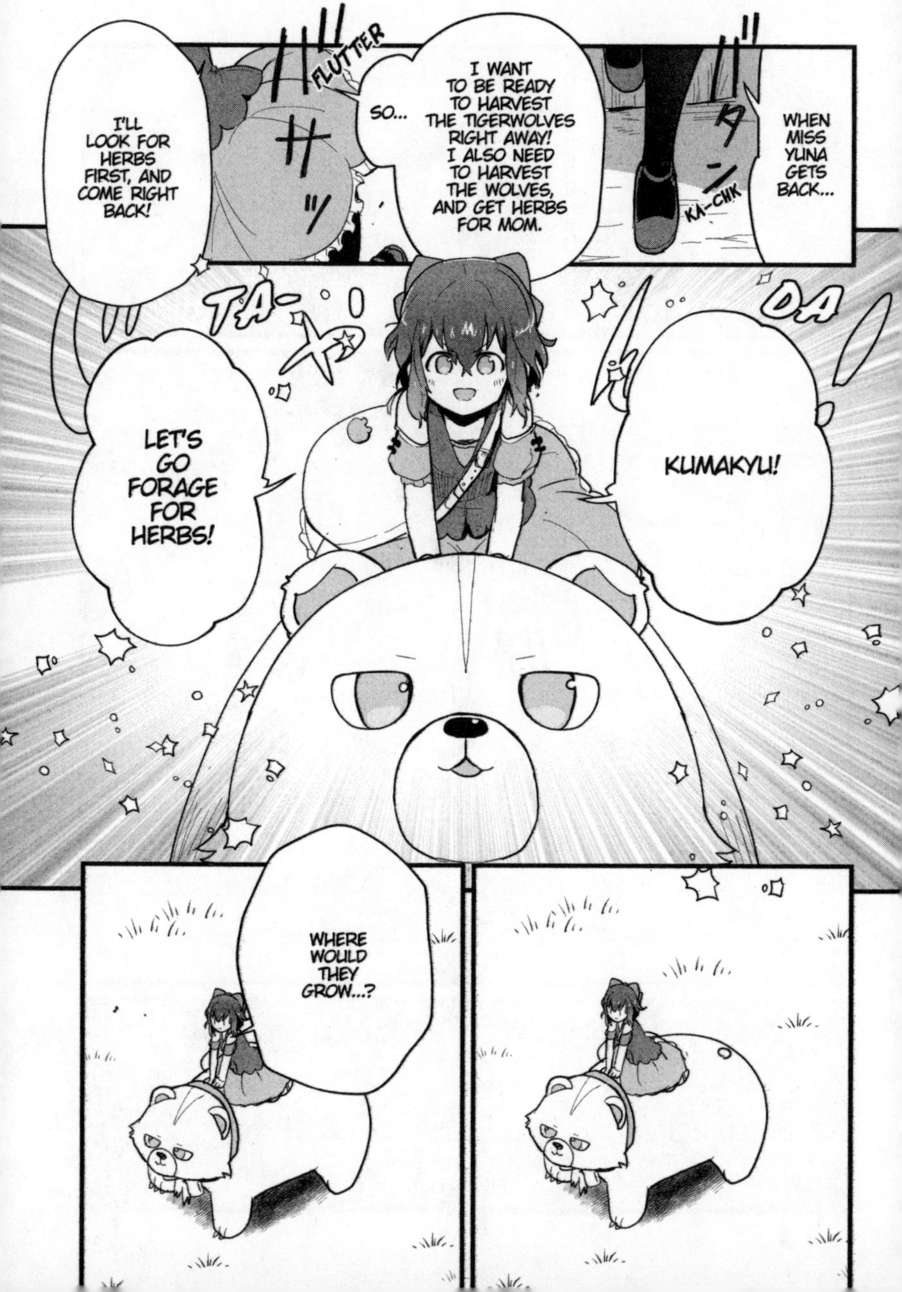
WHEN MISS YUNA GETS BACK...
KA-CHK
SO...
I WANT TO BE READY TO HARVEST THE TIGERWOLVES RIGHT AWAY! I ALSO NEED TO HARVEST THE WOLVES, AND GET HERBS FOR MOM.
FLUTTER
I'LL LOOK FOR HERBS FIRST, AND COME RIGHT BACK!
TA- DA
KUMAKYU!
LET'S GO FORAGE FOR HERBS!
WHERE WOULD THEY GROW...?

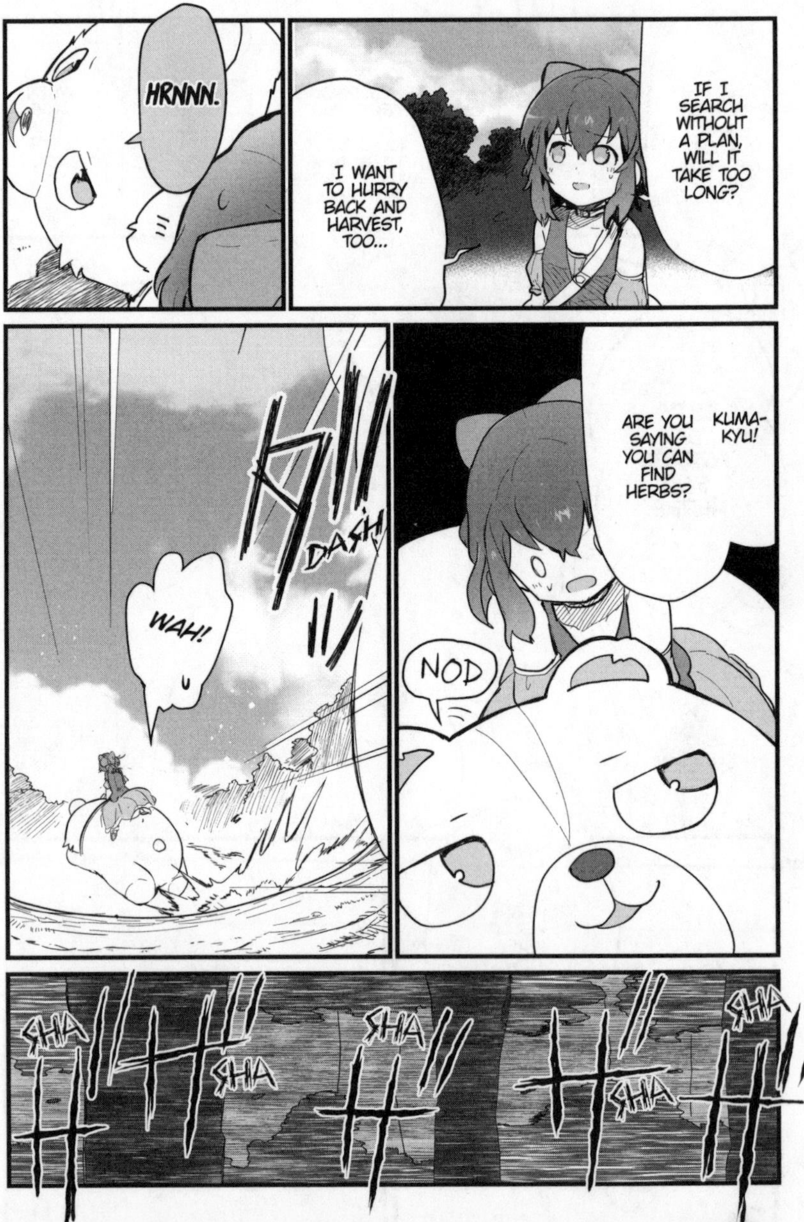
IF I SEARCH WITHOUT A PLAN, WILL IT TAKE TOO LONG?
I WANT TO HURRY BACK AND HARVEST, TOO...
HRNNN.
KUMA-KYU!
ARE YOU SAYING YOU CAN FIND HERBS?
NOD
DASH!!
WAH!

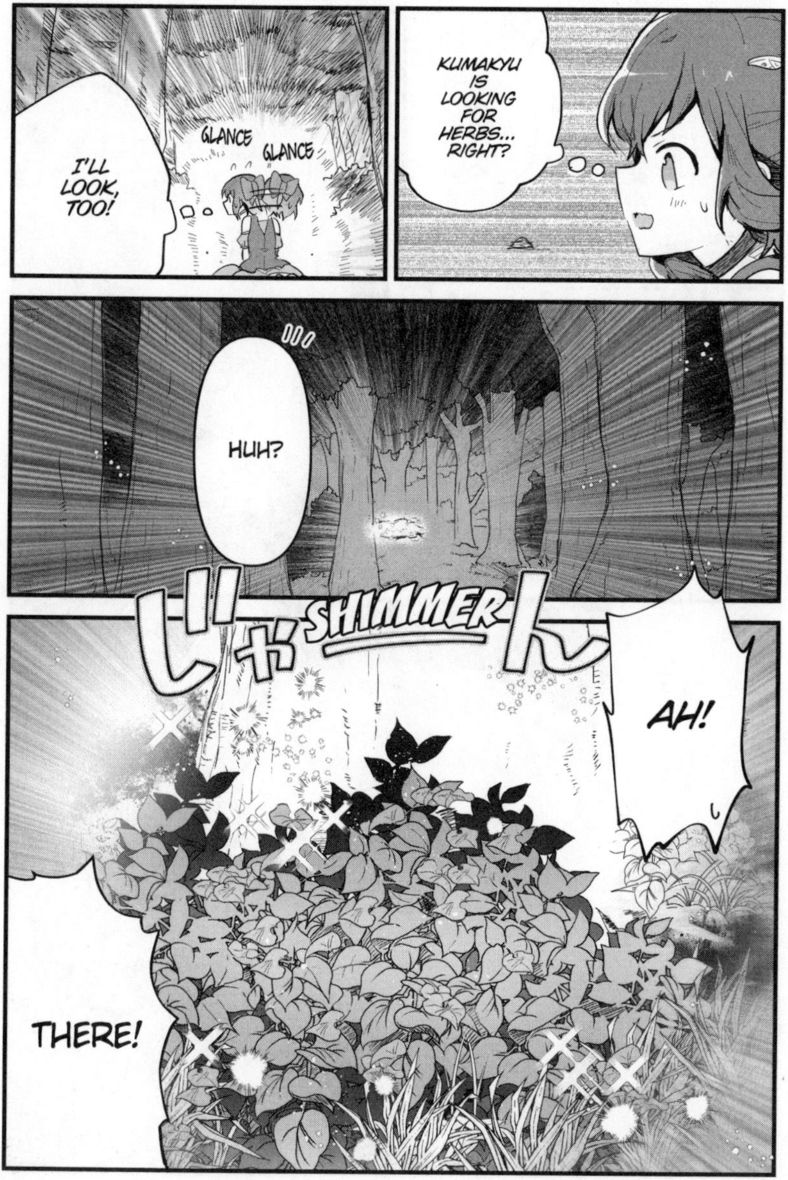
KUMAKYU IS LOOKING FOR HERBS... RIGHT?
GLANCE
GLANCE
I'LL LOOK, TOO!
HUH?
SHIMMER
AH!
THERE!

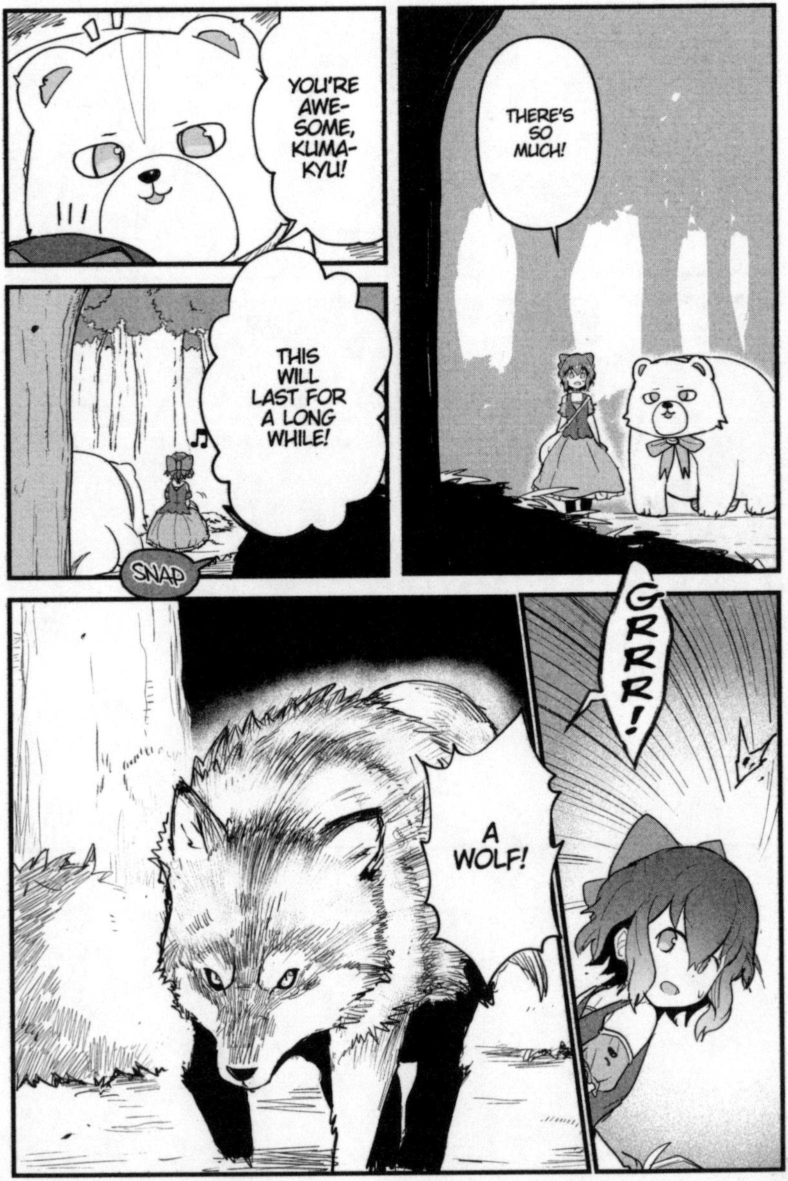
THERE'S SO MUCH!
YOU'RE AWE-SOME, KUMA-KYU!
THIS WILL LAST FOR A LONG WHILE!
SNAP
GRRR!
A WOLF!

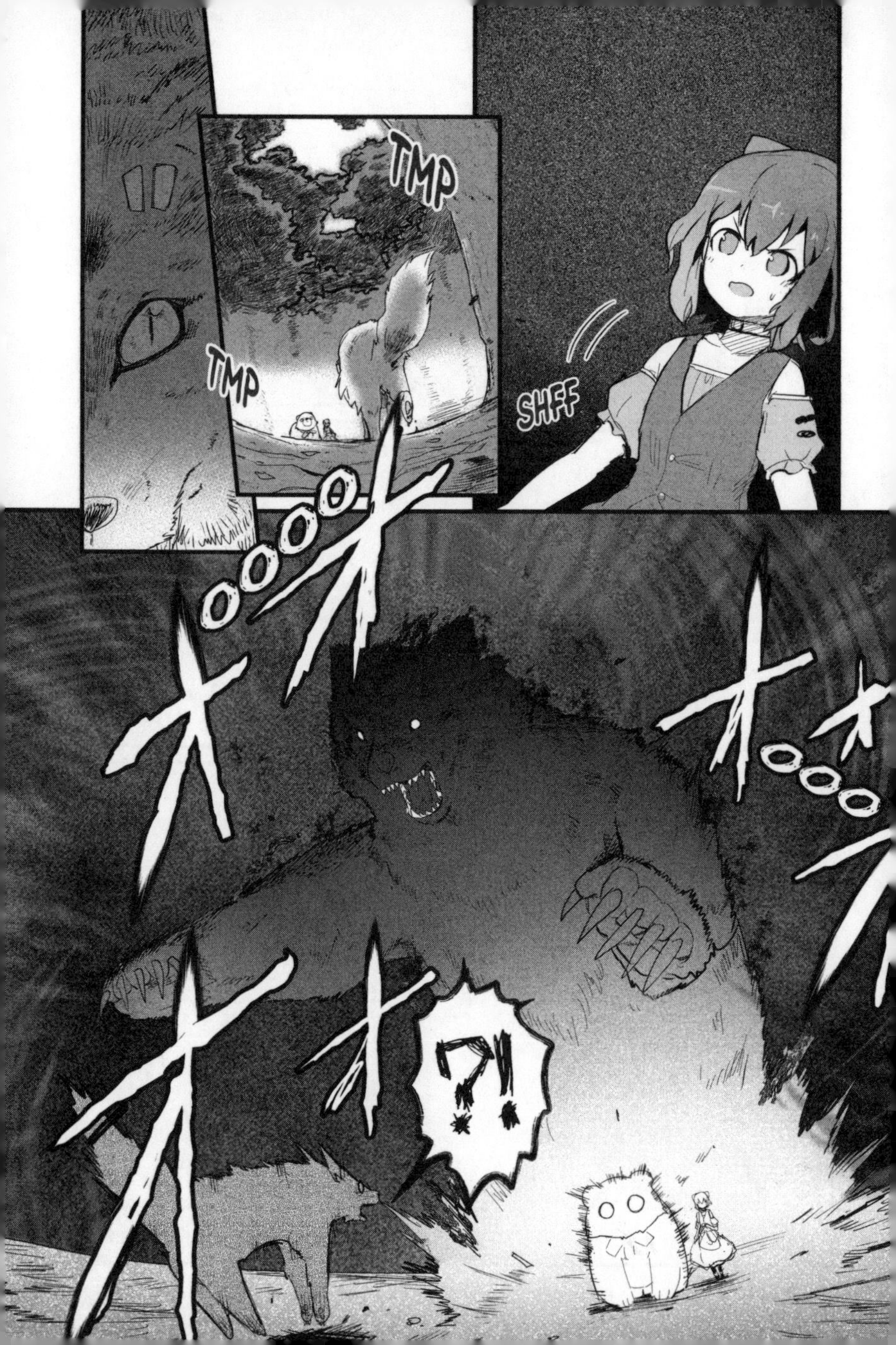
SHFF
TMP
TMP
OOOO
OOOOO
?!

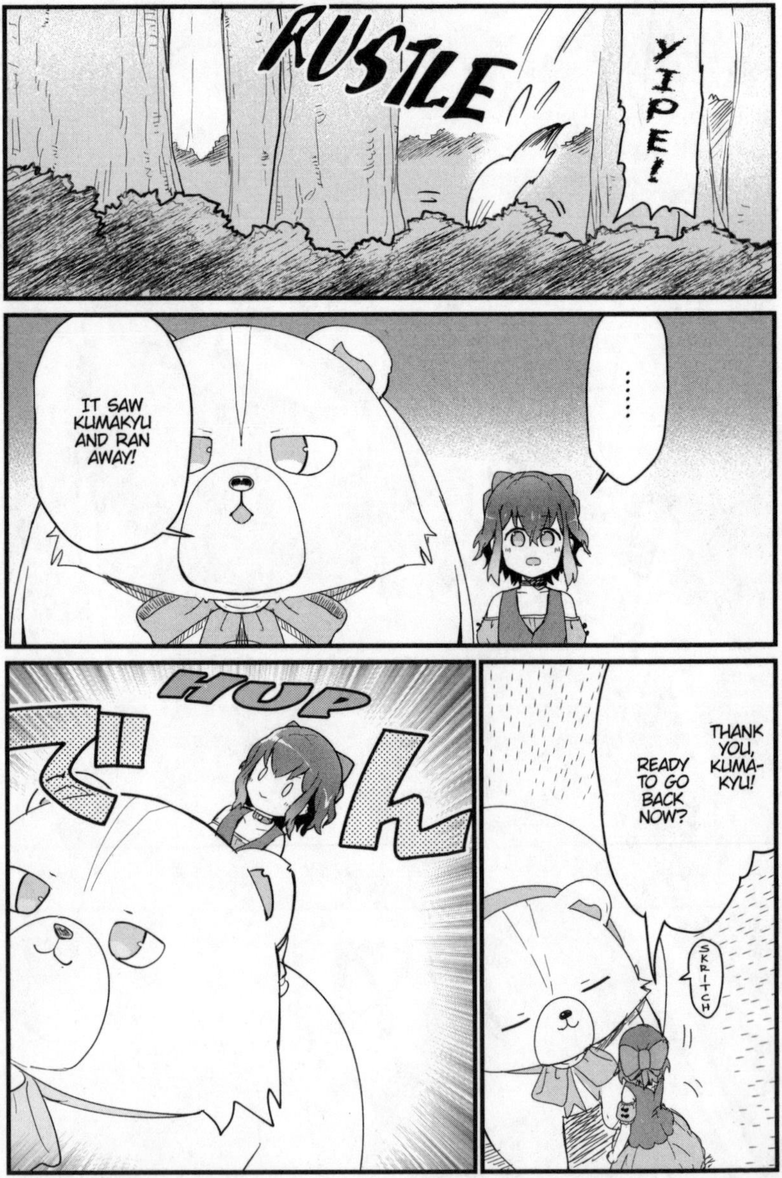

RUSTLE
YIPE!
......
IT SAW KUMAKYU AND RAN AWAY!
THANK YOU, KUMAKYU!
READY TO GO BACK NOW?
SKRITCH
HUP
でん

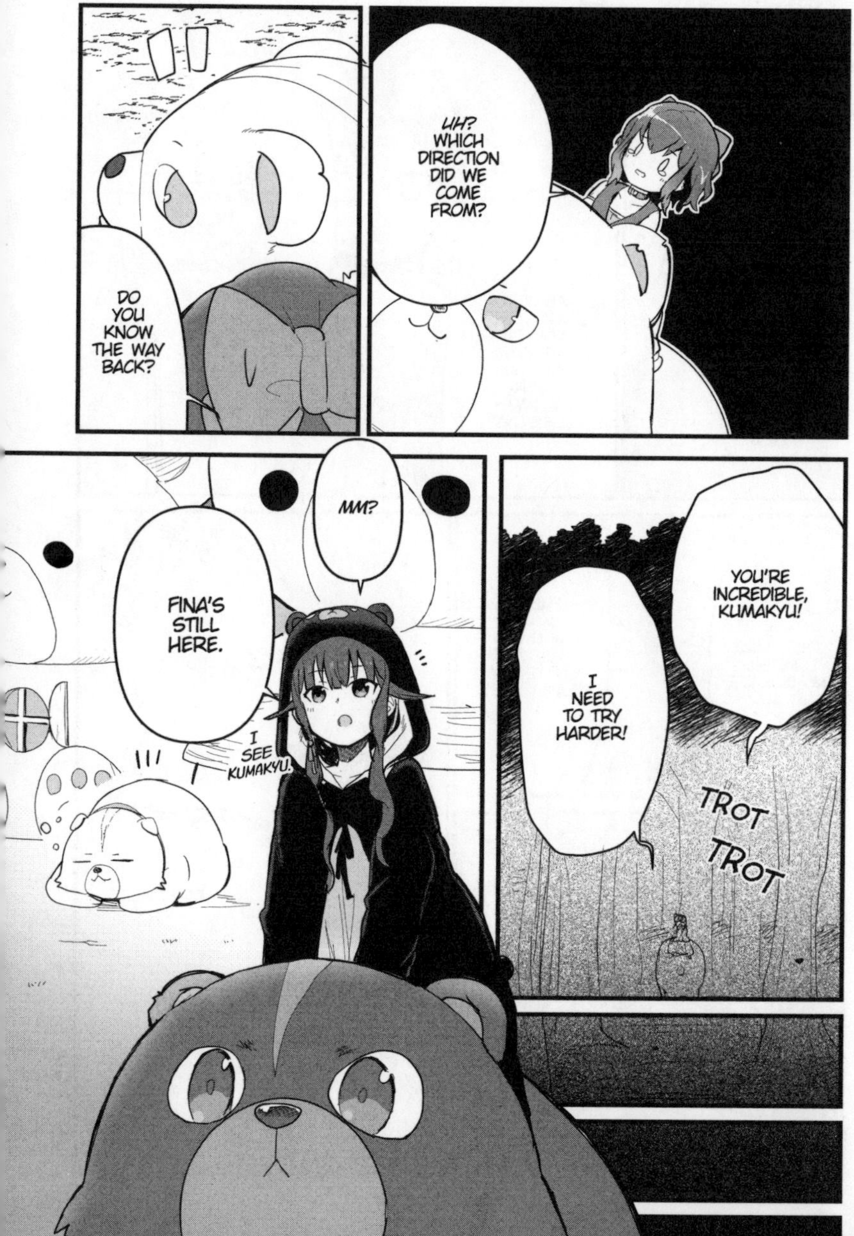
UH? WHICH DIRECTION DID WE COME FROM?
DO YOU KNOW THE WAY BACK?
YOU'RE INCREDIBLE, KUMAKYU!
I NEED TO TRY HARDER!
TROT
TROT
MM?
FINA'S STILL HERE.
I SEE KUMAKYU.

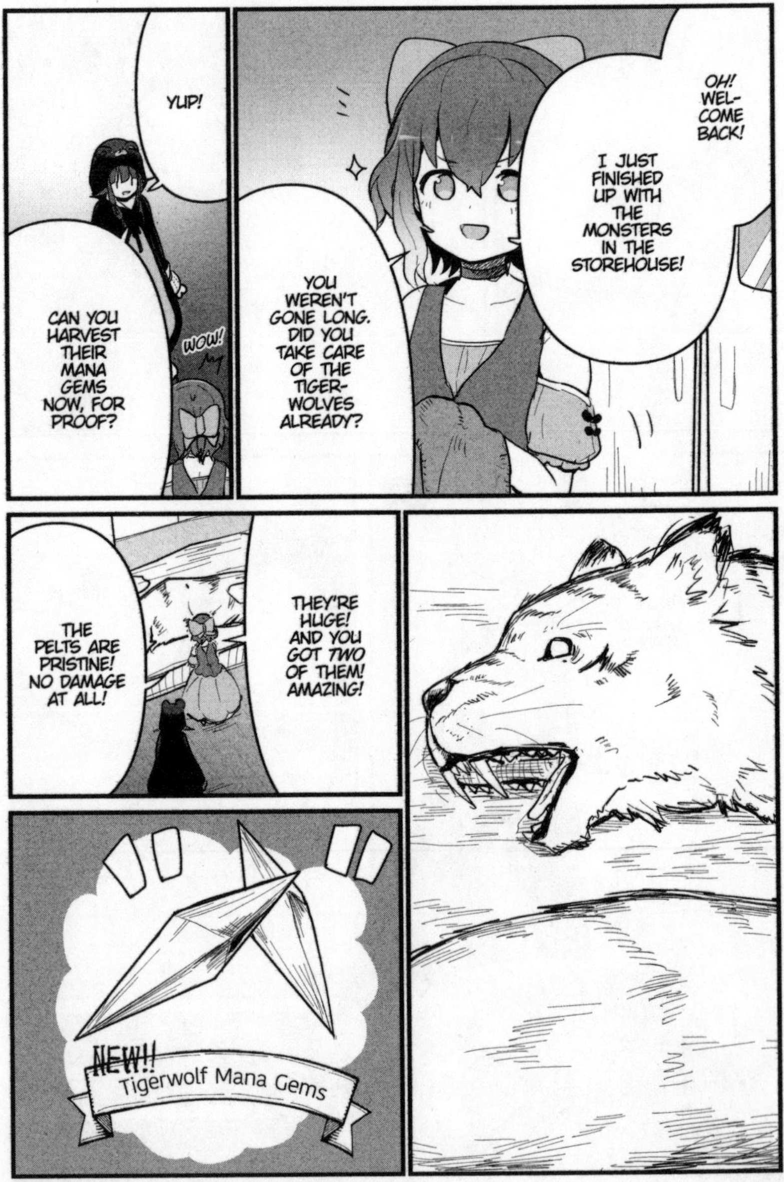
OH! WEL-COME BACK!
I JUST FINISHED UP WITH THE MONSTERS IN THE STOREHOUSE!
YOU WEREN'T GONE LONG. DID YOU TAKE CARE OF THE TIGER-WOLVES ALREADY?
YUP!
WOW!
CAN YOU HARVEST THEIR MANA GEMS NOW, FOR PROOF?
THEY'RE HUGE! AND YOU GOT *TWO* OF THEM! AMAZING!
THE PELTS ARE PRISTINE! NO DAMAGE AT ALL!
NEW!!
Tigerwolf Mana Gems

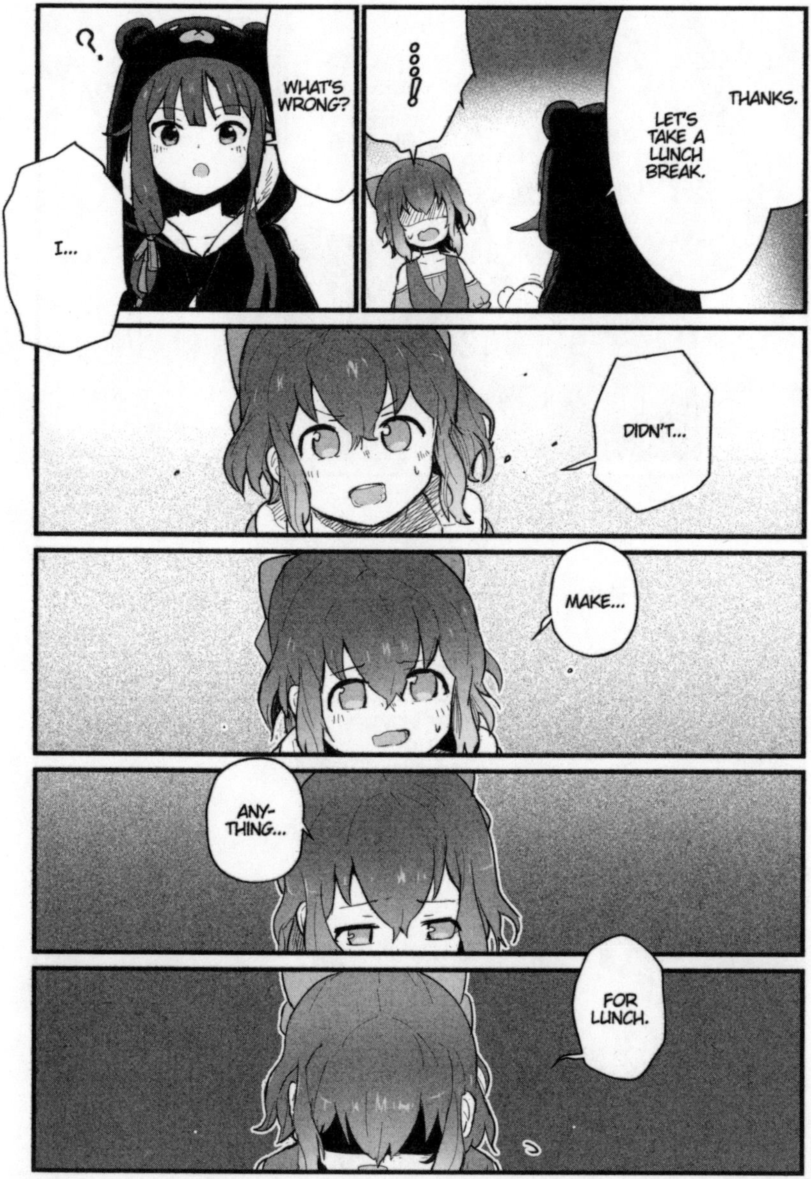
THANKS.
LET'S TAKE A LUNCH BREAK.
...!
?
WHAT'S WRONG?
I...
DIDN'T...
MAKE...
ANY-THING...
FOR LUNCH.

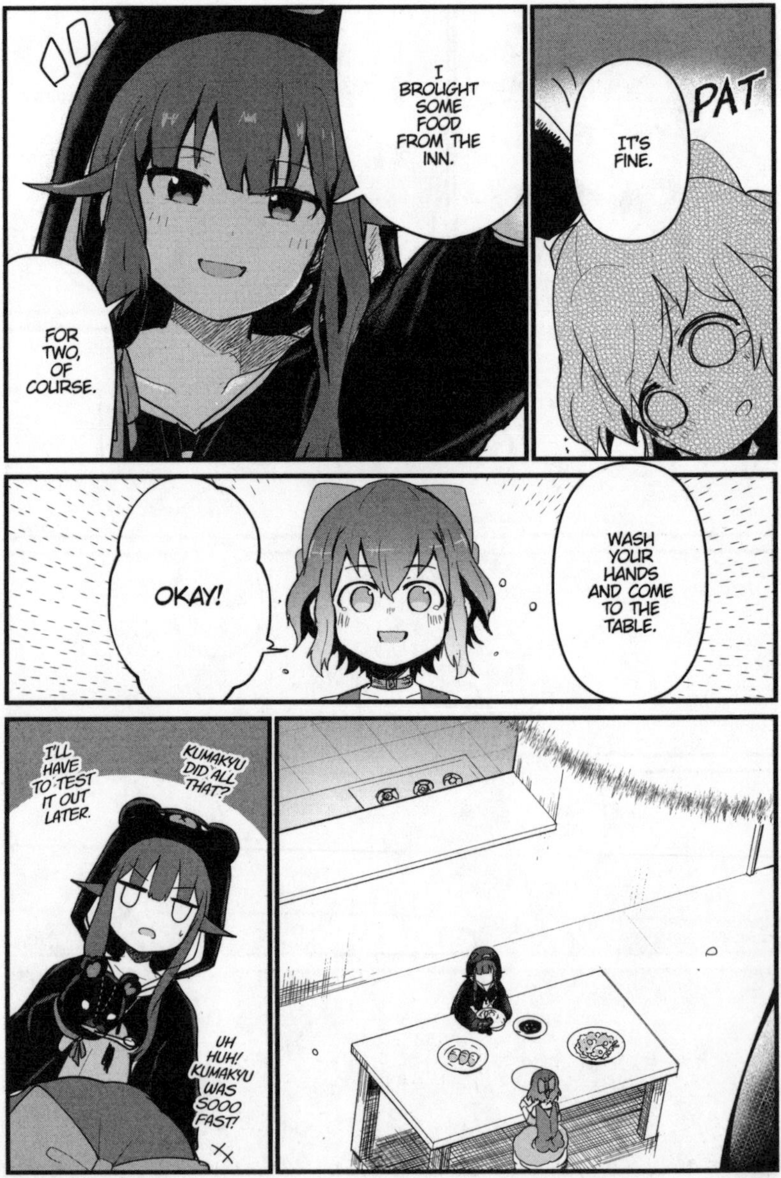
PAT
IT'S FINE.
I BROUGHT SOME FOOD FROM THE INN.
FOR TWO, OF COURSE.
WASH YOUR HANDS AND COME TO THE TABLE.
OKAY!
KUMAKYU DID ALL THAT?
I'LL HAVE TO TEST IT OUT LATER.
UH HUH! KUMAKYU WAS SOOO FAST!

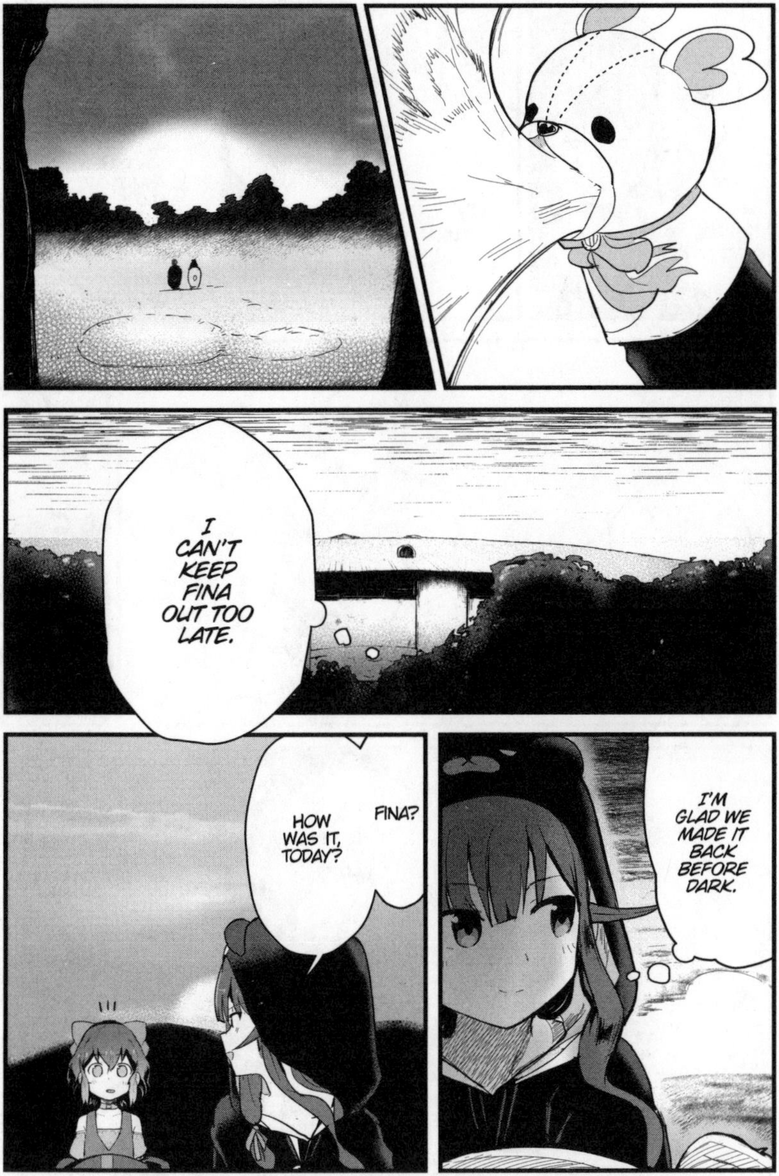
I CAN'T KEEP FINA OUT TOO LATE.
I'M GLAD WE MADE IT BACK BEFORE DARK.
FINA?
HOW WAS IT, TODAY?

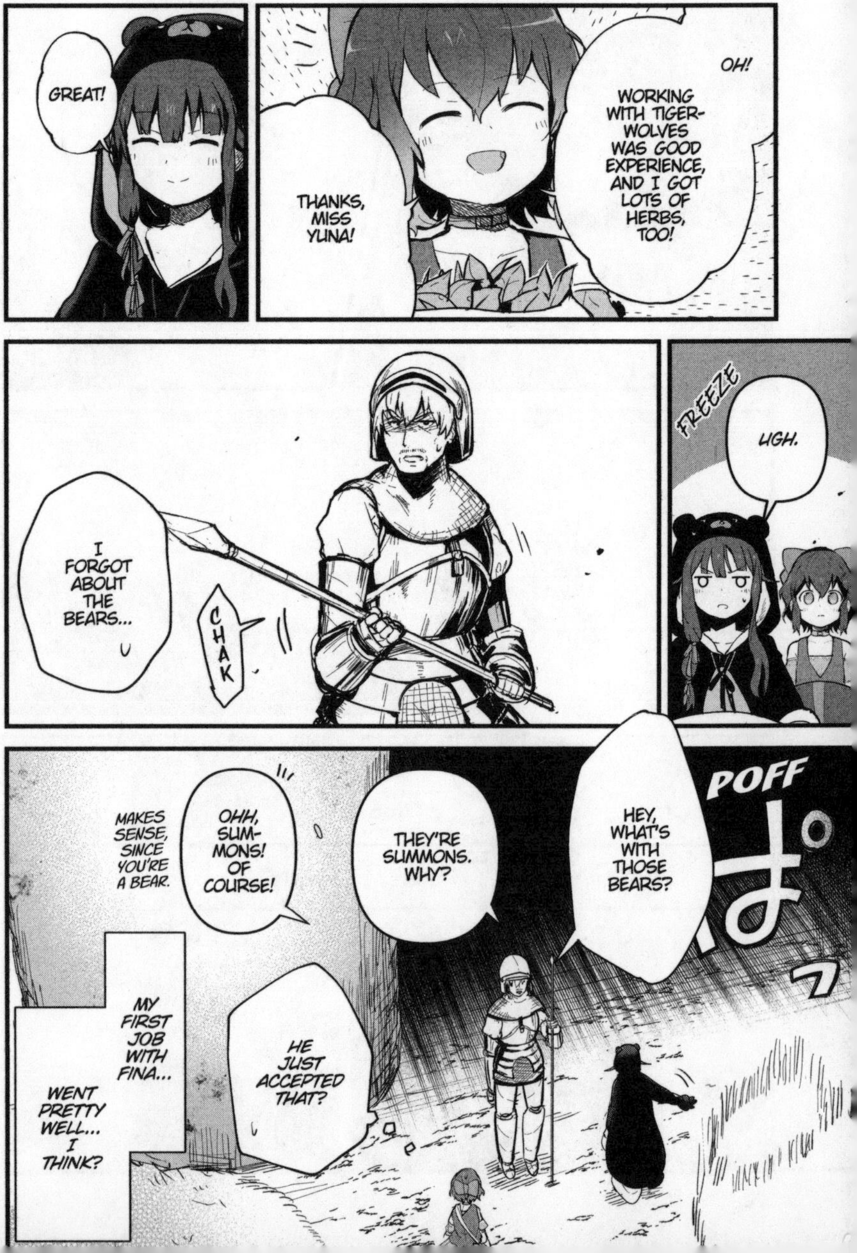
OH!
WORKING WITH TIGER-WOLVES WAS GOOD EXPERIENCE, AND I GOT LOTS OF HERBS, TOO!
THANKS, MISS YUNA!
GREAT!
FREEZE
UGH.
I FORGOT ABOUT THE BEARS...
CHAK
POFF
ぽ
HEY, WHAT'S WITH THOSE BEARS?
THEY'RE SUMMONS. WHY?
OHH, SUMMONS! OF COURSE!
MAKES SENSE, SINCE YOU'RE A BEAR.
HE JUST ACCEPTED THAT?
MY FIRST JOB WITH FINA...
WENT PRETTY WELL... I THINK?

Chapter 19

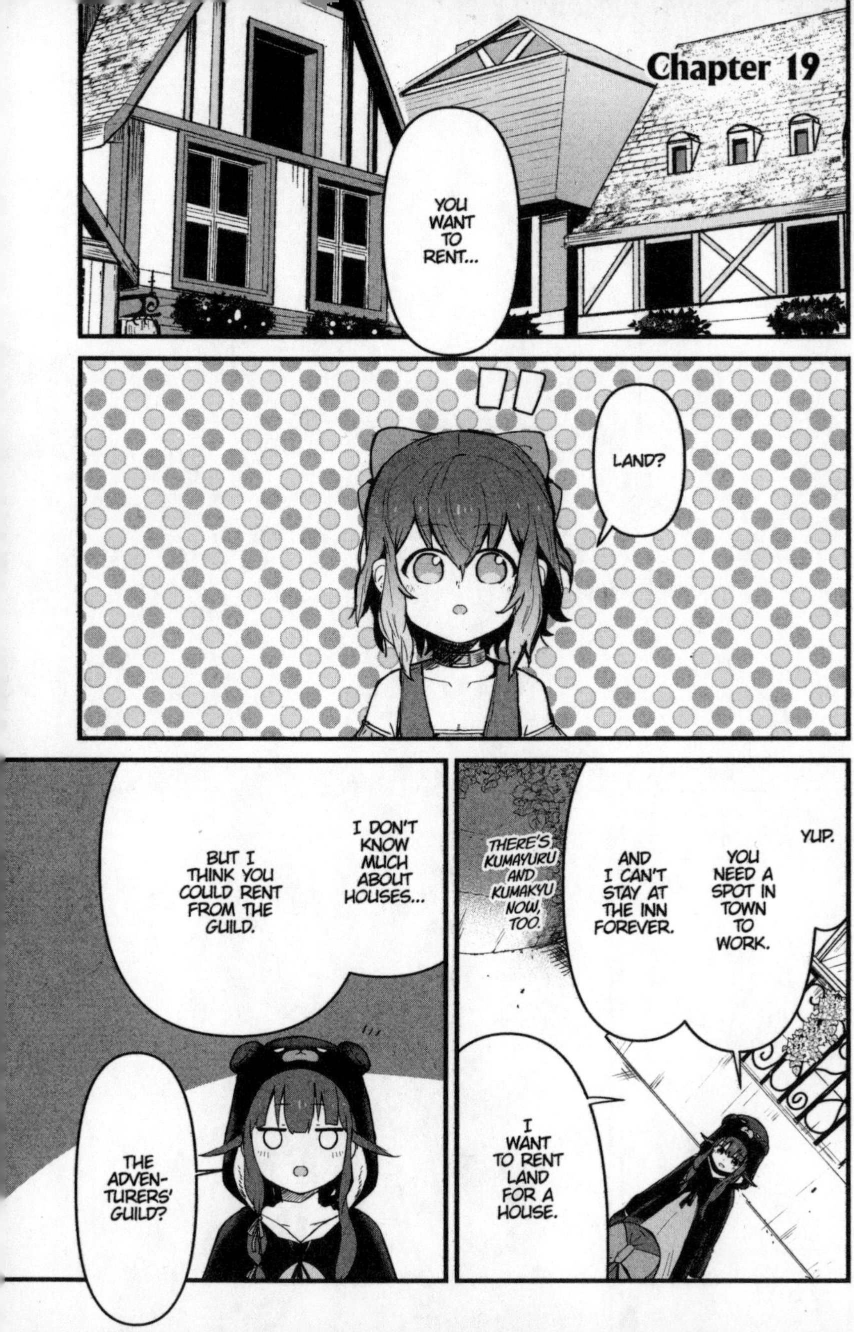
YOU WANT TO RENT...
LAND?
YUP.
YOU NEED A SPOT IN TOWN TO WORK.
AND I CAN'T STAY AT THE INN FOREVER.
THERE'S KUMAYURU AND KUMAKYU NOW, TOO.
I WANT TO RENT LAND FOR A HOUSE.
I DON'T KNOW MUCH ABOUT HOUSES...
BUT I THINK YOU COULD RENT FROM THE GUILD.
THE ADVENTURERS' GUILD?

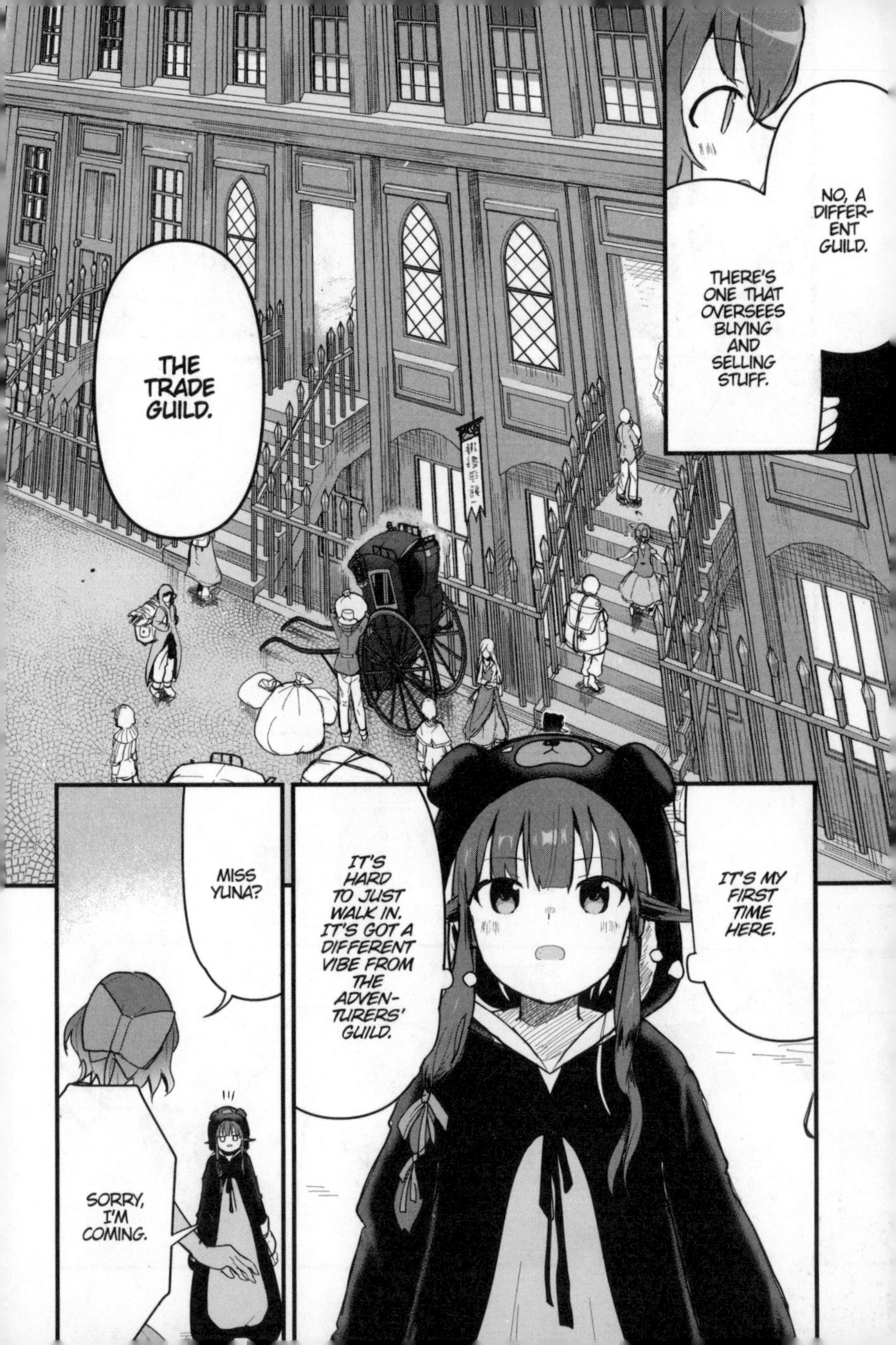
NO, A DIFFERENT GUILD.
THERE'S ONE THAT OVERSEES BUYING AND SELLING STUFF.
THE TRADE GUILD.
IT'S MY FIRST TIME HERE.
IT'S HARD TO JUST WALK IN. IT'S GOT A DIFFERENT VIBE FROM THE ADVENTURERS' GUILD.
MISS YUNA?
SORRY, I'M COMING.

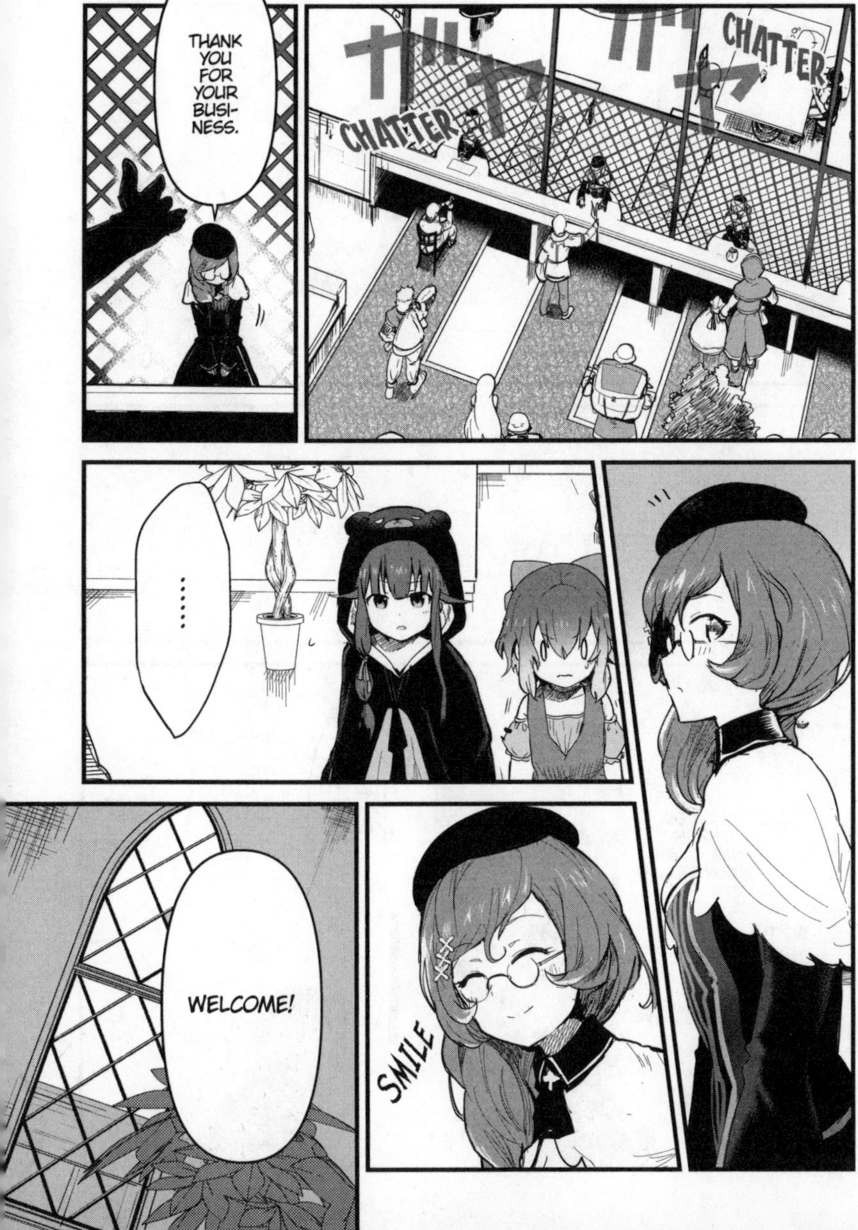
CHATTER
CHATTER
THANK YOU FOR YOUR BUSINESS.
......
SMILE
WELCOME!

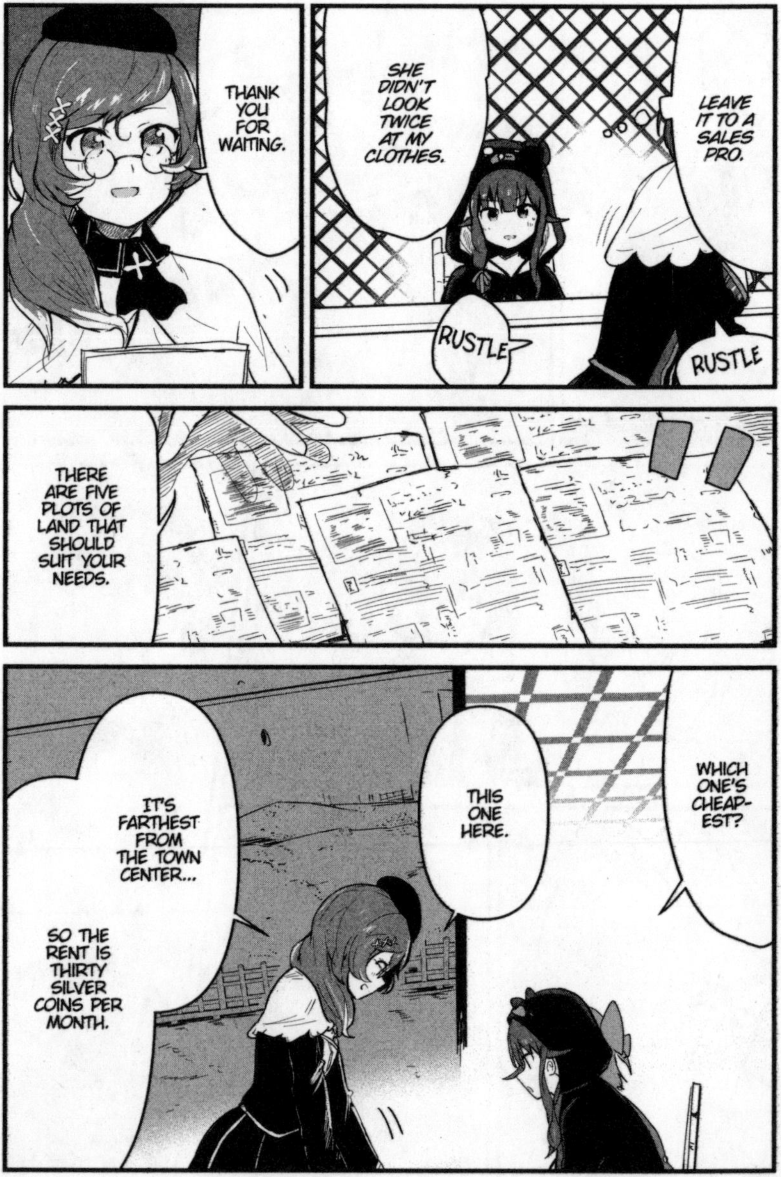
LEAVE IT TO A SALES PRO.
SHE DIDN'T LOOK TWICE AT MY CLOTHES.
RUSTLE
RUSTLE
THANK YOU FOR WAITING.
THERE ARE FIVE PLOTS OF LAND THAT SHOULD SUIT YOUR NEEDS.
WHICH ONE'S CHEAP-EST?
THIS ONE HERE.
IT'S FARTHEST FROM THE TOWN CENTER...
SO THE RENT IS THIRTY SILVER COINS PER MONTH.

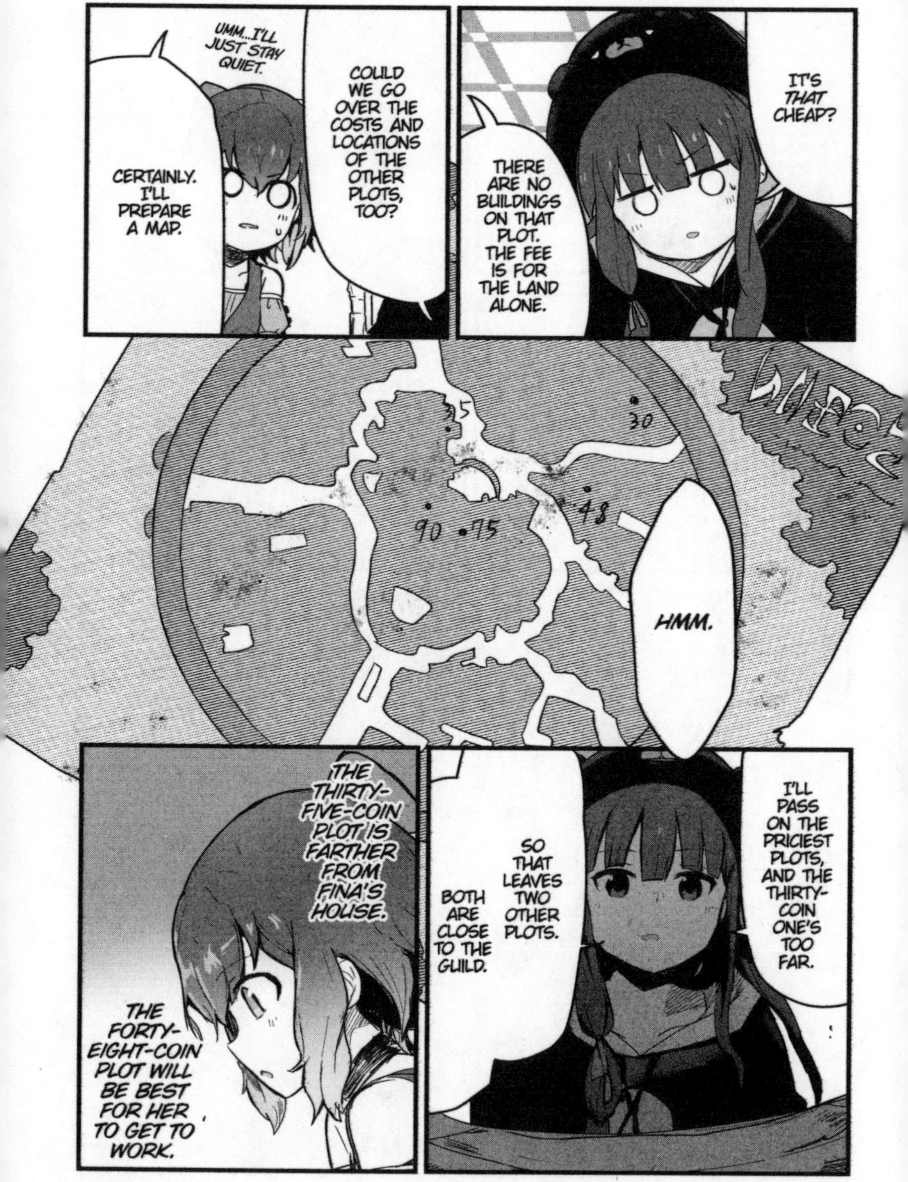
IT'S THAT CHEAP?
THERE ARE NO BUILDINGS ON THAT PLOT. THE FEE IS FOR THE LAND ALONE.
COULD WE GO OVER THE COSTS AND LOCATIONS OF THE OTHER PLOTS, TOO?
UMM...I'LL JUST STAY QUIET.
CERTAINLY. I'LL PREPARE A MAP.
35
30
48
90
75
HMM.
I'LL PASS ON THE PRICIEST PLOTS, AND THE THIRTY-COIN ONE'S TOO FAR.
SO THAT LEAVES TWO OTHER PLOTS.
BOTH ARE CLOSE TO THE GUILD.
THE THIRTY-FIVE-COIN PLOT IS FARTHER FROM FINA'S HOUSE.
THE FORTY-EIGHT-COIN PLOT WILL BE BEST FOR HER TO GET TO WORK.

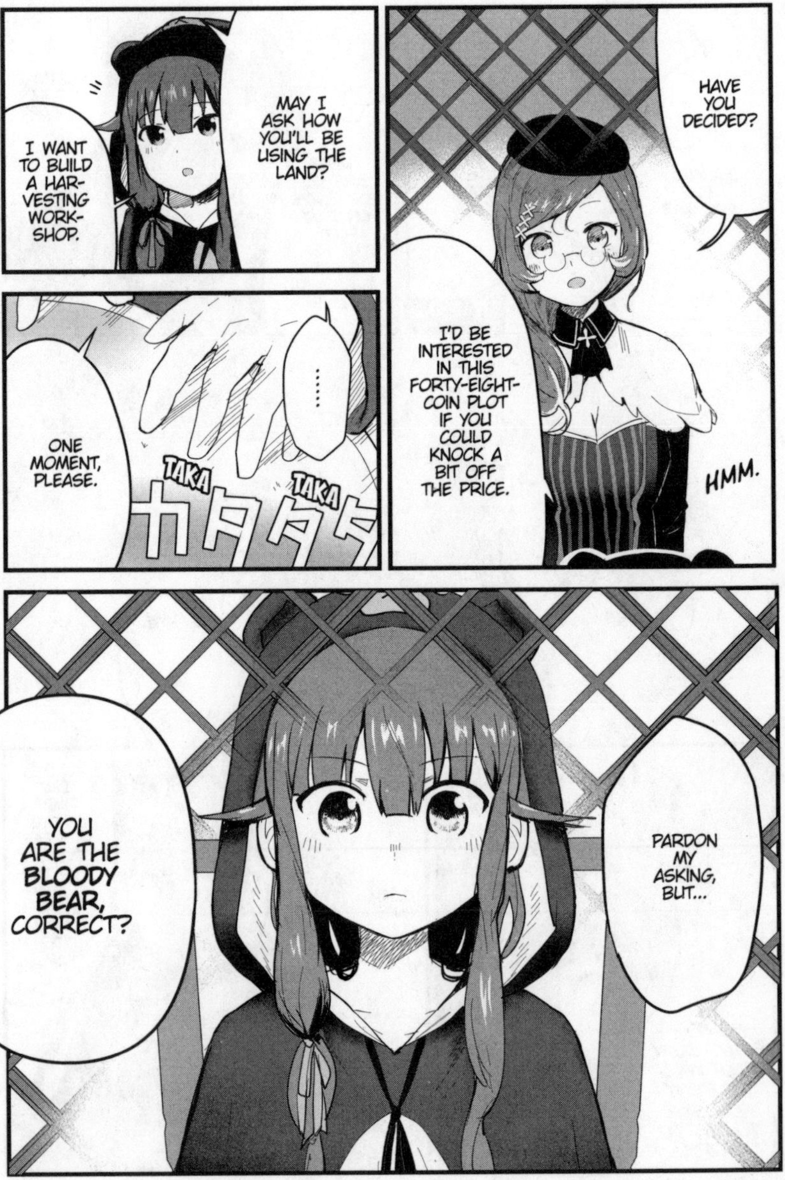
HAVE YOU DECIDED?
I'D BE INTERESTED IN THIS FORTY-EIGHT-COIN PLOT IF YOU COULD KNOCK A BIT OFF THE PRICE.
HMM.
MAY I ASK HOW YOU'LL BE USING THE LAND?
I WANT TO BUILD A HARVESTING WORKSHOP.
......
ONE MOMENT, PLEASE.
TAKA
TAKA
PARDON MY ASKING, BUT...
YOU ARE THE BLOODY BEAR, CORRECT?

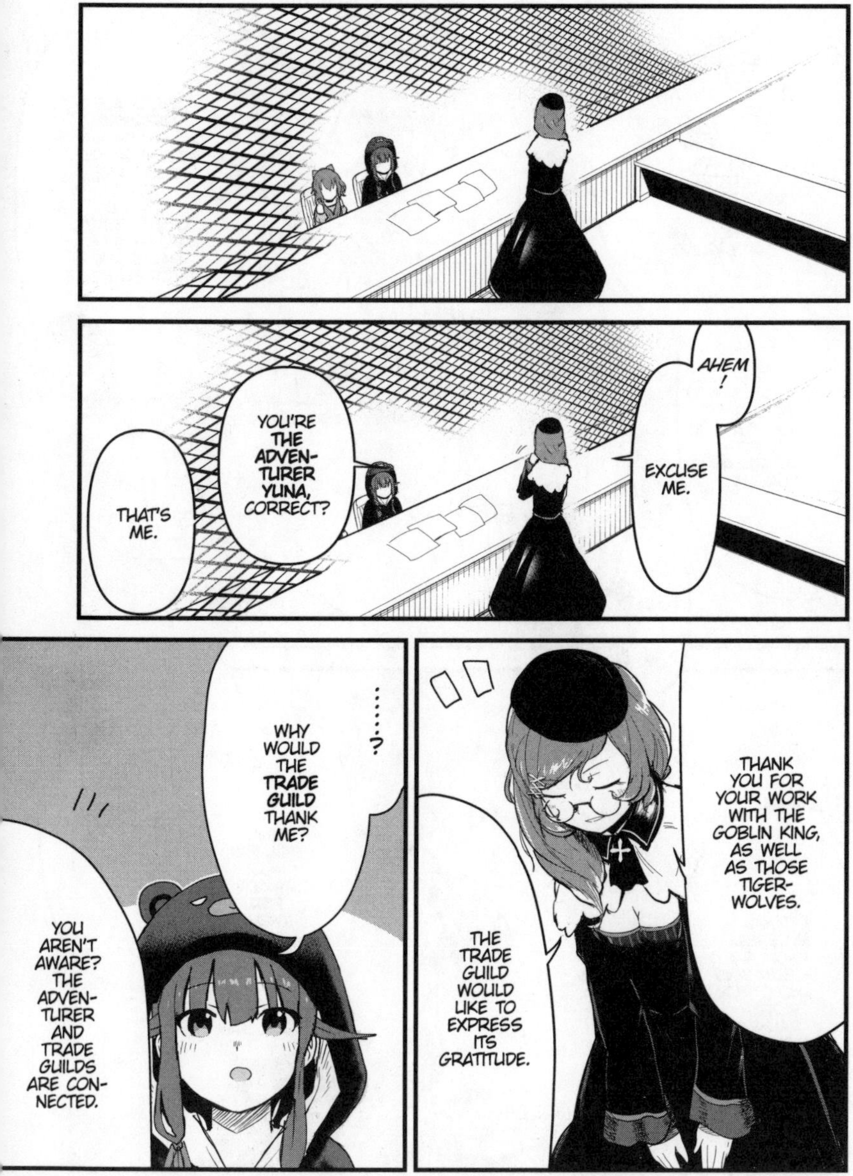
AHEM!
EXCUSE ME.
YOU'RE THE ADVENTURER YUNA, CORRECT?
THAT'S ME.
THANK YOU FOR YOUR WORK WITH THE GOBLIN KING, AS WELL AS THOSE TIGER-WOLVES.
THE TRADE GUILD WOULD LIKE TO EXPRESS ITS GRATITUDE.
......?
WHY WOULD THE TRADE GUILD THANK ME?
YOU AREN'T AWARE? THE ADVENTURER AND TRADE GUILDS ARE CONNECTED.

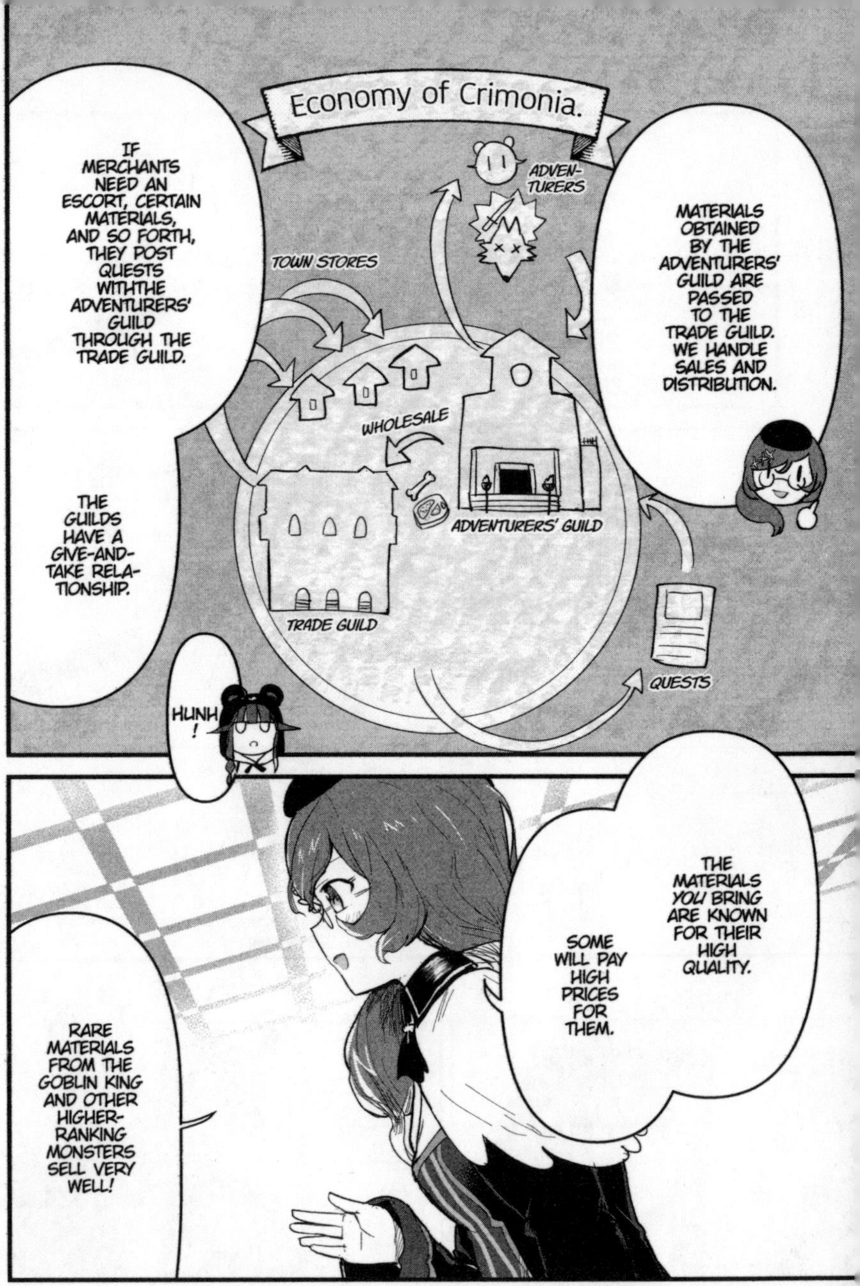
Economy of Crimonia.
ADVENTURERS
TOWN STORES
WHOLESALE
ADVENTURERS' GUILD
TRADE GUILD
QUESTS
MATERIALS OBTAINED BY THE ADVENTURERS' GUILD ARE PASSED TO THE TRADE GUILD. WE HANDLE SALES AND DISTRIBUTION.
IF MERCHANTS NEED AN ESCORT, CERTAIN MATERIALS, AND SO FORTH, THEY POST QUESTS WITHTHE ADVENTURERS' GUILD THROUGH THE TRADE GUILD.
THE GUILDS HAVE A GIVE-AND-TAKE RELATIONSHIP.
HUNH!
THE MATERIALS *YOU* BRING ARE KNOWN FOR THEIR HIGH QUALITY.
SOME WILL PAY HIGH PRICES FOR THEM.
RARE MATERIALS FROM THE GOBLIN KING AND OTHER HIGHER-RANKING MONSTERS SELL VERY WELL!

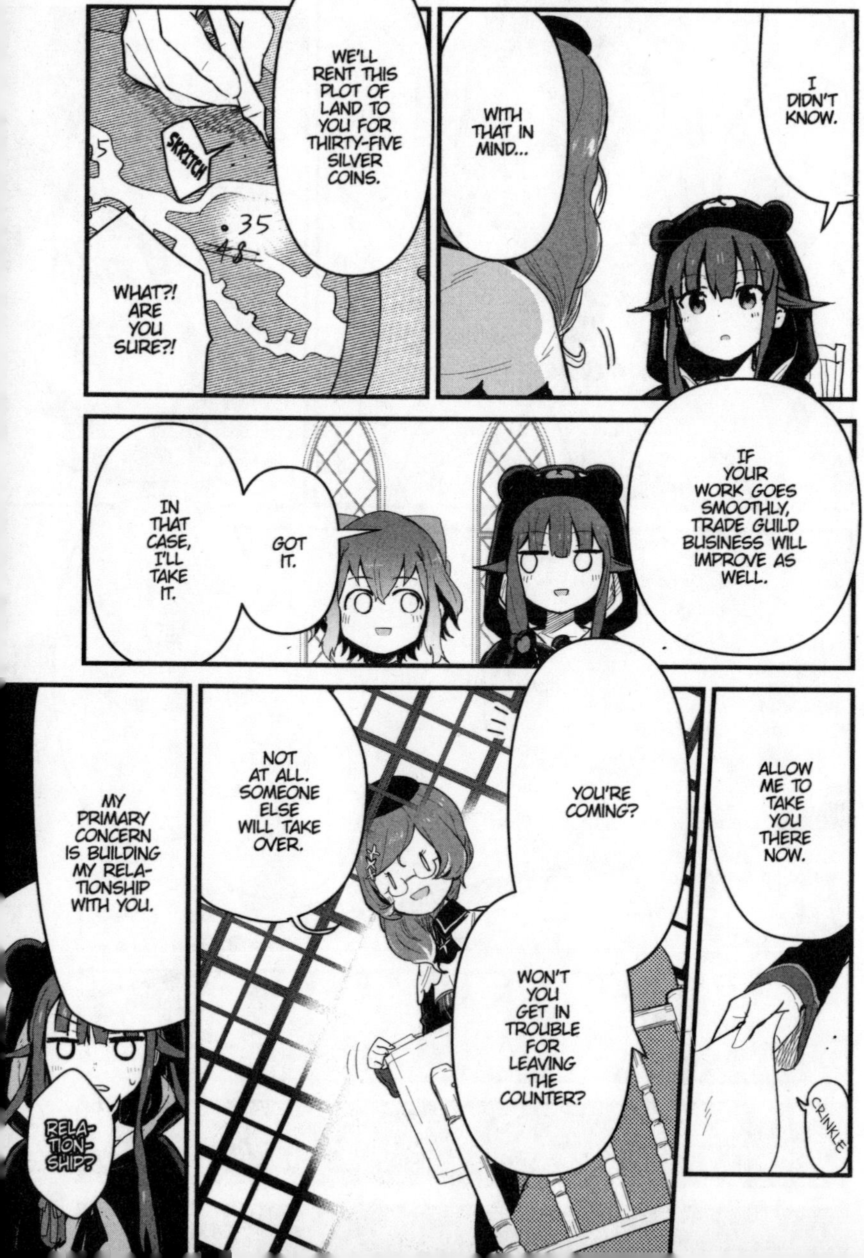
I DIDN'T KNOW.
WITH THAT IN MIND...
WE'LL RENT THIS PLOT OF LAND TO YOU FOR THIRTY-FIVE SILVER COINS.
SKRITCH
35
WHAT?! ARE YOU SURE?!
IF YOUR WORK GOES SMOOTHLY, TRADE GUILD BUSINESS WILL IMPROVE AS WELL.
GOT IT.
IN THAT CASE, I'LL TAKE IT.
ALLOW ME TO TAKE YOU THERE NOW.
CRINKLE
YOU'RE COMING?
WON'T YOU GET IN TROUBLE FOR LEAVING THE COUNTER?
NOT AT ALL. SOMEONE ELSE WILL TAKE OVER.
MY PRIMARY CONCERN IS BUILDING MY RELATIONSHIP WITH YOU.
RELATIONSHIP?

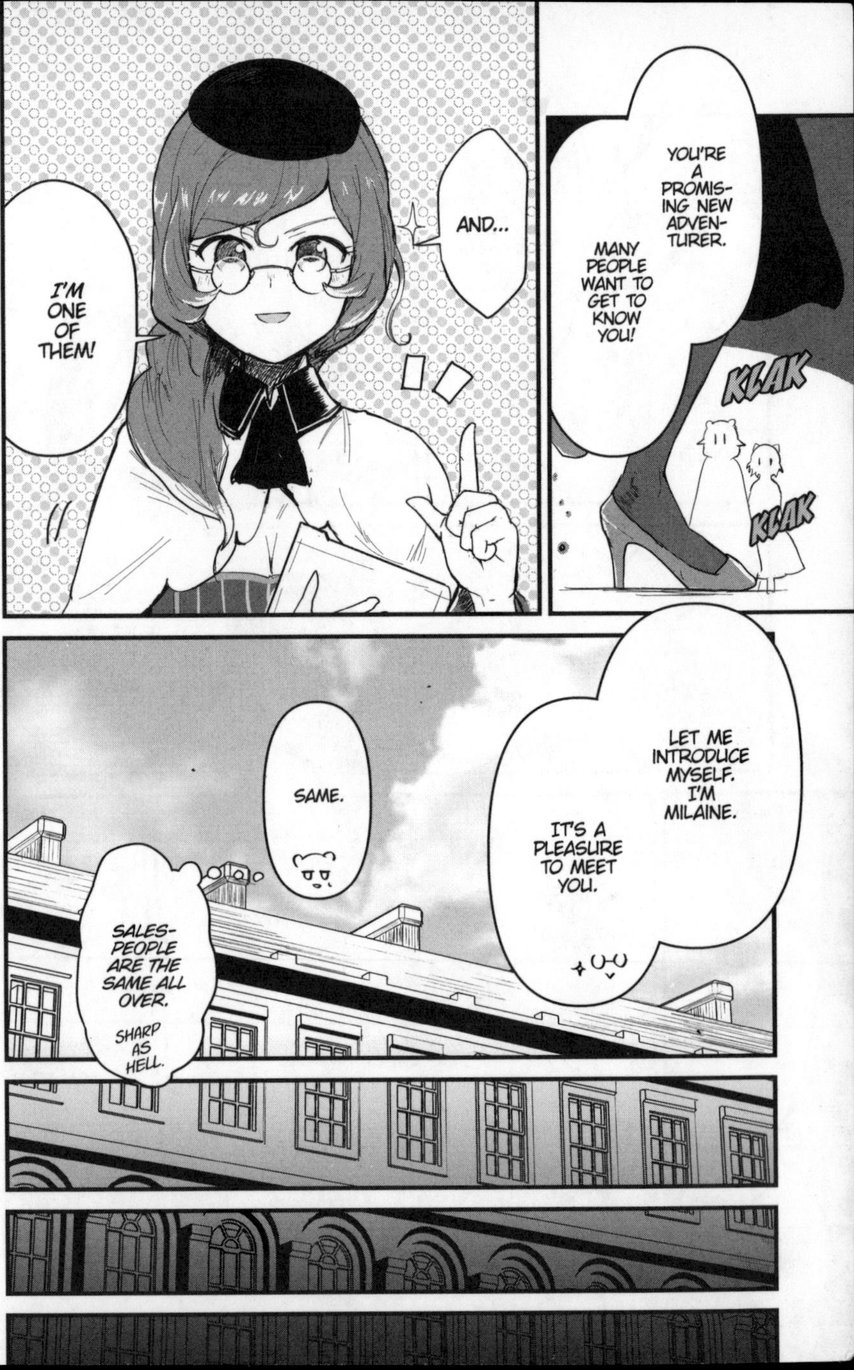
YOU'RE A PROMISING NEW ADVENTURER.
MANY PEOPLE WANT TO GET TO KNOW YOU!
KLAK
KLAK
AND...
I'M ONE OF THEM!
LET ME INTRODUCE MYSELF. I'M MILAINE.
IT'S A PLEASURE TO MEET YOU.
SAME.
SALES-PEOPLE ARE THE SAME ALL OVER.
SHARP AS HELL.

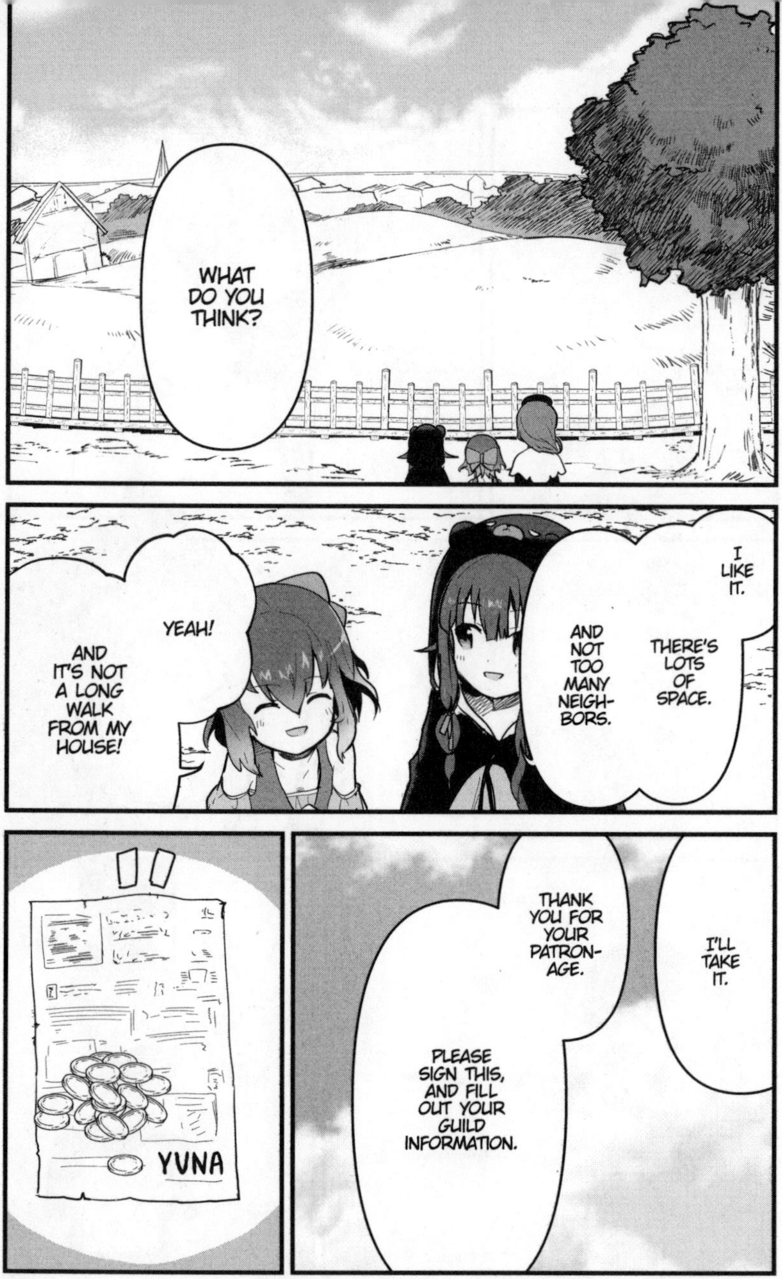
WHAT DO YOU THINK?
I LIKE IT.
THERE'S LOTS OF SPACE.
AND NOT TOO MANY NEIGH-BORS.
YEAH!
AND IT'S NOT A LONG WALK FROM MY HOUSE!
I'LL TAKE IT.
THANK YOU FOR YOUR PATRON-AGE.
PLEASE SIGN THIS, AND FILL OUT YOUR GUILD INFORMATION.
YUNA

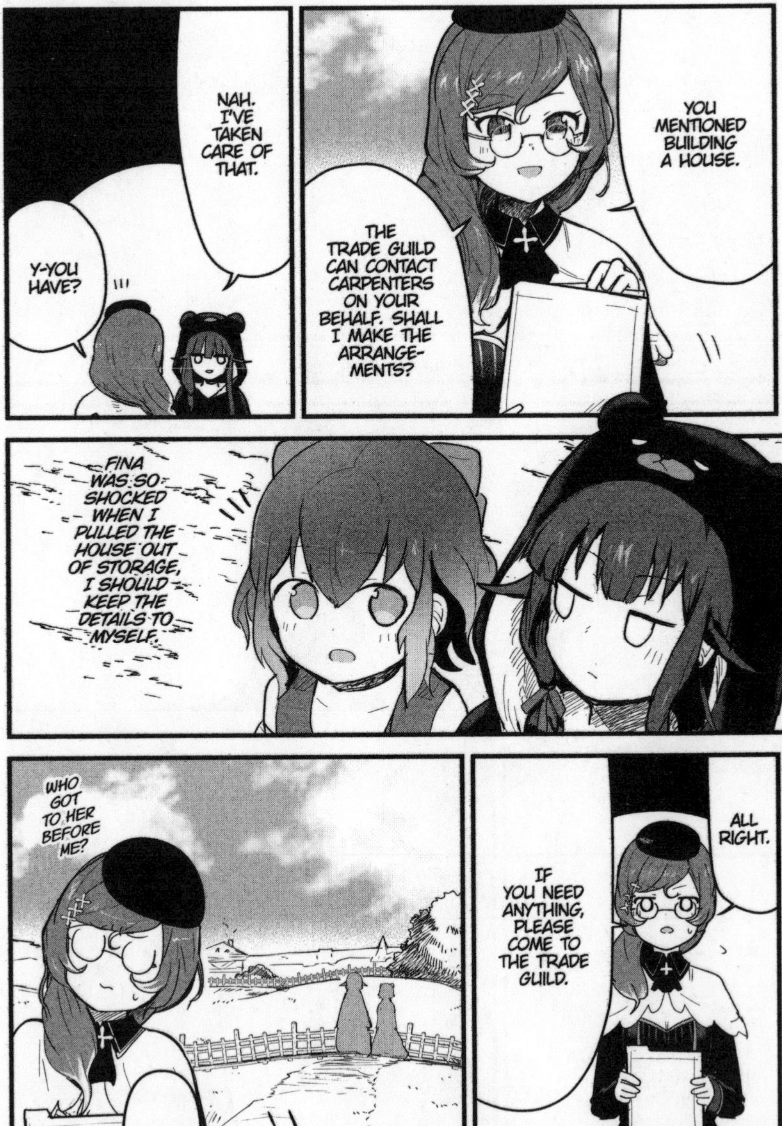
YOU MENTIONED BUILDING A HOUSE.
THE TRADE GUILD CAN CONTACT CARPENTERS ON YOUR BEHALF. SHALL I MAKE THE ARRANGE-MENTS?
NAH. I'VE TAKEN CARE OF THAT.
Y-YOU HAVE?
FINA WAS SO SHOCKED WHEN I PULLED THE HOUSE OUT OF STORAGE, I SHOULD KEEP THE DETAILS TO MYSELF.
ALL RIGHT.
IF YOU NEED ANYTHING, PLEASE COME TO THE TRADE GUILD.
WHO GOT TO HER BEFORE ME?
RIGHT!

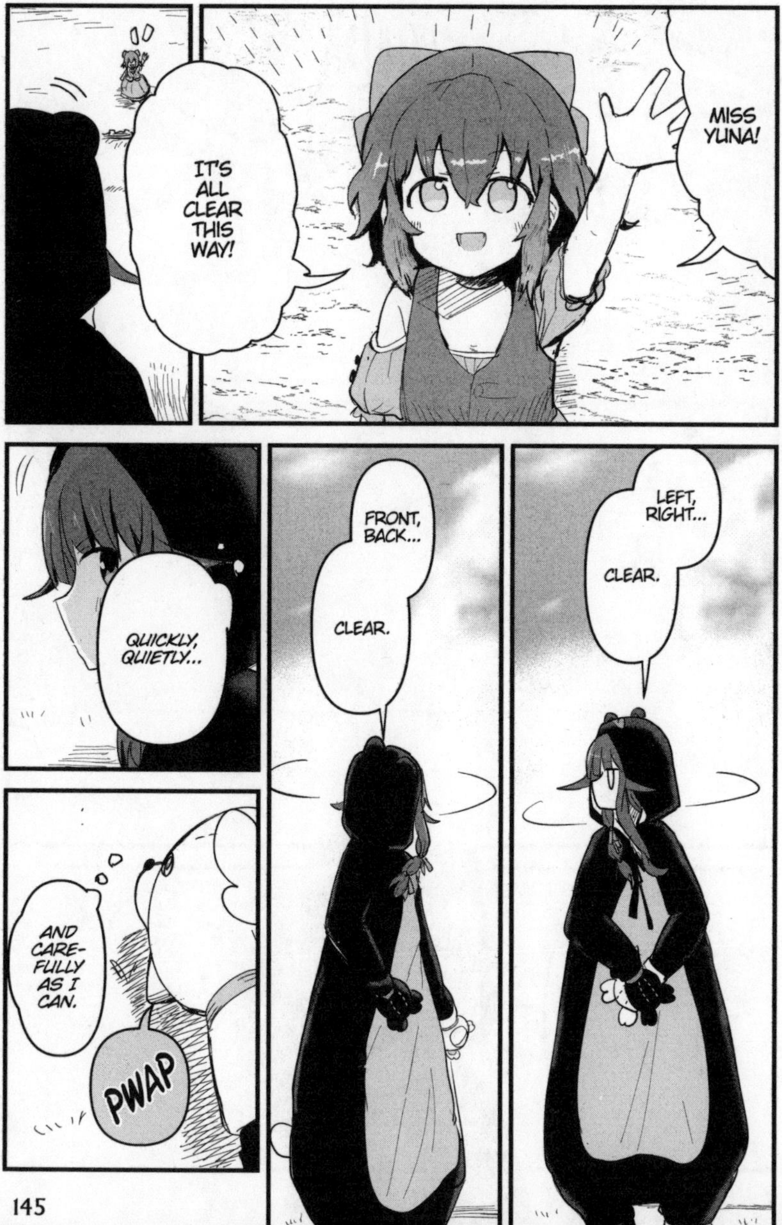
MISS YUNA!
IT'S ALL CLEAR THIS WAY!
LEFT, RIGHT...
CLEAR.
FRONT, BACK...
CLEAR.
QUICKLY, QUIETLY...
AND CARE-FULLY AS I CAN.
PWAP

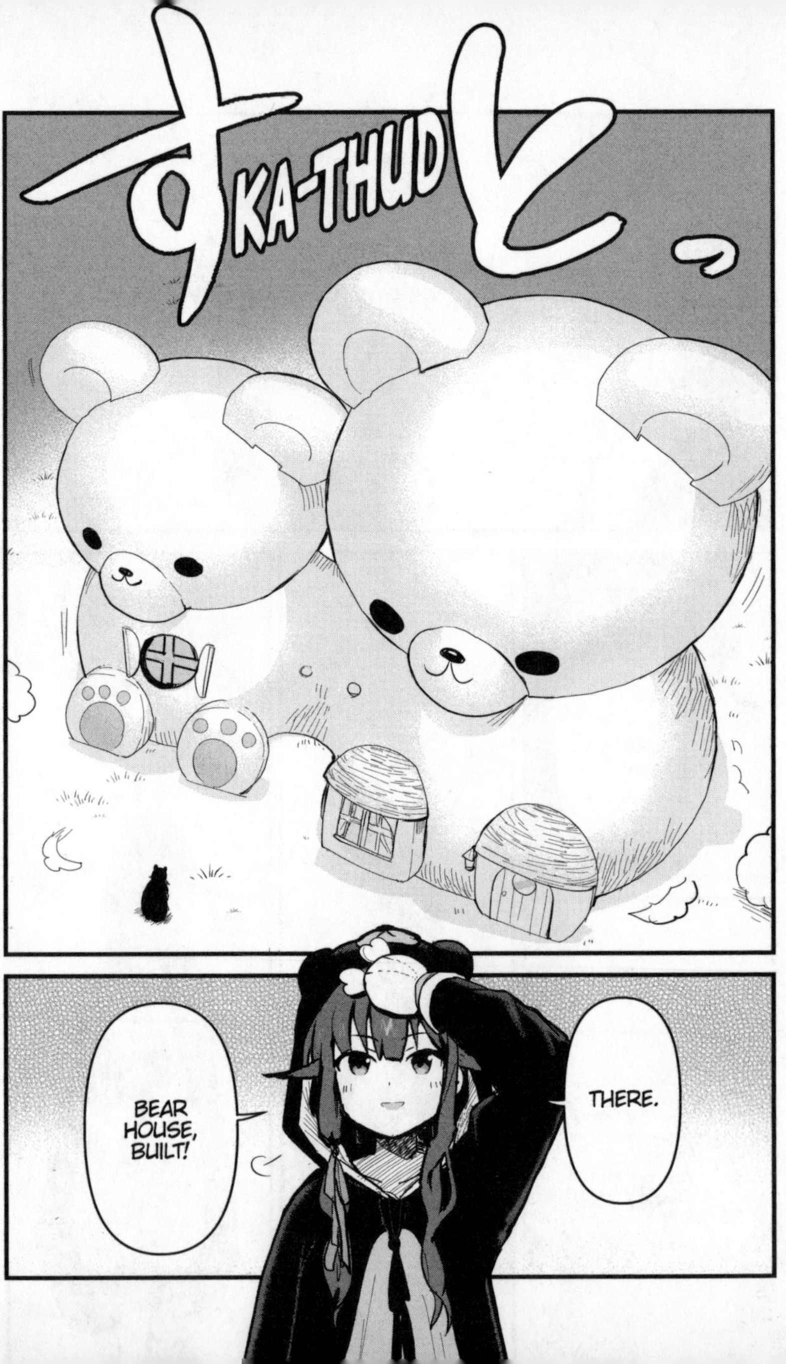
すKA-THUDとっ
THERE.
BEAR HOUSE, BUILT!

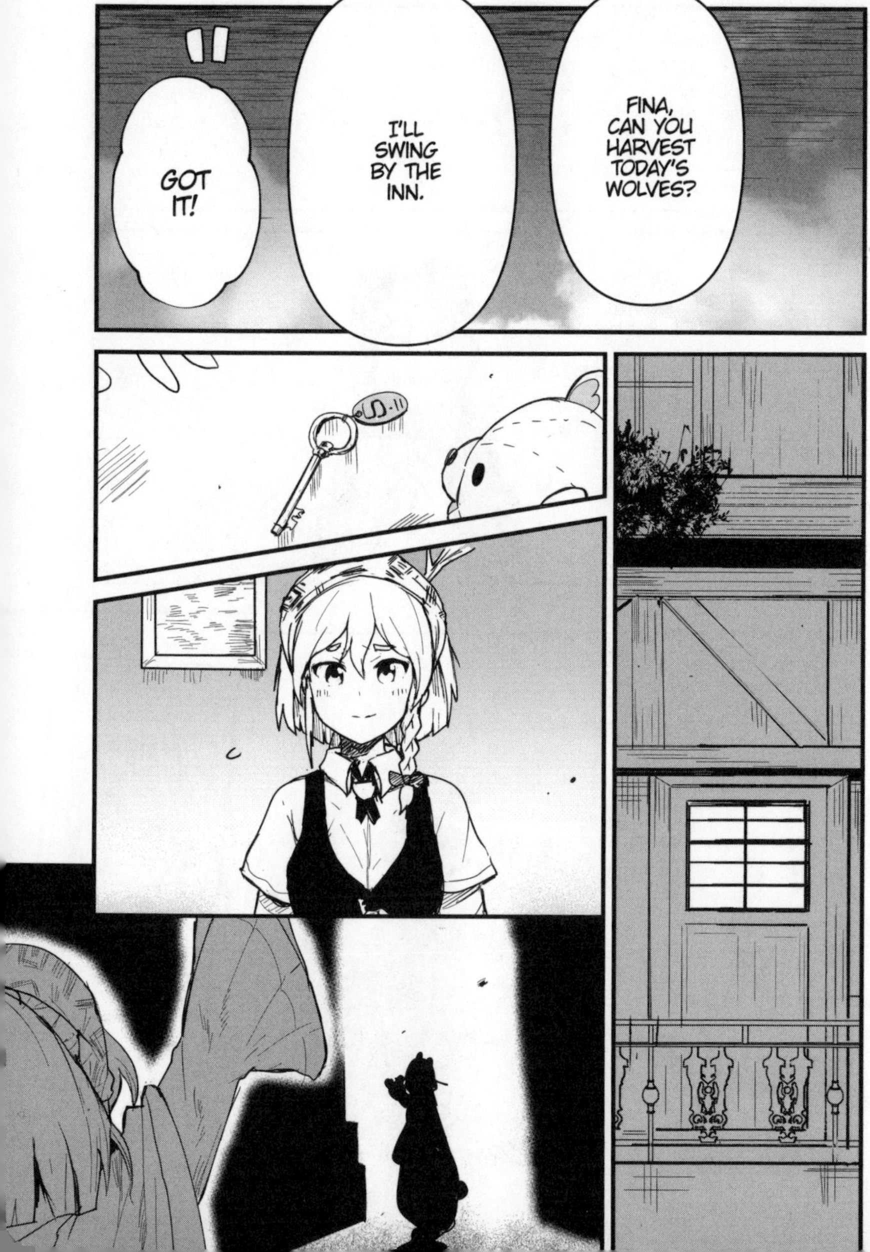
FINA, CAN YOU HARVEST TODAY'S WOLVES?
I'LL SWING BY THE INN.
GOT IT!

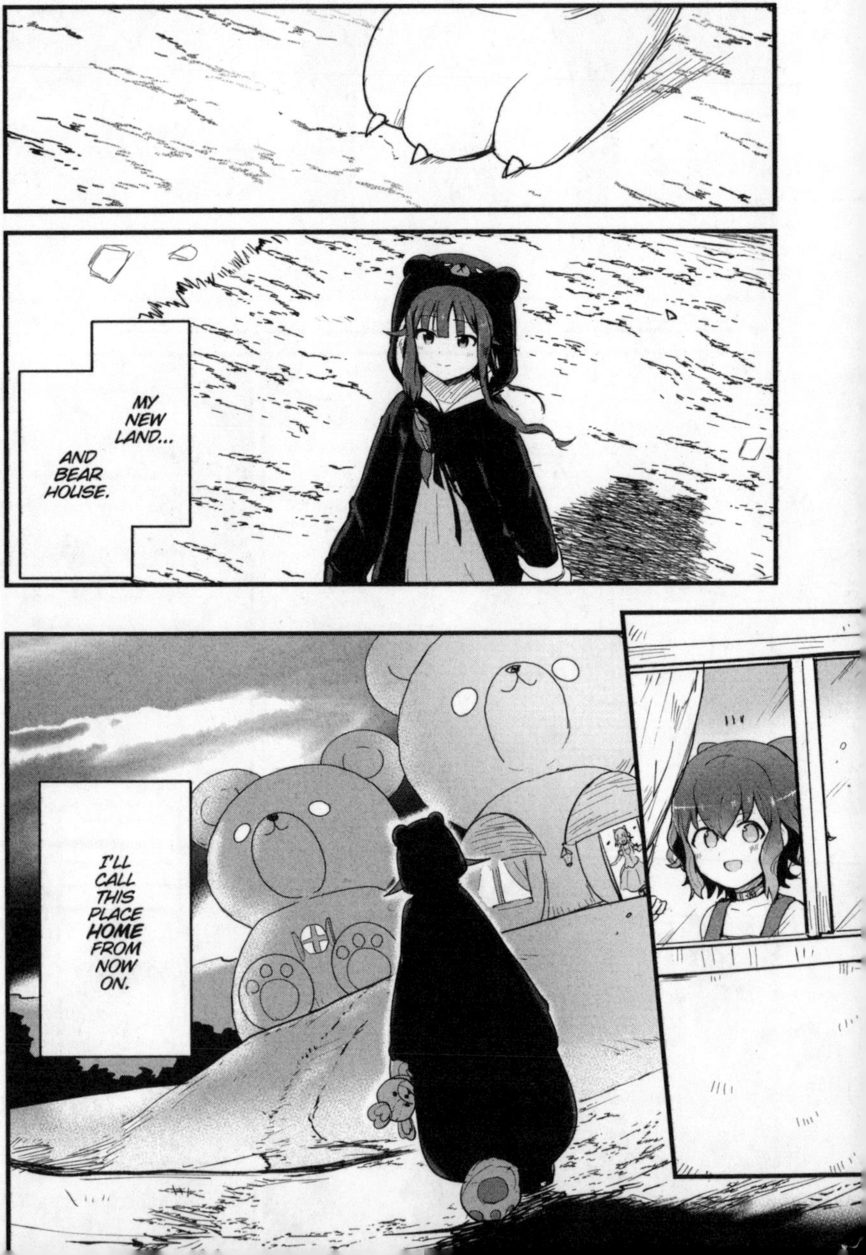
MY NEW LAND...
AND BEAR HOUSE.
I'LL CALL THIS PLACE HOME FROM NOW ON.

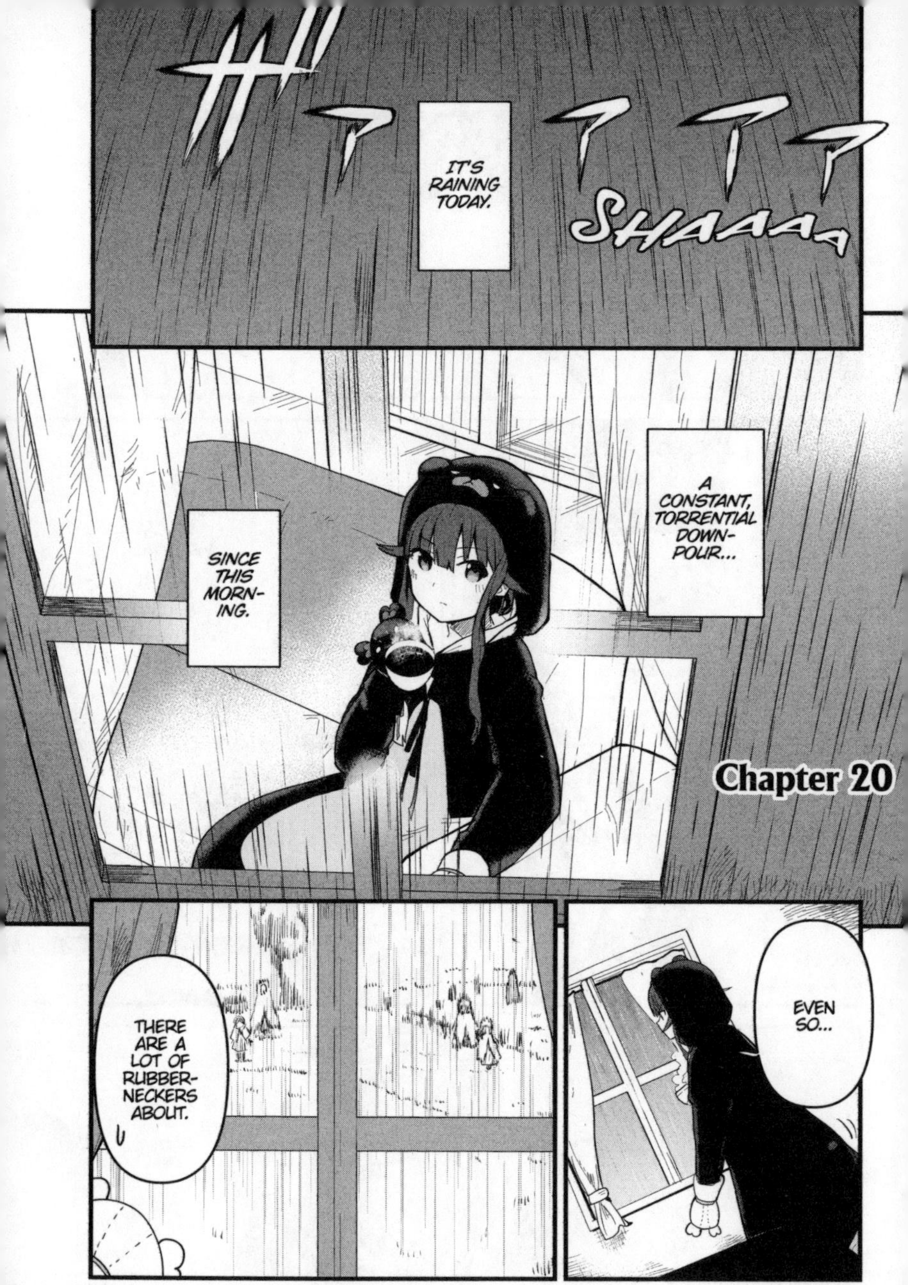
ザァァァァ
SHAAAA
IT'S RAINING TODAY.
A CONSTANT, TORRENTIAL DOWNPOUR...
SINCE THIS MORNING.
Chapter 20
EVEN SO...
THERE ARE A LOT OF RUBBERNECKERS ABOUT.

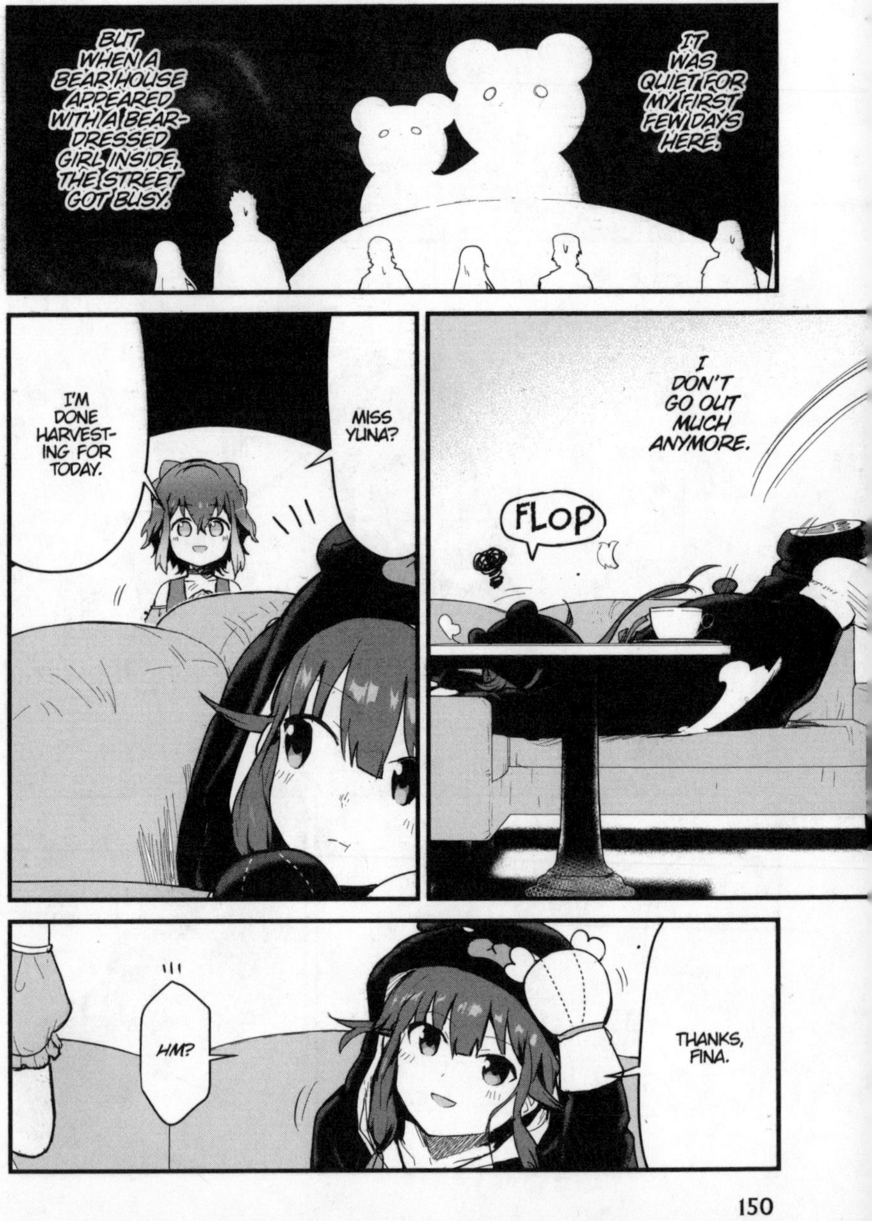
IT WAS QUIET FOR MY FIRST FEW DAYS HERE.
BUT WHEN A BEAR HOUSE APPEARED WITH A BEAR-DRESSED GIRL INSIDE, THE STREET GOT BUSY.
I DON'T GO OUT MUCH ANYMORE.
FLOP
MISS YUNA?
I'M DONE HARVESTING FOR TODAY.
THANKS, FINA.
HM?

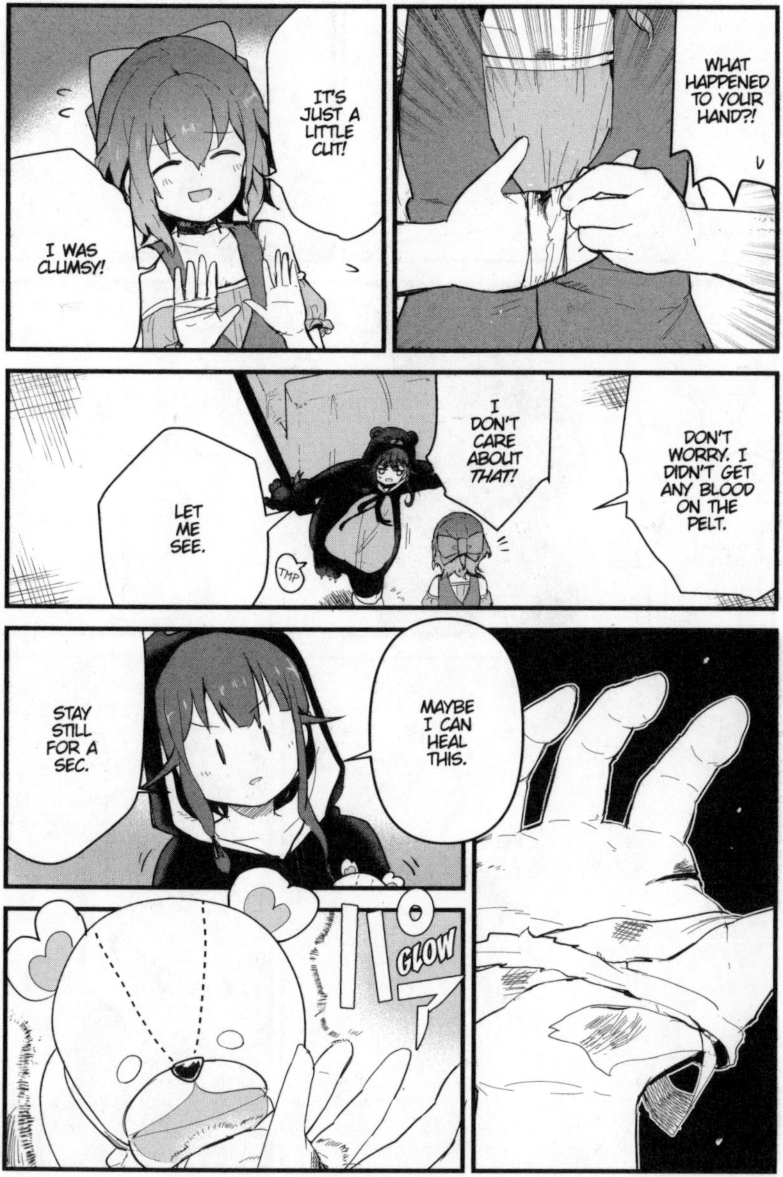
WHAT HAPPENED TO YOUR HAND?!
IT'S JUST A LITTLE CUT!
I WAS CLUMSY!
DON'T WORRY. I DIDN'T GET ANY BLOOD ON THE PELT.
I DON'T CARE ABOUT *THAT!*
TMP
LET ME SEE.
MAYBE I CAN HEAL THIS.
STAY STILL FOR A SEC.
GLOW

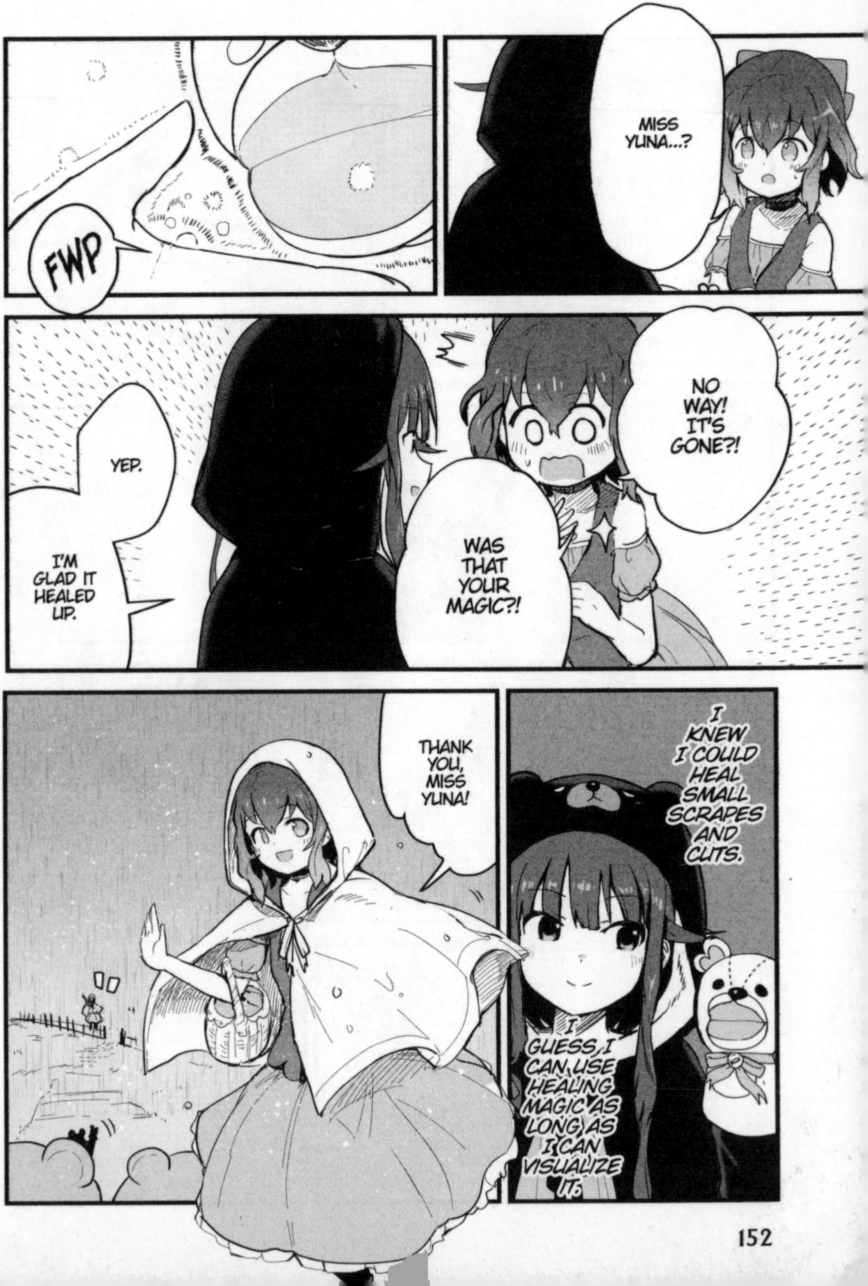
MISS YUNA...?
FWP
NO WAY! IT'S GONE?!
WAS THAT YOUR MAGIC?!
YEP.
I'M GLAD IT HEALED UP.
I KNEW I COULD HEAL SMALL SCRAPES AND CUTS.
I GUESS I CAN USE HEALING MAGIC AS LONG AS I CAN VISUALIZE IT.
THANK YOU, MISS YUNA!

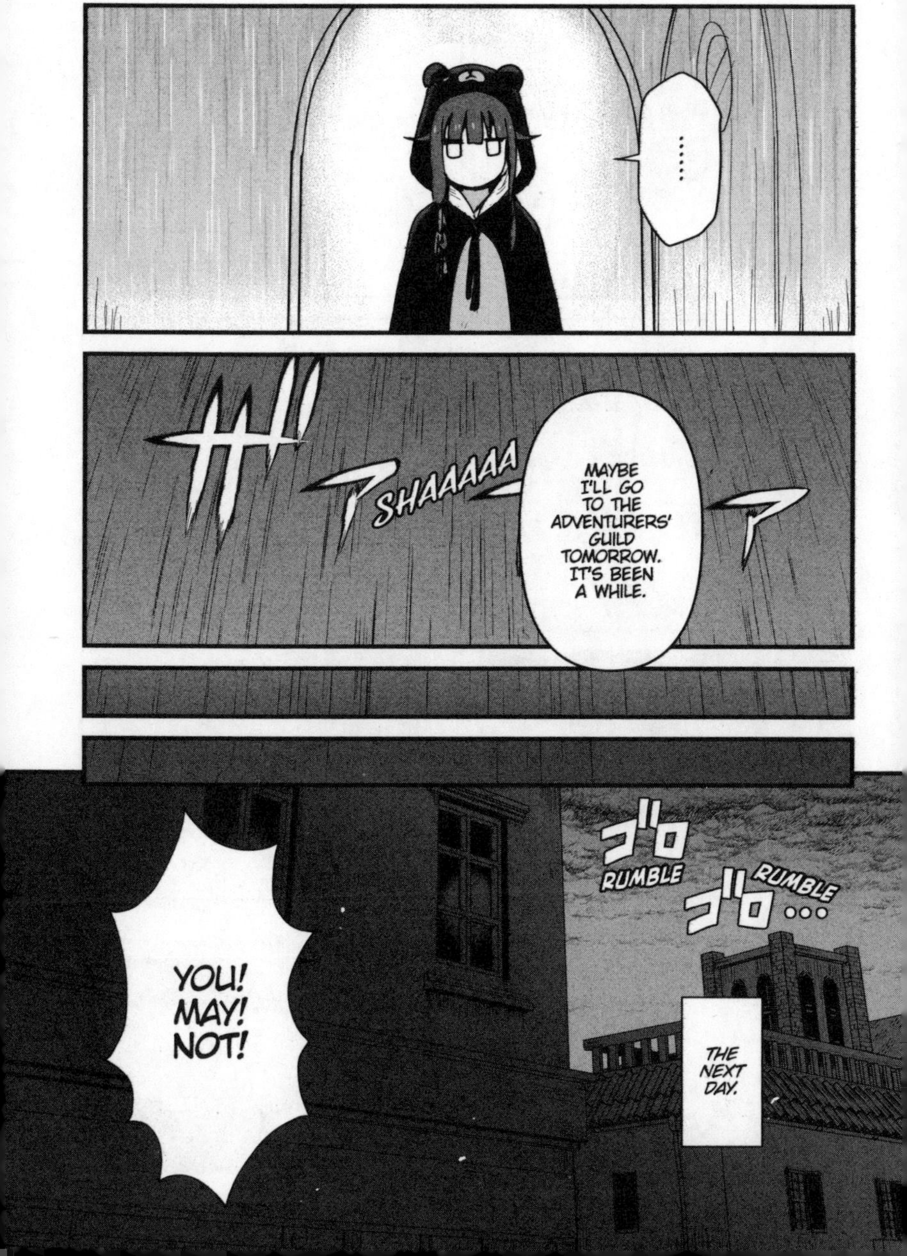
……
MAYBE I'LL GO TO THE ADVENTURERS' GUILD TOMORROW. IT'S BEEN A WHILE.
SHAAAAA
ゴロ
RUMBLE
RUMBLE
ゴロ…
THE NEXT DAY.
YOU! MAY! NOT!

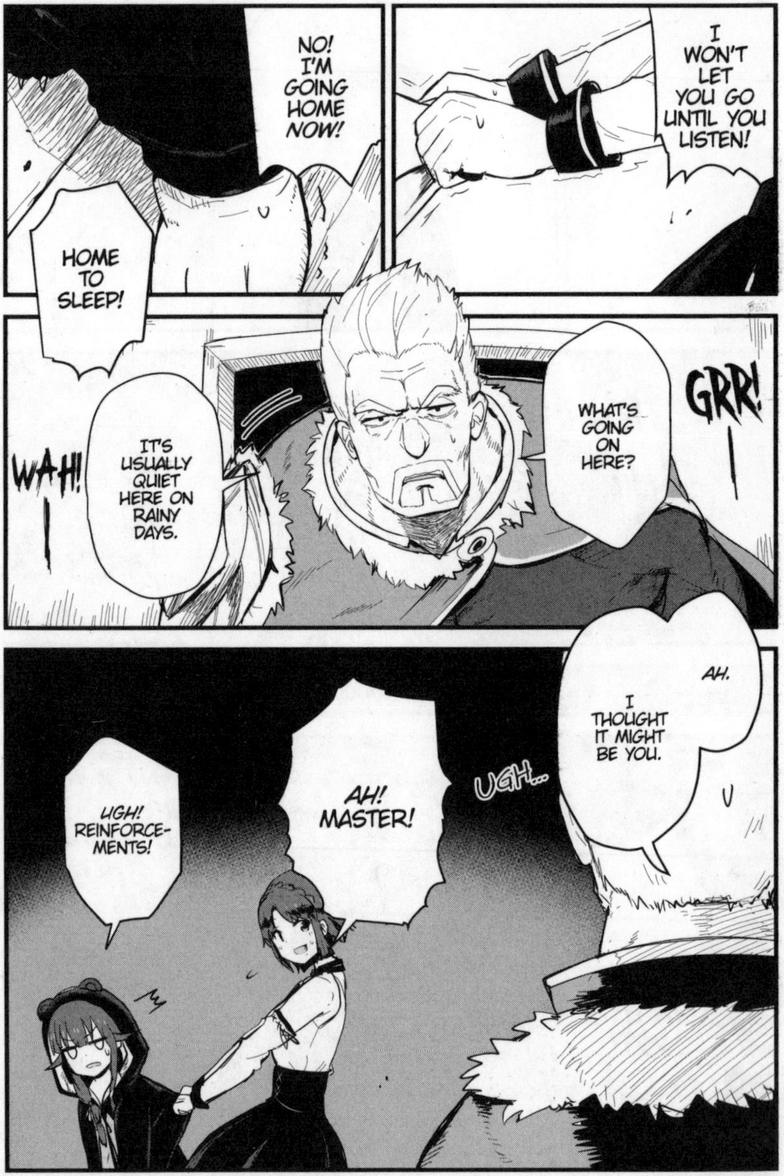
I WON'T LET YOU GO UNTIL YOU LISTEN!
NO! I'M GOING HOME NOW!
HOME TO SLEEP!
GRR!
WHAT'S GOING ON HERE?
IT'S USUALLY QUIET HERE ON RAINY DAYS.
WAH!
AH.
I THOUGHT IT MIGHT BE YOU.
UGH...
AH! MASTER!
UGH! REINFORCEMENTS!

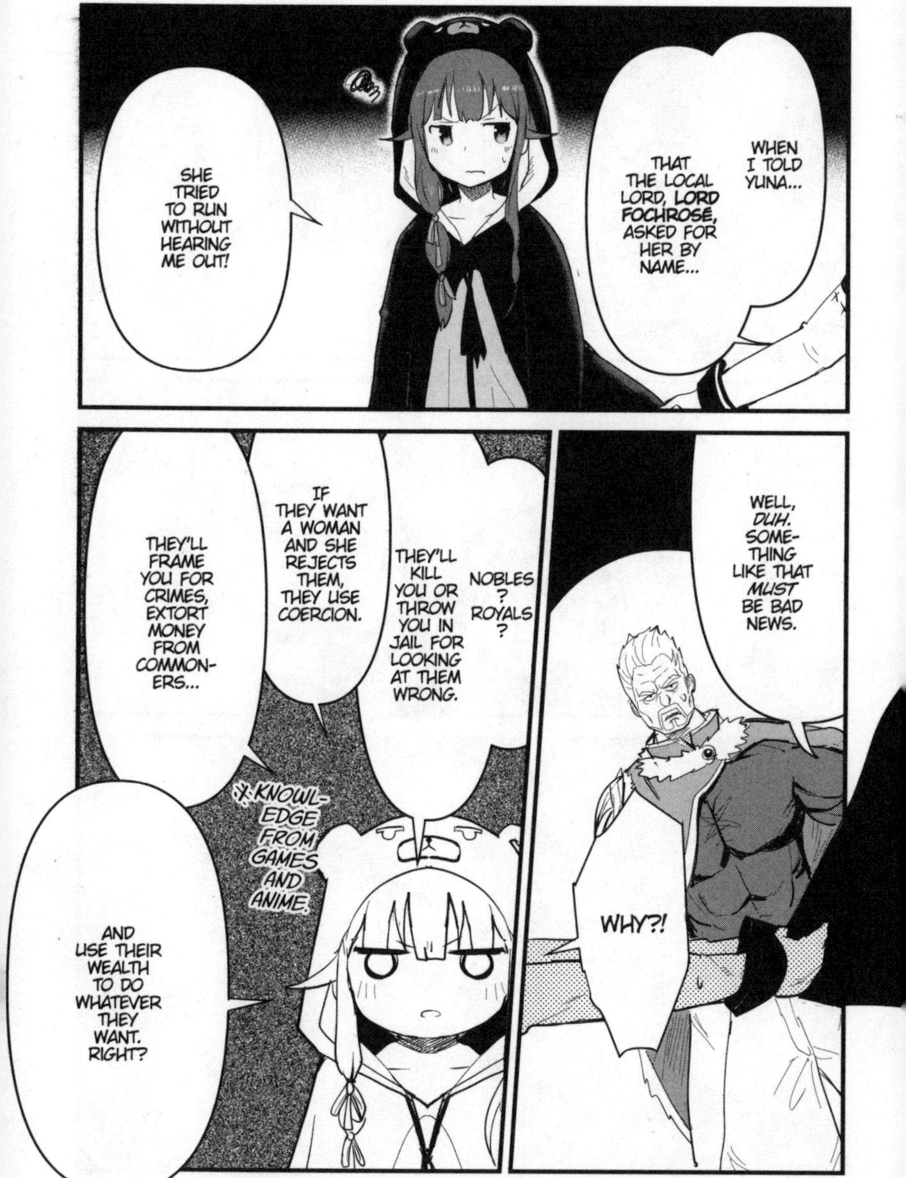
WHEN I TOLD YUNA...
THAT THE LOCAL LORD, LORD FOCHROSE, ASKED FOR HER BY NAME...
SHE TRIED TO RUN WITHOUT HEARING ME OUT!
WELL, DUH. SOMETHING LIKE THAT MUST BE BAD NEWS.
WHY?!
NOBLES? ROYALS?
THEY'LL KILL YOU OR THROW YOU IN JAIL FOR LOOKING AT THEM WRONG.
IF THEY WANT A WOMAN AND SHE REJECTS THEM, THEY USE COERCION.
THEY'LL FRAME YOU FOR CRIMES, EXTORT MONEY FROM COMMONERS...
※KNOWLEDGE FROM GAMES AND ANIME.
AND USE THEIR WEALTH TO DO WHATEVER THEY WANT. RIGHT?

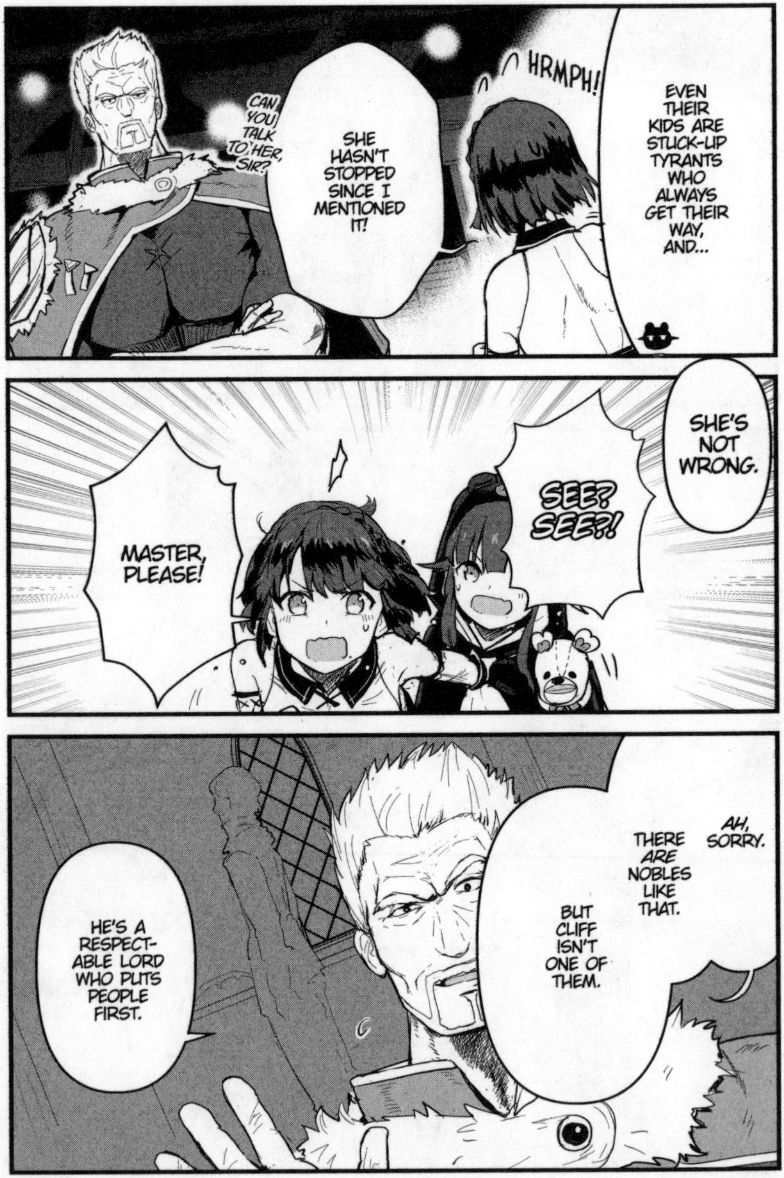
EVEN THEIR KIDS ARE STUCK-UP TYRANTS WHO ALWAYS GET THEIR WAY, AND...
HRMPH!
SHE HASN'T STOPPED SINCE I MENTIONED IT!
CAN YOU TALK TO HER, SIR?
SHE'S NOT WRONG.
SEE? SEE?!
MASTER, PLEASE!
AH, SORRY.
THERE *ARE* NOBLES LIKE THAT.
BUT CLIFF ISN'T ONE OF THEM.
HE'S A RESPECTABLE LORD WHO PUTS PEOPLE FIRST.

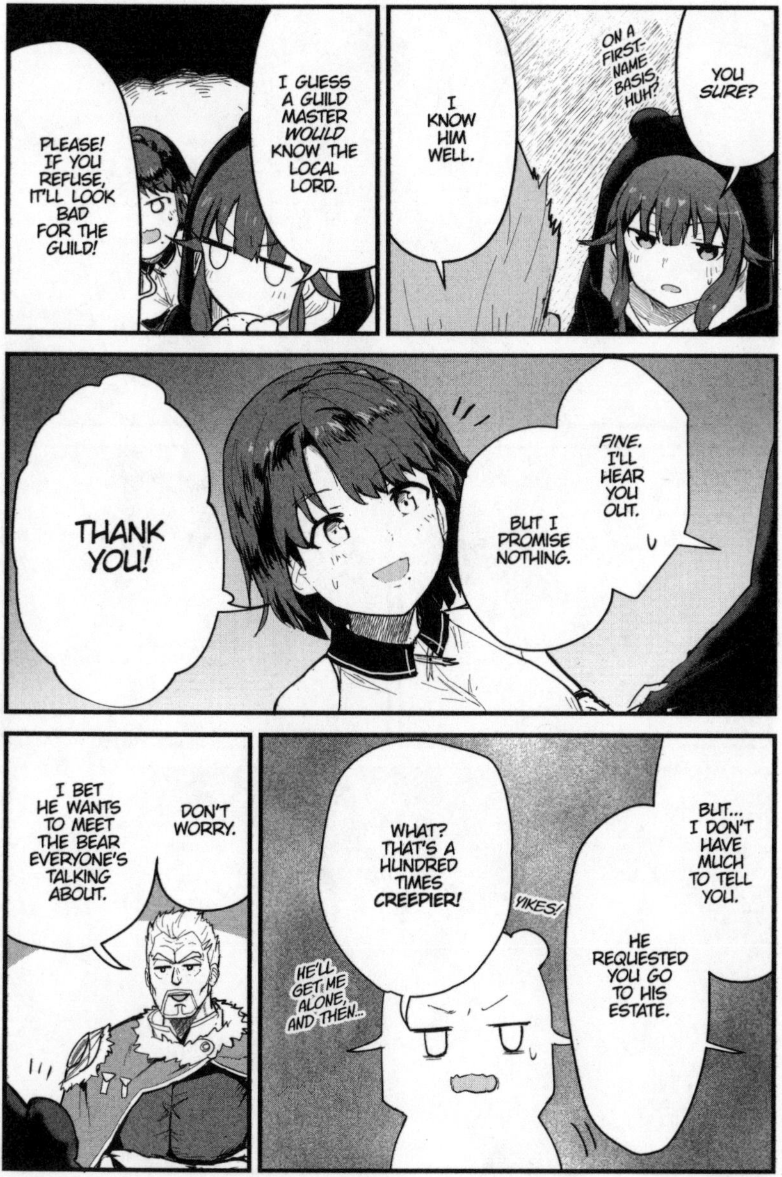
YOU SURE?
ON A FIRST-NAME BASIS, HUH?
I KNOW HIM WELL.
I GUESS A GUILD MASTER WOULD KNOW THE LOCAL LORD.
PLEASE! IF YOU REFUSE, IT'LL LOOK BAD FOR THE GUILD!
FINE. I'LL HEAR YOU OUT.
BUT I PROMISE NOTHING.
THANK YOU!
BUT... I DON'T HAVE MUCH TO TELL YOU.
HE REQUESTED YOU GO TO HIS ESTATE.
YIKES!
WHAT? THAT'S A HUNDRED TIMES CREEPIER!
HE'LL GET ME ALONE, AND THEN...
DON'T WORRY.
I BET HE WANTS TO MEET THE BEAR EVERYONE'S TALKING ABOUT.

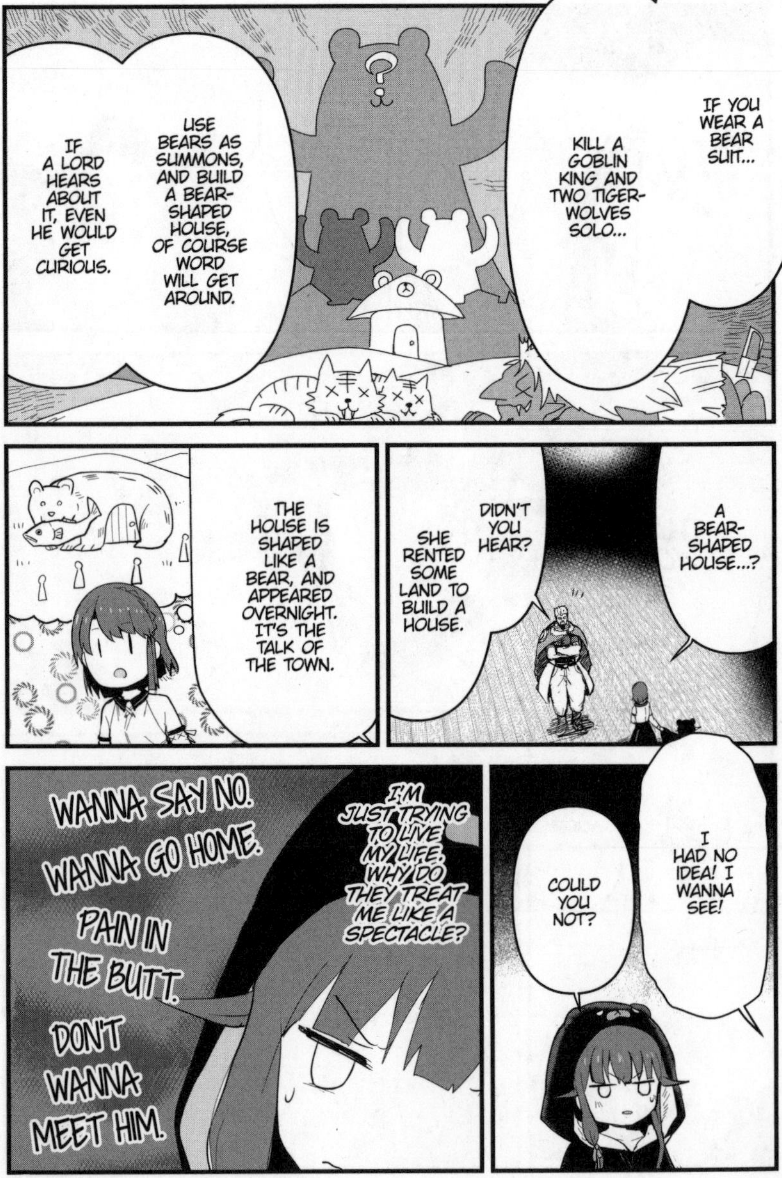
IF YOU WEAR A BEAR SUIT...
KILL A GOBLIN KING AND TWO TIGER-WOLVES SOLO...
USE BEARS AS SUMMONS, AND BUILD A BEAR-SHAPED HOUSE, OF COURSE WORD WILL GET AROUND.
IF A LORD HEARS ABOUT IT, EVEN HE WOULD GET CURIOUS.
A BEAR-SHAPED HOUSE...?
DIDN'T YOU HEAR?
SHE RENTED SOME LAND TO BUILD A HOUSE.
THE HOUSE IS SHAPED LIKE A BEAR, AND APPEARED OVERNIGHT. IT'S THE TALK OF THE TOWN.
I HAD NO IDEA! I WANNA SEE!
COULD YOU NOT?
I'M JUST TRYING TO LIVE MY LIFE. WHY DO THEY TREAT ME LIKE A SPECTACLE?
WANNA SAY NO.
WANNA GO HOME.
PAIN IN THE BUTT.
DON'T WANNA MEET HIM.

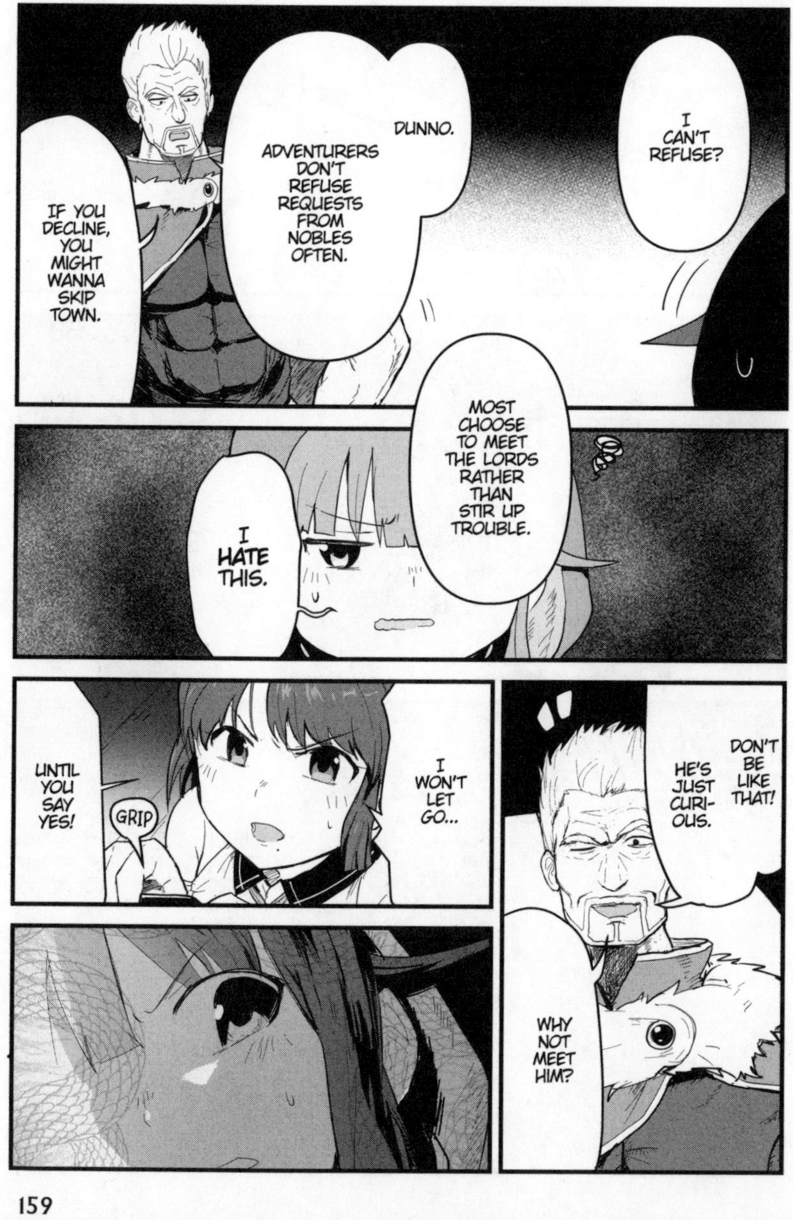
I CAN'T REFUSE?
DUNNO.
ADVENTURERS DON'T REFUSE REQUESTS FROM NOBLES OFTEN.
IF YOU DECLINE, YOU MIGHT WANNA SKIP TOWN.
MOST CHOOSE TO MEET THE LORDS RATHER THAN STIR UP TROUBLE.
I HATE THIS.
DON'T BE LIKE THAT!
HE'S JUST CURI-OUS.
WHY NOT MEET HIM?
I WON'T LET GO...
GRIP
UNTIL YOU SAY YES!

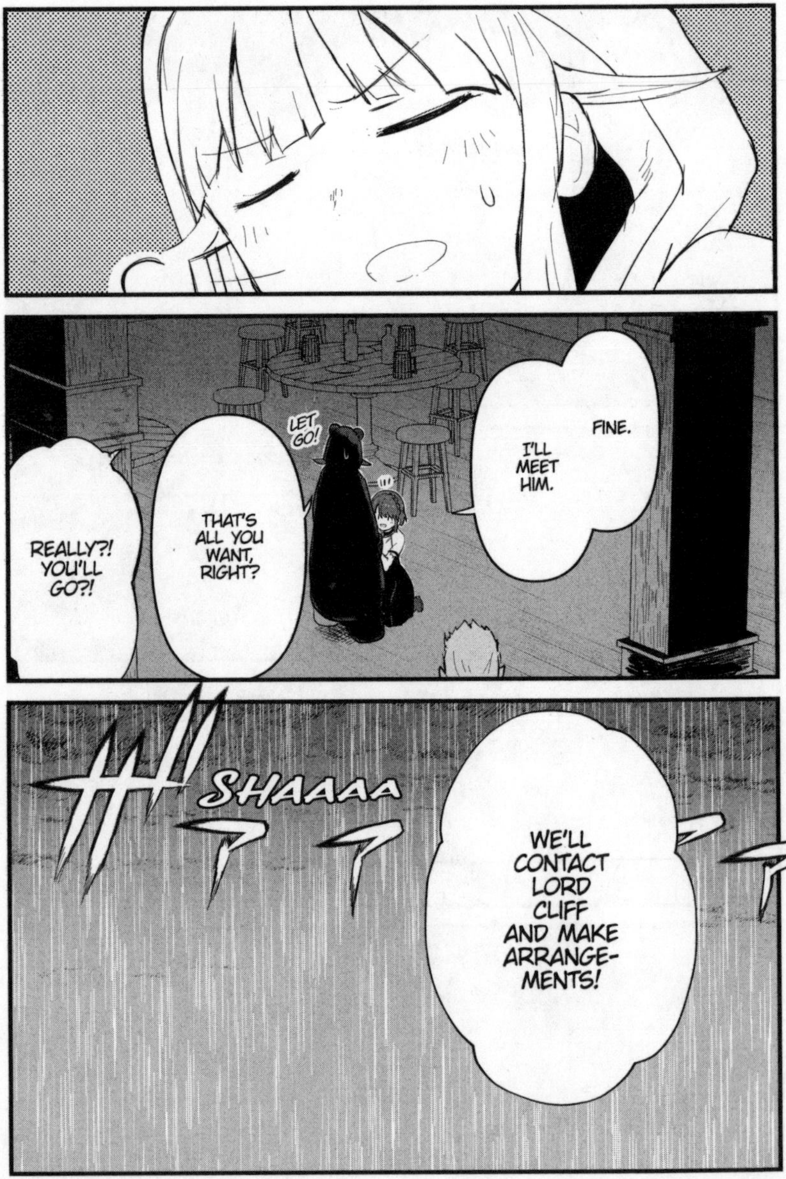
FINE.
I'LL MEET HIM.
LET GO!
THAT'S ALL YOU WANT, RIGHT?
REALLY?! YOU'LL GO?!
WE'LL CONTACT LORD CLIFF AND MAKE ARRANGE-MENTS!
SHAAAA

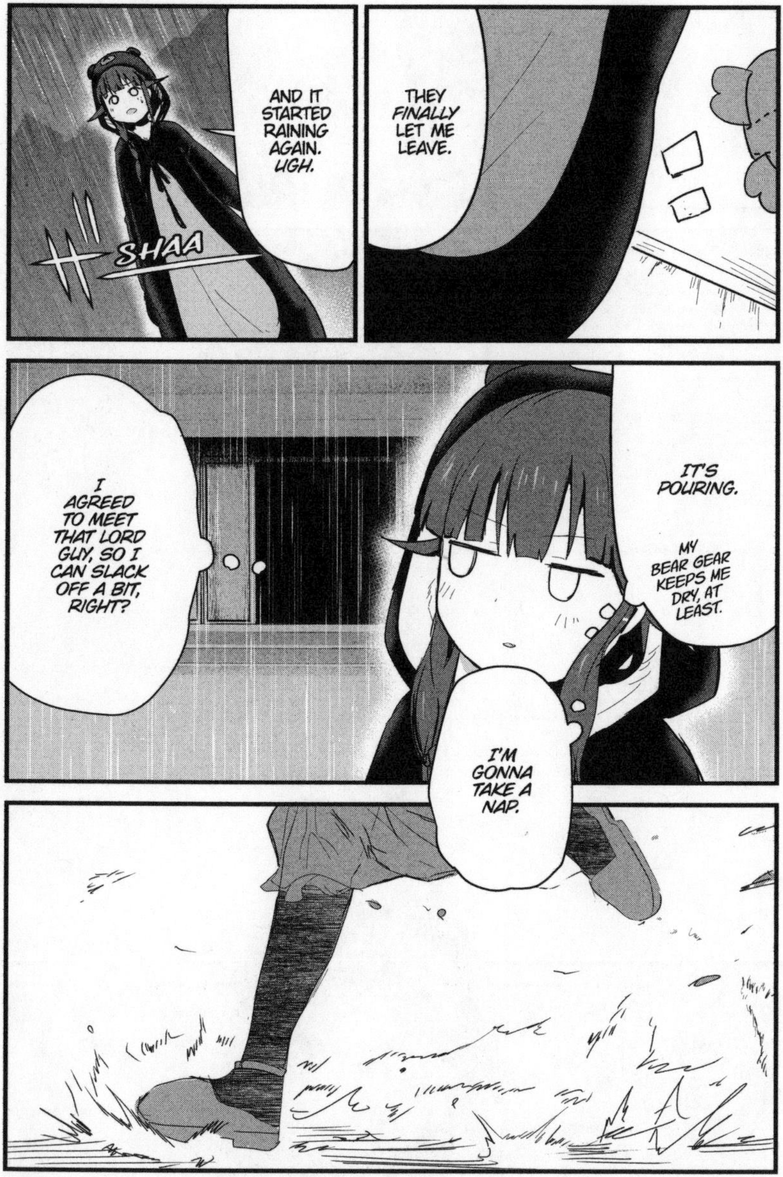
THEY FINALLY LET ME LEAVE.
AND IT STARTED RAINING AGAIN. UGH.
SHAA
IT'S POURING.
MY BEAR GEAR KEEPS ME DRY, AT LEAST.
I AGREED TO MEET THAT LORD GUY, SO I CAN SLACK OFF A BIT, RIGHT?
I'M GONNA TAKE A NAP.

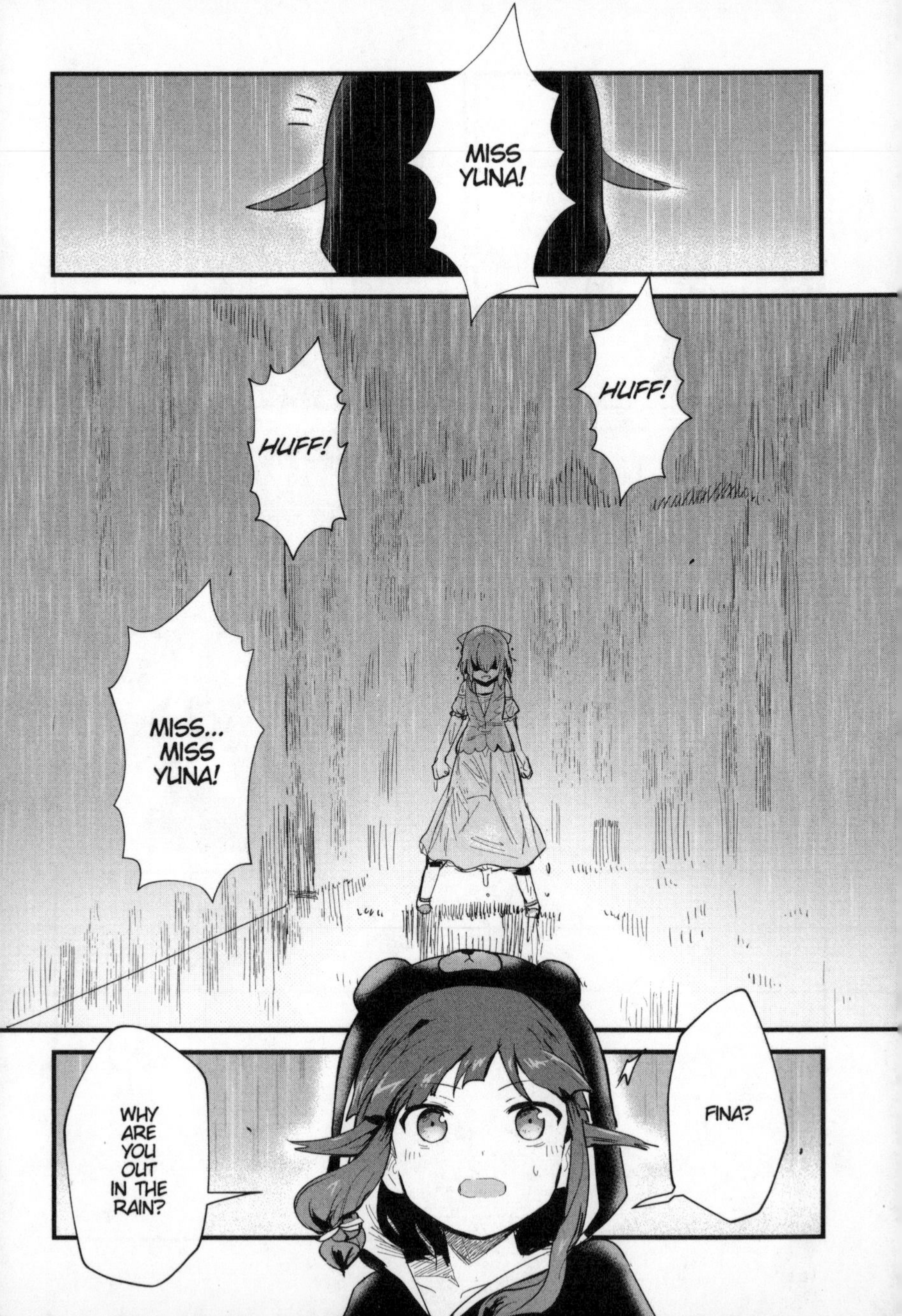
MISS YUNA!
HUFF!
HUFF!
MISS... MISS YUNA!
FINA?
WHY ARE YOU OUT IN THE RAIN?

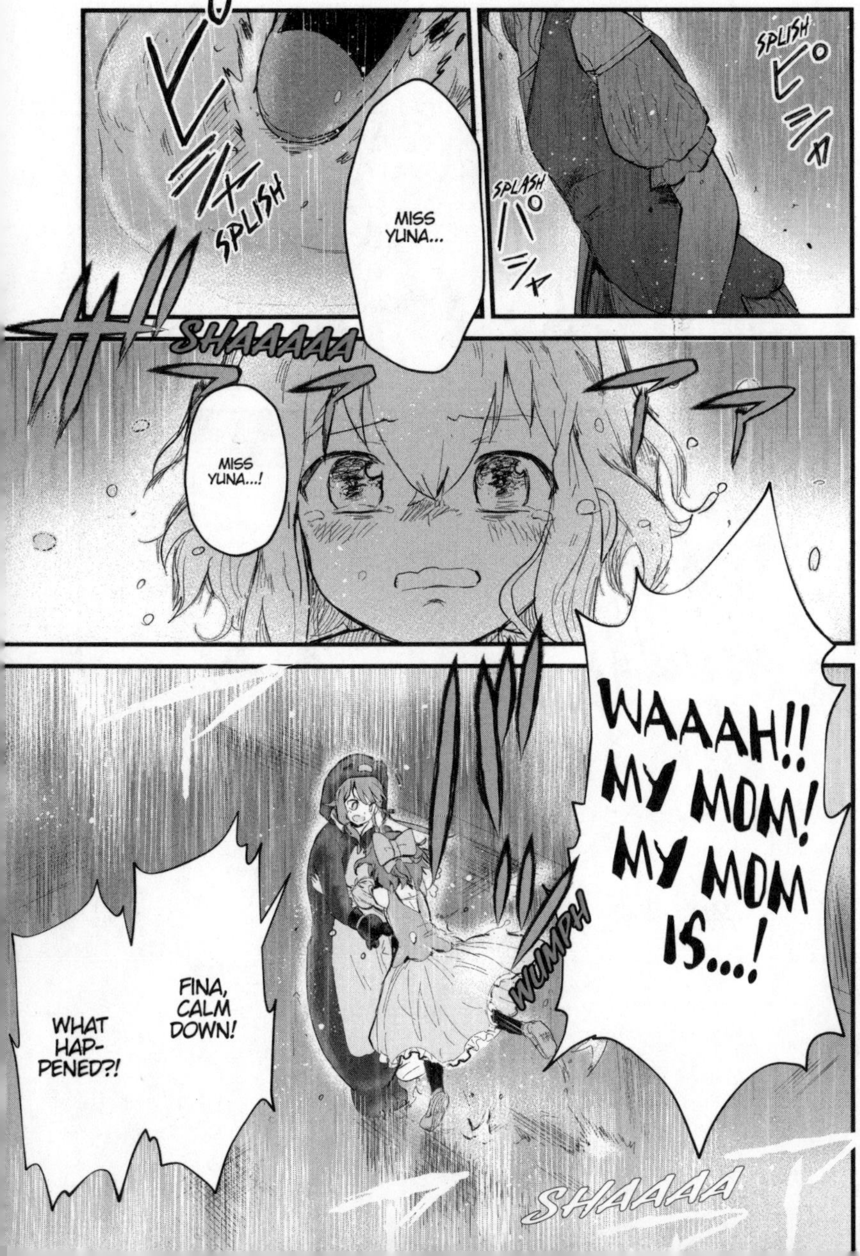
SPLISH
SPLASH
SPLISH
MISS YUNA...
SHAAAAAA
MISS YUNA...!
WAAAH!! MY MOM! MY MOM IS...!
WUMPH
FINA, CALM DOWN!
WHAT HAP-PENED?!
SHAAAA

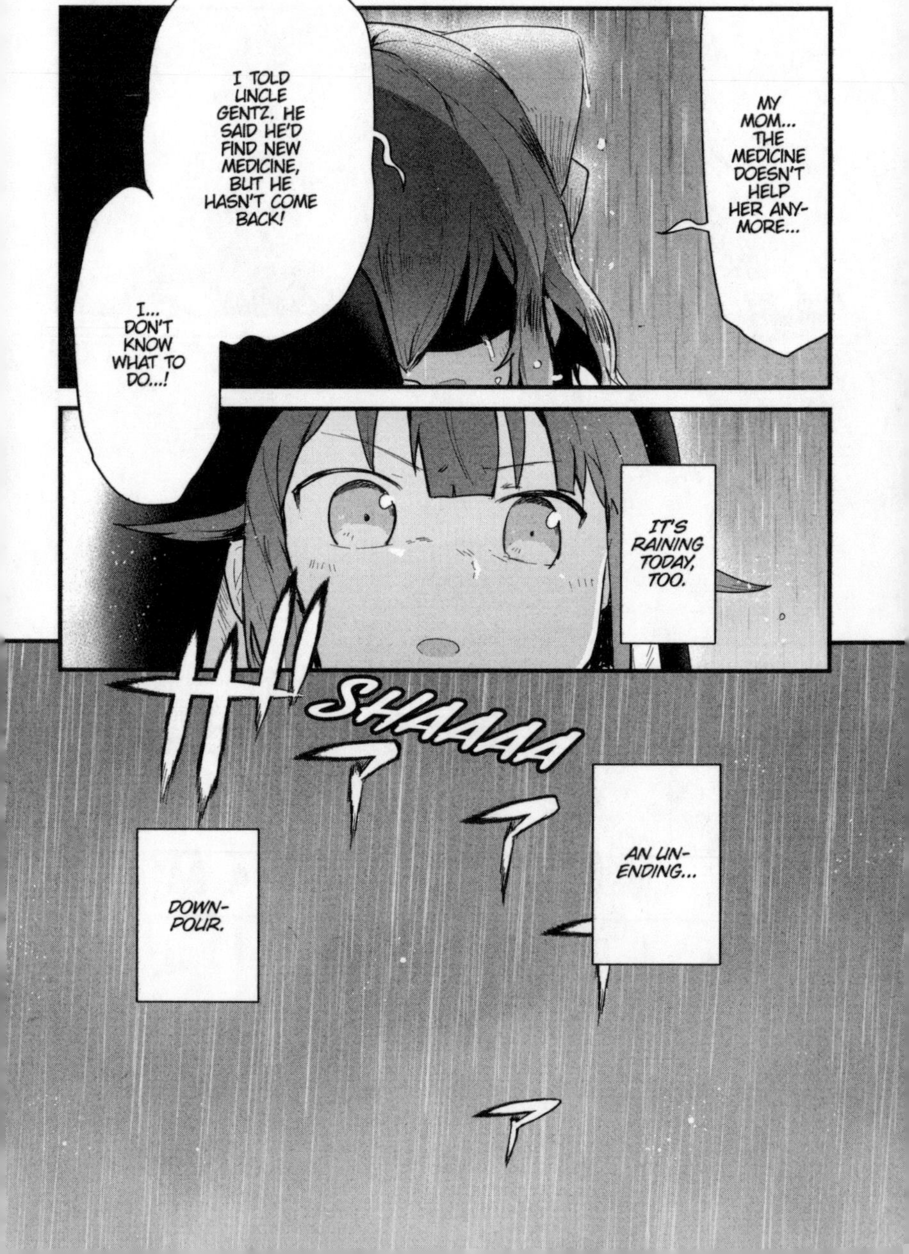
MY MOM... THE MEDICINE DOESN'T HELP HER ANY-MORE...
I TOLD UNCLE GENTZ. HE SAID HE'D FIND NEW MEDICINE, BUT HE HASN'T COME BACK!
I... DON'T KNOW WHAT TO DO...!
IT'S RAINING TODAY, TOO.
SHAAAAA
AN UN-ENDING...
DOWN-POUR.

Bear House

Written by Kumanano

My family has grown! Now I have cute bear summons at my side. I summon them every evening when I get back to the inn. They are two bears: one black, one white.

They're tame and adorable, but I can't just call them "bear." I needed a way to tell them apart, so I named the black bear Kumayuru, and the white bear Kumakyu. Why those names? No reason, they just felt right. I know I'm bad with names, but the bears seem fine with it.

"Kumayuru, Kumakyu! I hope we can all get along."

Kumayuru and Kumakyu reply with happy hums and cuddle up to me. They're so soft and fluffy, it's like being wrapped in top-of-the-line furs.

The only problem is that they're huge. It wouldn't be a problem if they were cubs, but summoning two full-grown bears into an inn room is pretty cramped. If I want to live with Kumayuru and Kumakyu, I need more space.

I head out of town, the trip doubling as a walk for Kumayuru and Kumakyu. I summon them as soon as I'm outside of the village walls. I climb up on Kumayuru, and Kumakyu gives me a sad look.

"I'll ride you on the way back, okay?"

Kumakyu hums happily in reply.

I've learned that I have to ride them both, or else the other will sulk. I summon both of them as much as I can, but there's only one of me. I can't ride them at the same time, so I alternate between them.

With me on their back, Kumayuru takes off into a run, and Kumakyu keeps pace beside us.

I love this. Riding feels great, and it saves time. At first, I thought the bears were a prank from God, but they were actually the perfect gift.

I look around. This is a good spot!

Once we're far enough from town, I hop off of Kumayuru's back.

I know that "bear storage" (what I like to call my item bag) can hold anything, no matter how much or how big. I tested it by putting fallen trees inside--a whole bunch of 'em. I had an idea: if I build a house and put it in storage, I could take it anywhere.

Standing in a clearing, I create the house I made when I was goblin slaying with Rulina-san.

Hmm. Not quite right. I want a second floor, so I add one. A rectangular box stacks on top of the house. It still doesn't feel right. I build a house in a different shape next to the first, but that doesn't do it for me, either. I try more shapes, but none of them feel quite right.

I stop to gather my thoughts. A two-story house would be good for the number of rooms I want. The first floor could be the kitchen, a living room to relax in, and maybe a bath? And the second floor could be the bedrooms. The bigger the better, so I can sleep with Kumayuru and Kumakyu.

Now that I've planned out the layout, I have to figure out the hard part: the exterior.

Since it's a fantasy world, danger is around every corner. I should cover my bases for the sake of safety. Magic works through visualization, and in my case, my magic is stronger when I visualize bears. So, the strongest house I can make would be based on the image of a bear.

I decide to give it a try, so I imagine a house with a bear shape. To strengthen the mental image, I look into the faces of Kumayuru and Kumakyu. They gaze sweetly back at me. The image becomes more concrete in my mind.

I build it, and...done!

Since I was looking at Kumayuru and Kumakyu for inspiration, the finished project is way cuter than intended. It looks like a sitting teddy bear. It turned out like some house from a fairy tale.

There's no point in having a bear-shaped house if it's not stronger than a normal house, so I decide to test that out.

I take turns attacking the normal-looking house I made and the bear-shaped one, hitting them with bear punches and magic. The regular house crumbles, but the bear house stands strong. So, it really is stronger! From the perspective of safety, the bear house is the winner.

But I'd be embarrassed to live in a house like that. It's just so *twee*. On the other hand, if I venture out into the wild and monsters attack in the night, I'd be safe inside the bear house. For all I know, there could be bandits out there, too. Staying alive is more important than avoiding embarrassment.

Why should I get hung up on that stuff now? I already wear a bear onesie everywhere. No one would be surprised by me living in a bear house, too. After reasoning it out, I commit to the bear-shaped house.

With the exterior complete, I go inside and get to work finalizing the floor plan. As I decided earlier, the first floor is a kitchen-slash-living room, plus a bathroom.

Thinking about the stone lion water fountains in rich people's homes, I make a bear water spout for the bath. If I'm the only one using it, it might as well be fun.

On the second floor, I make the bedrooms. After dividing the floor evenly, I end up with three rooms. If they don't get used as bedrooms, I could use them for storage, or I could make them into rooms for Kumayuru and Kumakyu.

Okay! That should do it. There should be enough space to summon Kumayuru and Kumakyu inside, and still be comfortable.

Although the house is finished, the interior is sparse. I'll have to get some furniture.

I put the bear house into the bear storage. I knew that it would work, but seeing an entire house fly into the storage space is surprising! It's so convenient, though. It's great to carry things around so easily!

I ride Kumakyu back to town to go furniture shopping.

Stares and gasps greet me everywhere I go, but I have no problem buying all I need. I get a chair, desk, bed, and bedding for my room. For the dining area, I get a table, chairs, and a sofa when I spot one. Now I can lie down after I eat! It's the way I thought when I was a shut-in, but oh well. No one else will see me, so who cares? With money to burn, I go ahead and buy everything else I might need, too.

After furniture shopping, I leave town, take out the bear house, and arrange the furniture inside. No matter how it might look on the outside, at least the inside is nice. Now, my house, Bear House, is complete!

Now, could I put it in town somewhere? I'll have to think on it some more.

Later, Gentz-san begs me to hire Fina as a personal monster-harvester. When I mention it to her, she bows and pleads, "Please let me work for you!" I planned on bringing the work back to her in town, but she says "I want to look for medicine for my mom, too. If it's not too much trouble, can I go with you?"

Remembering how I met her, and what Gentz-san told me about her mom, I accept her request.

Fina needs somewhere safe to work. The brand-new Bear House would be the safest place, but it doesn't have a spot for that. So, I resolve to add a workshop-slash-storehouse to the side of Bear House. If it's just a workshop, it doesn't need to be big.

I construct a small bear hut next to Bear House, so it looks like a mama bear and cub. I might as well own it at this point, so I don't let the appearance bother me.

I connect the interiors of the mama bear and cub, and enter the bear cub. First, I divide the rooms. I want to store monsters as well as harvest them. I *could* put them in bear storage, but there's no harm in having a space for that. Then I construct the workshop for Fina, and a separate storage space for her, too.

"If she's harvesting monsters, she'll also need a sink."

I set up a sink with a water gem like I did for the bath, so the workshop has running water. After that, I take out a worktable for monsters to be laid out on, and arrange all the things Fina told me she would need. A proper workshop starts to take shape.

And now the workshop-slash-storehouse is finished, too!

Later, I take a quest to hunt tigerwolves. When I show the Bear House to Fina, the stunned look on her face is priceless!

KUMA KUMA
KUMA BEAR
Volume.2

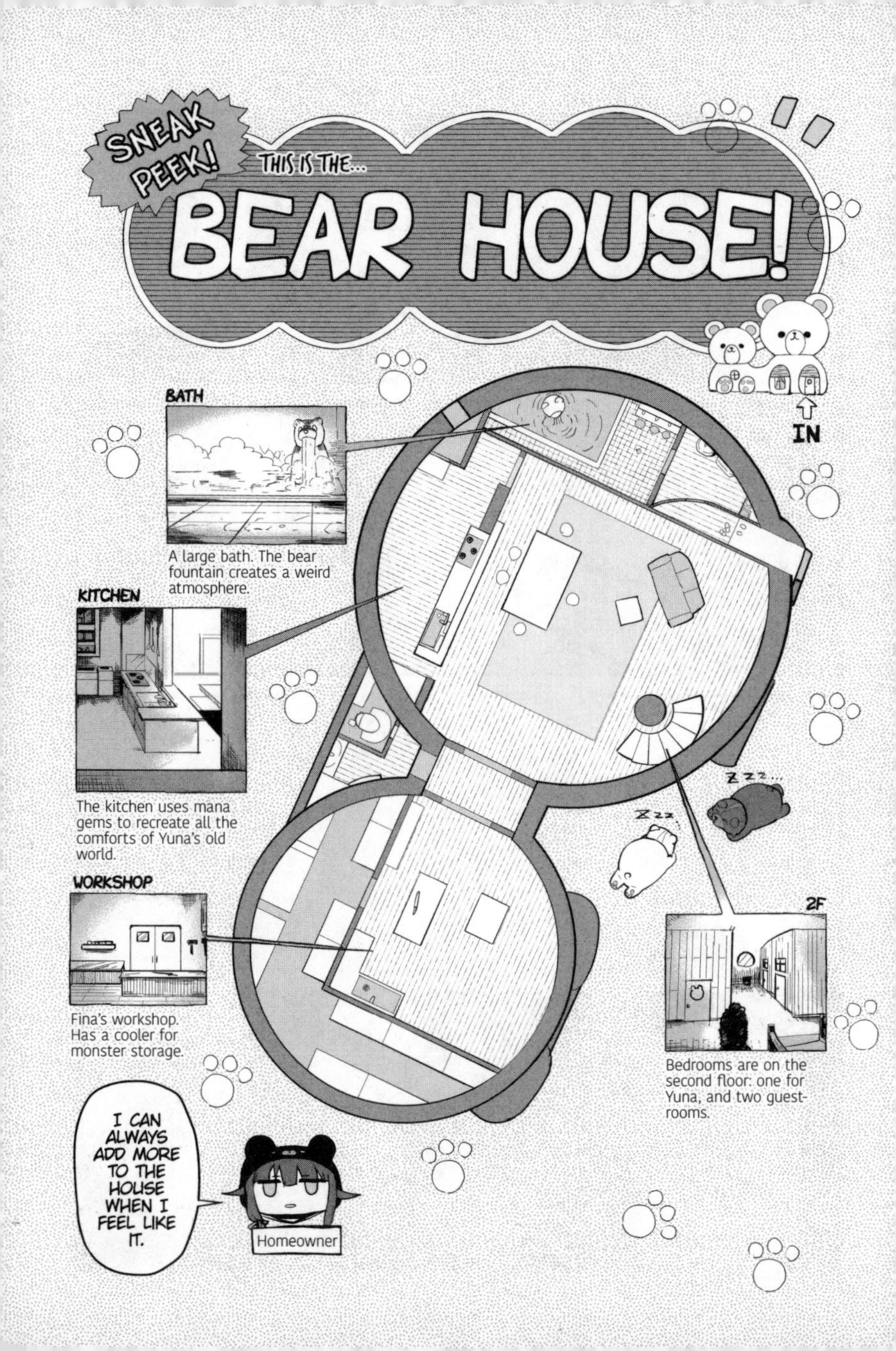
SNEAK PEEK!
THIS IS THE...
BEAR HOUSE!
IN
BATH
A large bath. The bear fountain creates a weird atmosphere.
KITCHEN
The kitchen uses mana gems to recreate all the comforts of Yuna's old world.
WORKSHOP
Fina's workshop. Has a cooler for monster storage.
2F
Bedrooms are on the second floor: one for Yuna, and two guest-rooms.
Z Z Z...
Z Z Z
I CAN ALWAYS ADD MORE TO THE HOUSE WHEN I FEEL LIKE IT.
Homeowner

GUILD MASTER PROBLEMS

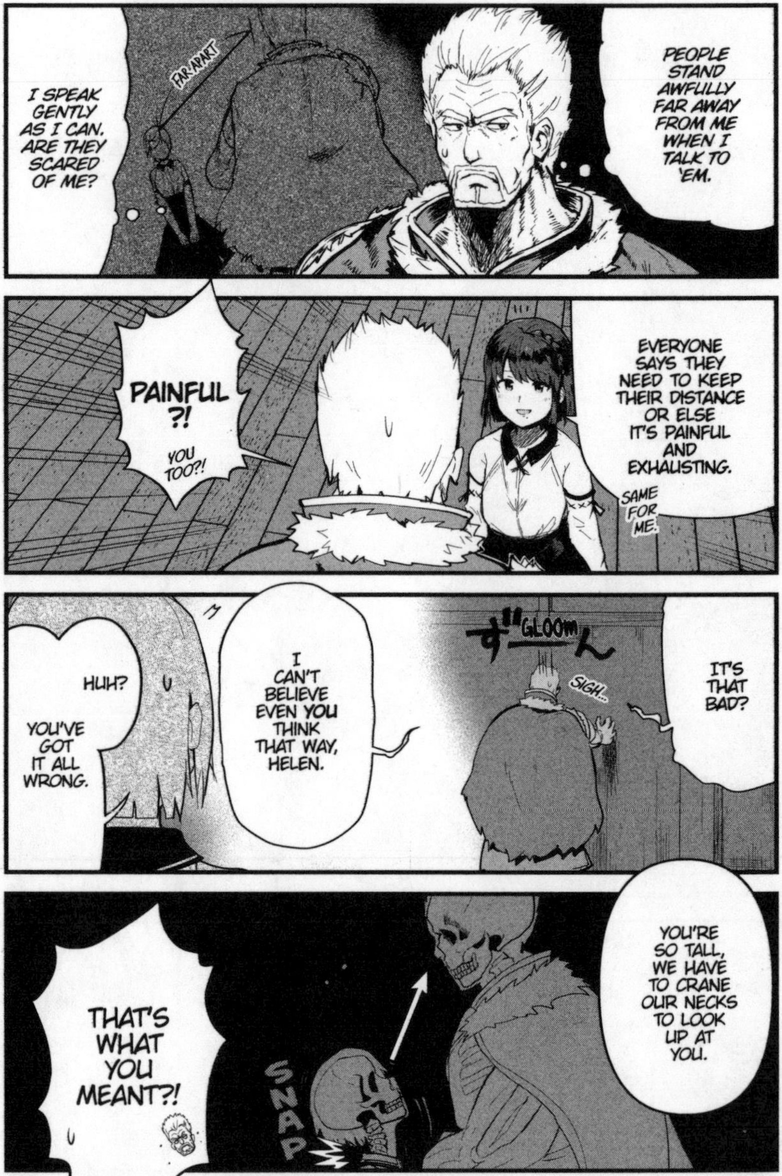
PEOPLE STAND AWFULLY FAR AWAY FROM ME WHEN I TALK TO 'EM.
FAR APART
I SPEAK GENTLY AS I CAN. ARE THEY SCARED OF ME?
EVERYONE SAYS THEY NEED TO KEEP THEIR DISTANCE OR ELSE IT'S PAINFUL AND EXHAUSTING.
SAME FOR ME.
PAINFUL?!
YOU TOO?!
IT'S THAT BAD?
ずーん GLOOM
SIGH...
I CAN'T BELIEVE EVEN YOU THINK THAT WAY, HELEN.
HUH?
YOU'VE GOT IT ALL WRONG.
YOU'RE SO TALL, WE HAVE TO CRANE OUR NECKS TO LOOK UP AT YOU.
SNAP
THAT'S WHAT YOU MEANT?!

THE LIFE OF A BEAR

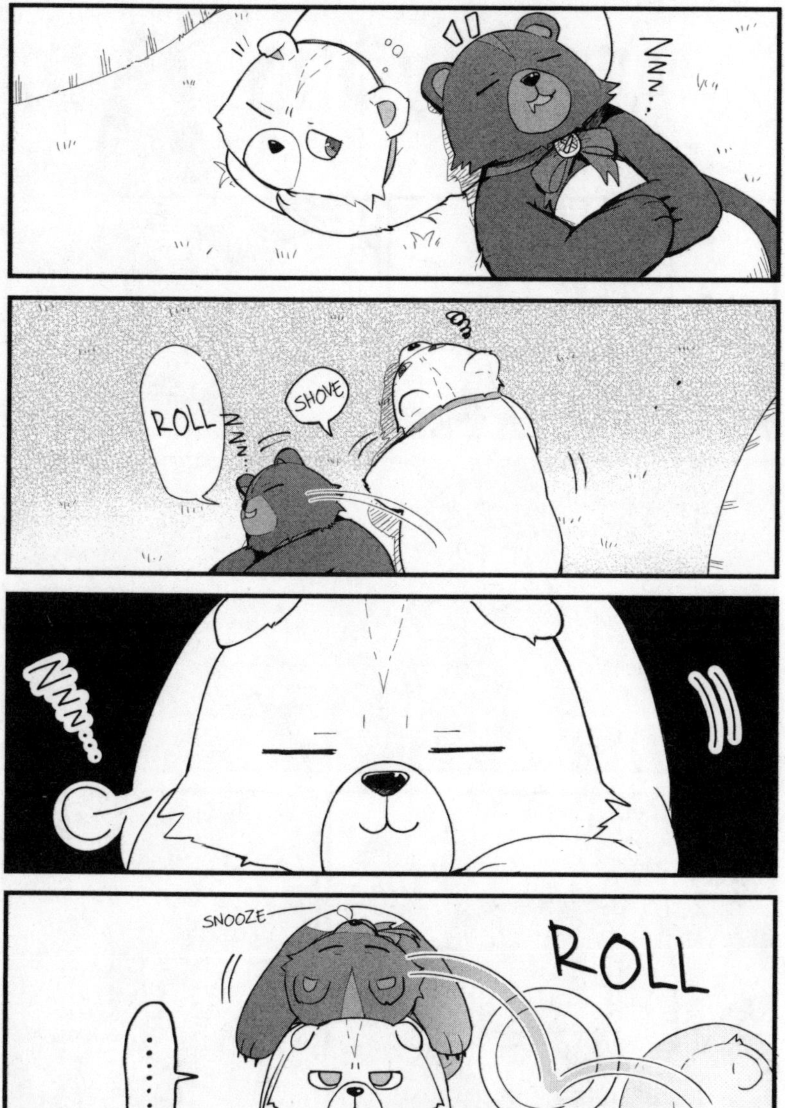

Zzz...
SHOVE
ROLL
Zzz...
ROLL
SNOOZE
......

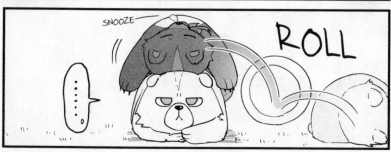

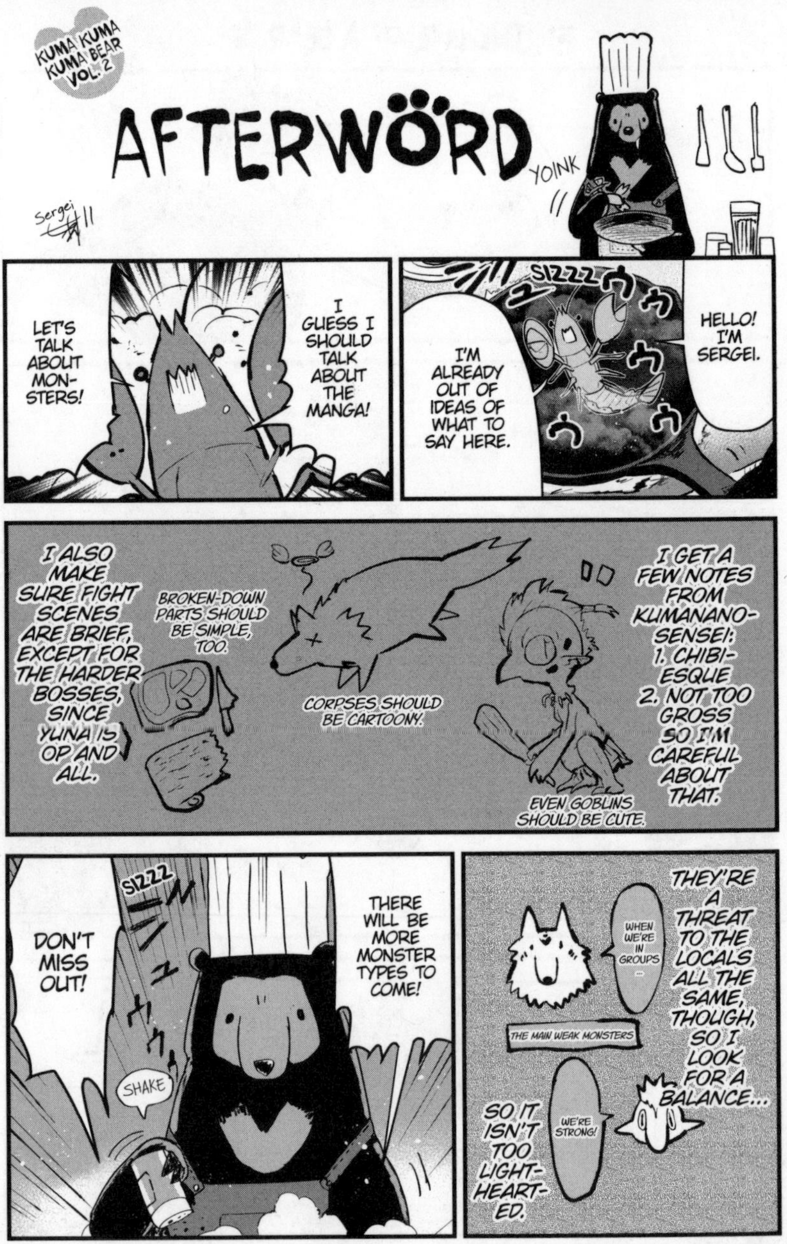
KUMA KUMA KUMA BEAR VOL. 2
AFTERWÖRD
YOINK
Sergei
SIZZZ
HELLO! I'M SERGEI.
I'M ALREADY OUT OF IDEAS OF WHAT TO SAY HERE.
I GUESS I SHOULD TALK ABOUT THE MANGA!
LET'S TALK ABOUT MONSTERS!
I GET A FEW NOTES FROM KUMANANO-SENSEI: 1. CHIBI-ESQUE 2. NOT TOO GROSS SO I'M CAREFUL ABOUT THAT.
EVEN GOBLINS SHOULD BE CUTE.
CORPSES SHOULD BE CARTOONY.
BROKEN-DOWN PARTS SHOULD BE SIMPLE, TOO.
I ALSO MAKE SURE FIGHT SCENES ARE BRIEF, EXCEPT FOR THE HARDER BOSSES, SINCE YUNA IS OP AND ALL.
THEY'RE A THREAT TO THE LOCALS ALL THE SAME, THOUGH, SO I LOOK FOR A BALANCE...
WHEN WE'RE IN GROUPS...
THE MAIN WEAK MONSTERS
WE'RE STRONG!
SO IT ISN'T TOO LIGHT-HEARTED.
SIZZZ
THERE WILL BE MORE MONSTER TYPES TO COME!
DON'T MISS OUT!
SHAKE

SEVEN SEAS ENTERTAINMENT PRESENTS

KUMA KUMA KUMA BEAR

story by **KUMANANO** / art by **SERGEI** / character designs by **029**

VOLUME 2

TRANSLATION
Amanda Haley

ADAPTATION
Dawn Davis

LETTERING AND RETOUCH
Laura Heo

COVER DESIGN
Nicky Lim

PROOFREADING
Kurestin Armada

EDITOR
Shannon Fay

PREPRESS TECHNICIAN
Rhiannon Rasmussen-Silverstein

PRODUCTION MANAGER
Lissa Pattillo

MANAGING EDITOR
Julie Davis

ASSOCIATE PUBLISHER
Adam Arnold

PUBLISHER
Jason DeAngelis

KUMA KUMA KUMA BEAR 2
© SERGEI   © KUMANANO 2019
Originally published in Japan in 2019 by SHUFU TO SEIKATSU SHA CO.,
LTD., Tokyo.
English translation rights arranged with SHUFU TO SEIKATSU SHA CO.,
LTD., Tokyo, through TOHAN CORPORATION, Tokyo.

Seven Seas press and purchase enquiries can be sent to Marketing Manager
Lianne Sentar at press@gomanga.com. Information regarding the distribution
and purchase of digital editions is available from Digital Manager CK Russell
at digital@gomanga.com.

Seven Seas and the Seven Seas logo are trademarks of
Seven Seas Entertainment. All rights reserved.

ISBN: 978-1-64505-529-7

Printed in Canada

First Printing: September 2020

10 9 8 7 6 5 4 3 2 1

FOLLOW US ONLINE: *www.sevenseasentertainment.com*

READING DIRECTIONS

This book reads from **_right to left_**, Japanese style.
If this is your first time reading manga, you start
reading from the top right panel on each page and
take it from there. If you get lost, just follow the
numbered diagram here. It may seem backwards at
first, but you'll get the hang of it! Have fun!!

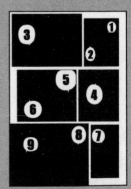